Praise for *Waiting fo*

This amazing book is about motherhood and fat............, ...
foster care. It interweaves three themes: the professional lives of Gary and
Helen Stephens as they founded the orphanages Mother's Choice in Hong
Kong and Mother's Care in China; the history and realities of adoption; and,
most importantly, the story of Jacob Lok Chi, the blind, nonverbal son they
adopted in 1998.

Gary and Helen have touched so many lives around the world. The
orphanages they founded have set standards of love and commitment that have
led to changes in government policies and attitudes in China. That alone is a
lifetime achievement. Building a life with their son Jacob has been an even
more profound one.

Gary and Helen, like so many adoptive and foster parents, have deliberately immersed their lives in the uncomfortable so as not to miss the exhilarating experience of Jacob as their son. Through the story of Jacob Lok Chi,
we learn that when we give ourselves wholly to the most vulnerable people
on earth, we truly discover the Jesus who washes our feet. This book is a challenge to every reader: what will we do to empty the orphanages of the world?

IAN STRACHAN, DIRECTOR OF SOCIAL WELFARE (RETIRED)
HONG KONG GOVERNMENT

Having worked in the field of intercountry adoption for nearly sixty years, I
highly recommend *Waiting for a Father* to anyone whose life has been touched
by adoption. Jacob Lok Chi Stephens' remarkable story is an inspiration to all,
and a testament to the power of love and family.

DR. DAVID H. KIM, PRESIDENT EMERITUS
HOLT INTERNATIONAL CHILDREN' SERVICES

It would be impossible for anyone with a human heart not to be moved by
this wonderful true story of a man who—after a lifetime of taking on other
peoples' burdens—decides to take on just one more. And readers sharing this
amazing journey will learn a wonderful lesson: that "tough cases" often perceived as burdens are actually the source of life's deepest joys. Recommended.

NURY VITTACHI, AUTHOR OF *THE CURIOUS DIARY OF MR. JAM*

WAITING FOR A FATHER

WAITING FOR A
FATHER

Hearing the Heart-Cry of the Orphans of the World

GARY STEPHENS AND CARMEN RADLEY

Waiting for a Father:
Hearing the Heart-Cry of the Orphans of the World

Copyright © 2013 by Gary Stephens and Carmen Radley

DEEP RIVER BOOKS
Sisters, Oregon
www.deepriverbooks.com

ISBN-13: 9781937756789
ISBN-10: 1937756785

Library of Congress: 2013931167

Cover Design by Jason Enterline

*For children
without families.*

Gary and Helen with Jacob Lok Chi outside Mother's Choice, with Hong Kong's many high rises and part of Victoria Peak in background, 1996.

CONTENTS

PREFACE
Hearing Jacob's Heart-Cry

❧

The child must be given the means requisite for its normal development, both materially and spiritually. The child that is hungry must be fed, the child that is sick must be nursed, the child that is backward must be helped, the delinquent child must be reclaimed, and the orphan and the waif must be sheltered and succored. The child must be the first to receive relief in times of distress. The child must be put in a position to earn a livelihood, and must be protected against every form of exploitation. The child must be brought up in the consciousness that its talents must be devoted to the service of its fellow men.

"DECLARATION OF THE RIGHTS OF THE CHILD"
EGLANTYNE JEBB, FOUNDER OF SAVE THE CHILDREN, 1923

I was living in Hong Kong.

On a summer day hotter than blazes, I visited a large group home for orphans on the Kowloon Peninsula. The building was low and squat and made of cinder blocks, as was the fence surrounding it. High-rises thirty stories tall glistened in the sun around us, and heat radiated up from the cement like steam.

I was working as the managing director of Mother's Choice, a social service organization founded in 1987 by my wife Helen and me, and another couple, Ranjan and Phyllis Marwah. We ran a hostel for pregnant teenagers and child-care facilities for infants and children with special needs. But after all we had done, after caring for thousands of children, we had only become more and more passionate about getting children out of institutions and into permanent, loving families, both locally and internationally. Though we ran orphanages, we didn't—and still don't—believe they meet the emotional, physical, spiritual, and psychological needs of the child. Studies show it, and the children who came through our homes were evidence of it.

So this hot summer day in 2000, I was visiting a group home to meet a nine-year-old boy whose English name was Jacob. That morning, one of our adoption social workers, a beautiful Chinese woman named Suzanne Luk, had stuck her head into my office and asked if I would come with her to visit a child. Suzanne had met Jacob a few times. He'd been referred to Mother's Choice by the Social Welfare Department of Hong Kong, who asked if we could find an adoptive family for him, and though Suzanne had experience getting children in *our* care adopted, this was a very different situation. She didn't know much about him—his personality or demeanor or the problems an adoptive family might encounter with him, things we knew about children in our care. She said to me, "Gary, you're a father. I would like your perspective on whether or not this young boy has a chance at adoption."

Once we made it inside, we were relieved to find ceiling fans, but otherwise the place wasn't very welcoming. It was sterile and institutional, of concrete and cinder block construction like the outside, with bare walls. We were directed to a conference room to wait, and as we walked through the facility, I didn't see any garden or lawn, only paved courtyards. In terms of enjoying nature, the only thing you could do was listen to the wind, hoping it would blow through some trees outside the facility.

Suzanne and I waited in the conference room for a few minutes, and then suddenly the door opened and in walked this handsome little boy in his school uniform, typical of school-aged children in Hong Kong, in navy blue shorts and a white shirt with a patch on the pocket, wearing a tie that he immediately unclipped and tossed up in the air, where it caught on the overhead ceiling fan. I laughed to myself and thought, *Typical kid.* Maybe he was trying to diffuse some of the tension of meeting with these unfamiliar people, or maybe, after seeing her a few times, he already understood that Suzanne could help him somehow. But whatever it was, he was savvy and quick, and he walked straight past Suzanne, sat beside me, put his arm around my shoulder, and looked up into my face.

This next moment is imprinted in my brain like the glare of a lightbulb when you look away. Jacob had his dark eyes fixed on mine, his chin lifted and confident, and suddenly, it was as if he turned on some kind of high white light between his eyes and his smile. I'll never forget it. And then he spoke. Out of the side of his mouth, he asked Suzanne in Cantonese, "Is he my daddy?" Without waiting for a response, he looked at me and asked in English, "Are you my daddy?"

I quickly pointed at Suzanne and said, "No, Jacob, I'm her boss."

Jacob kept his arm around me and said, "Don't you want to be my daddy?"

My heart was in pieces, but I couldn't say what I was thinking—yes and no at the same time—that yes, I wanted him to have a father, but that my hands were already full. I began explaining to Jacob that only a few months earlier, my wife and I had completed our own process of adopting a young Chinese boy. He was a few years younger, and his English name was also Jacob. I explained that my son Jacob was blind and wore prosthetic eyes, and I told him a few stories of Jacob taking his eyes out at inconvenient times, of him rolling an eye across the church floor during prayer, of him taking them out on the escalator in the shopping mall. And then I told him my favorite, of a time when we were in the waiting room of an eye doctor's office in the heart of Hong Kong Island with a number of other patients. I was sitting down and my Jacob was standing between my legs when an older Australian woman said "Hello" to him.

"Ma'am," I said, "he doesn't speak. And he's actually blind."

"But he's looking straight at me," she replied.

"Those are prosthetic eyes," I said. The woman furrowed her brow in doubt. Yet within two minutes, Jacob had taken one of his eyes out and thrown it onto the middle of the waiting room floor. I quickly grabbed a tissue out of a box and picked up the eye and tucked it in my shirt pocket. "I told you!" I said.

When I finished telling him all this, Jacob just sat there, looking up at me. Then he asked, "Don't you want another?"

In the decade that has passed, I have recalled his words thousands upon thousands of times, and I have come to understand that at that moment in that office, I heard the heart-cry of every orphaned and abandoned child in the world: "I want a mommy and daddy." This Jacob was still hugging me and searching my face. He wasn't comparing skin tones or the fact that he was Chinese and I was Caucasian. He was looking at me as a father, and in a moment of profound revelation, I realized that this boy was saying to me what my son Jacob couldn't say but what millions of children across the world hope for every day.

As Suzanne and I drove back to Mother's Choice that morning, I told her, "Yes, I certainly believe it is not only possible, but probable for Jacob to find an adoptive family."

To that end, Suzanne and her husband began fostering him within weeks, preparing him for the transition to a permanent, loving family. Less than a year later, Jacob went to live in the southern United States with a mother, father, and older brother. As we do with many of the children we have helped through the process of adoption, Helen and I hear of Jacob's progress in small bits, in a couple of paragraphs every other year. We got an update when Jacob toured the White

House with some other students from his school district as a reward for academic achievement, and over the years, we heard that he was excelling in sports. Last year we watched twenty minutes of film highlights of him playing quarterback for his high school football team his junior year, and it looks like he'll be continuing when he goes to college. Despite spending his early life without the safety and security of a family, and despite the challenges of integrating with a new family in a new country after that, Jacob has prevailed.

Yet the heart-cry of the orphaned and abandoned children of the world continues, especially in countries that have suffered war, natural disasters, political oppression, and extreme poverty. Since that profound morning when I traveled with Suzanne to meet Jacob and heard *his* cry, I have taken up the mantle to be an advocate and a voice for these children without families.

In part, this book's purpose is to share my own heart, which has for many years been heavy with the weight of the most vulnerable among us. But I have also taken up this calling because inherent in my belief system is that at the center of the universe is a Creator God who inspires love and who gave rise to many different institutions that humans use to care for each other, ranging from governments to religious institutions to civil institutions to families. But of all these institutions, there is only one that is natural for a child to be raised in. Children are born inside the family, and my passion, which has grown over the years as I have worked with orphaned and abandoned children, is to move children out of institutions and into loving families, which is the highest and best way to care for them.

I am convinced that if we as willing and able adults, living anywhere on the globe, would open our hearts and homes, we could empty the orphanages of the world.

GARY STEPHENS, JANUARY 2013
MONTROSE, COLORADO

CHAPTER 1

A STORY OF DEPRIVATION

❧

There is nothing in the cosmos, nothing known to man, that comes remotely close to the complexity and the elegance of the architecture of every child's brain as it is developing.

DR. DAVID ARREDONDO

Hong Kong

The crib where Jacob lay was his territory, something predictable, a space he could measure with his body. With his hands and his feet, he could detect the size of the space and the objects and textures in it, the cool metal bars, and the coarse cotton sheet on the mattress.

But everything outside it was unknown. From that void, the hands of a caregiver would materialize suddenly and press upon his skin and pick him up, removing him from the familiar space of the crib to change him, to bathe him, or to take him to therapy. He could not see her coming. He could not anticipate where her hands would land, or, as the caregivers rotated through morning, afternoon, and night shifts, the gentleness or force with which she would grasp him. What other babies could measure with their eyes as they watched a woman cross the room toward their beds and reach in to lift them by the armpits onto her hip, Jacob could only try to do with his ears. But if she walked softly on the tile floors, if she did not speak as she traversed the room, or if other children were crying so loudly it drowned out her sounds, he could not prepare himself for her touch. In an instant, a person would exist where previously there was no one. Abruptly she was removing him from a small place that he knew and exposing him to a vast expanse of objects and spaces and people and sounds he could not make sense of, all of which were potentially hostile. Sickly and weak, he could resist only feebly through his cries, but to little effect.

Those hands cared for forty children in his ward, and because of it, Jacob received scant individual attention. Everything from bathing to feeding was, by necessity, done in the most perfunctory way. Jacob spent most of his time lying on his back in the crib, and when it came time to eat, a caregiver would put a bottle filled with a rice gruel called *congee* in his mouth, then place a rolled-up towel near his head to keep the bottle inverted. If he refused the nipple and turned his head away, it would press against his cheek or his ear or the side of his head, and the congee would trickle out and down his face, drying to form a white crust.

All day long, the wails of other children filled the air, and with little other stimulus, with no familiar hands cradling his head and no familiar voice assuring him of his intrinsic worth, with no one encouraging him to sit, crawl, or explore the world, Jacob languished. When he was nineteen months old, he needed help to roll over. He could sit only momentarily with his hands in front supporting his torso, and only if he was placed in that position. Hospitalized for chest infections, bronchitis, croup, and the adverse effects of antibiotics an unbelievable sixteen times before his second birthday, Jacob developed a flat spot on the back of his head from lying on his back, and he never learned to speak.

This was where Helen and Gary Stephens found him, when he was twenty-seven months old. He'd lived in one other large child-care facility before this one under similar conditions of neglect, and before that, in two different hospitals. Not surprisingly, there are no photographs of him as a baby, and his first two years are told mostly through hospital records and the notes of social workers. Born six weeks prematurely on May 26, 1994, at Queen Elizabeth Hospital in the Kowloon section of peninsular Hong Kong, Jacob weighed 5.2 pounds and suffered from a rare congenital condition called anophthalmia, which results in the absence of eyes. He also was born with a hole in the lining of his stomach, which had caused infection and inflammation. To remedy this, doctors performed emergency surgery when he was only six days old. He never went home but lived in the hospital until he was seven months old.

Jacob's biological parents are sketches in a series of documents from hospital psychologists and social workers. Some details are trivial, banal even: the fact that they both enjoyed basketball and pop music, that he played squash and she liked to bicycle. But through them, one can piece together an outline that helps explain why, after naming this little boy *Lok Chi*—Persistent Happiness—they stepped back and eventually walked away. They were in their early twenties and had married when she became pregnant, which on its own could put a young marriage under strain. But other problems compounded that. They struggled financially: she was a quality controller in a garment factory, he was a clerk in a hospital, and together they made less than US $2000 a month. She had a visible abnormality in her left eye, some sort of congenital condition like a cataract, which peers, neighbors, schoolmates, and teachers had teased her about throughout her childhood and adolescence. As a consequence, she was overwhelmingly self-conscious. A psychologist's assessment said she hardly dared to look at others directly; instead, she walked past quietly with her face lowered toward the ground.

As for her attitude toward the baby, records say she showed some affection toward him soon after he was born, yet if she held him or spoke to him isn't mentioned. What is mentioned is that she had difficulty accepting him. She was educated in China, which through propaganda and education in the cities, and through more coercive tactics in rural areas, had pushed a birth planning policy not only of quantity—the well-known and widely excoriated one-child-for-all—but also of *quality*. In the late 1970s, the state began a eugenics campaign, *yousheng youyu* or "superior birth and child rearing," which promoted the cultivation of children who were physically and mentally excellent. Leaders hoped that a combination of lowering the population and cultivating well-educated, high-performing, globally-savvy young people would help China become a modern, developed nation by the year 2000, but there were many unintended consequences. One was that by the 1990s, the perfect child had become a national obsession.

Of course, Jacob's mother was now in Hong Kong, but crossing the blurred and porous border did not mean she'd left China behind. Its culture and values pervaded life in the city. Her child was not perfect, and she felt that others, particularly her relatives and in-laws, would think it her fault that the baby had been born without eyes. Perhaps she was just too fragile for such judgment. Records say that over time, she grew more determined in relinquishing her parental rights.

Certainly her husband was an influence. He was younger than she, less mature, and offered little support. Records say that he was unwilling to ask relatives for help, and from day one, he was very firm in his decision to cut all ties to the baby, a decision owing almost totally to the child's disability. Maybe he too was influenced by campaigns asserting the need for a child without blemish, or maybe he was scared and ill equipped to be a father to anyone, incapable of taking on the considerable responsibility that role entails. The psychologist assessing him seemed to think this was the case. Citing their "inadequate personalities," the unstable marriage, and the father's refusal to look to others for help, the psychologist determined that they would struggle to parent a child even without special needs, and more so Jacob. Therefore he approved their request to "sign off on the child."

They had visited him only twice, when he was seven months old and again on his first birthday, precisely recorded as December 20, 1994, and May 26, 1995, but had no other contact. And then the ties that, though tenuous from the beginning, should have been the means for him to learn the world and secure the confidence to be a part of it were cut. He had already been named a ward of the state in July of 1995, but on October 24, Jacob's parents signed the official Form 4A and Statutory Declaration, waiving their parental rights, and the director of social welfare in Hong Kong became his legal guardian. Records show that Jacob had only one other visitor: they say a student nurse at Queen Elizabeth Hospital—a Miss Choi—came "regularly," without quantifying how often, to help clean his prosthetic eyes and to play with him. Otherwise, he stayed in his crib. He attended occasional occupational and physical therapy sessions, but he had no steady, close, affectionate contact with another person.

The social worker's notes about Jacob's demeanor during this time amount to a lifeless assessment a few steps removed. It is plain that he was a difficult baby. She describes his "hot temper" and his propensity to cry when he was first admitted to the first of his two institutional placements. "Later when he adjusted to the environment," she continues, "he came to enjoy a stable emotion. He would make some monosounds when he was happy." The phrasing is vague and suggests there was little positive to report, but Gary and Helen believe she was probably being delicate to protect him, since a negative file would only be more of a barrier to his finding a home. His "stable emotion" is thus portrayed as positive adjustment rather than the alternative: that he might be resigning himself to the fact that his cries would not be heard, that he could not rely on the world to respond to him and meet his needs, that he was shifting from protest to despair.

There is no doubt Jacob suffered serious neglect, but his neurological development during these formative years was not charted, so the effects can only be conjectured. Though neurologists once thought genetics played the major role in brain function, they now know a child's environment also has a huge impact on how the brain develops. Thousands of pathways are built every second, and a young child requires copious and continuous stimulation in order to use all parts of the brain, which later will shape the child's abilities with language and mathematics as well as his ability to navigate social spaces. To maximize efficiency, the brain prunes away connections that are not used, and through neglect, a genetically normal child can become mentally disabled. A 2006 report of children in Romanian orphanages produced such conclusions; a nurse assessing children in the study believed that by neglecting the children, the authorities in the institutions she visited were "manufacturing disability."

Whether this was the case with Jacob is difficult to prove after the fact, but undoubtedly, the deprivation he suffered through the first two years of his life impeded his neurological development to some degree. A brain scan at birth read normal, but after months of severe illness in a hospital, then several months in his first residential facility, Jacob was given an IQ test based on visual norms and was consequently labeled "mentally retarded." Afterward he was moved to a ward for mentally disabled children on the third floor of a large hospital, a white block of cement above a rushing freeway, where Gary and Helen found him a year later—a sickly, skinny, stressed, and tactile-defensive child with little hope of finding a home.

❋ ❋ ❋

In 1969, a young Welsh social worker named James Robertson released a film to the psychiatric community that, in the years and decades to come, had powerful and far-reaching consequences for children in situations like Jacob's. *John* is a simple film, documenting the experience of a dark-haired, seventeen-month-old British boy sent to a residential nursery while his mother gave birth to a second baby. As recent transplants to London, John's parents had no friends or family to care for him during the mother's delivery and recovery, and the father couldn't work and take care of John too. So they chose to admit him, and though it wasn't an ideal situation, they were encouraged by the appearance of the place. "The nursery and training center was a handsome building in a leafy suburb," Robertson explains in a book coauthored with his wife, Joyce, called *Separation and the Very Young.* "The setting, together with the pretty picture of young nurses walking well-dressed children in the nearby park, gave the establishment a deceptive aura of charm." John's parents thought this would be better than a foster care situation, given that "the nursery was open to view."

But in nine days, the "sturdy, good-looking boy who ate and slept well and said a few words" underwent a startling transformation. At first, he was steady and quiet and was open to Mary, the friendly, eighteen-year-old nurse who came to dress him the first morning, and to Christine, who fed him breakfast. Yet the turnover of nurses—four in one day—was unsettling to John, as were the constant commotion and the slaps and pinches he sustained from the other children, who had spent most of their lives there. The nurses overlooked him for the children who cried louder than he, and by day three John had abandoned his early attempts to connect with the other children or his caregivers.

"On the fourth day there was marked deterioration," Robertson writes. "There were lengthy spells of sad crying which merged with the din of the other children and went unnoticed by the nurses. His play was listless; he sucked more, and his fingers often strayed over his face and eyes." Several times, he crawled under a table to cry by himself. By day five, instead of reaching for a human, he found a teddy bear larger than himself for comfort, and he spent his time twisting and pulling the bear's arms around himself in an attempt at solace. When his father visited that night, John slapped and pinched him.

John refused to eat for the duration of his stay, which he spent alternately crying, huddling against the bear, falling to the ground in despair, and squirming away from nurses who tried to hold him. When John's mother finally returned on the ninth day, he struggled against her embrace, arching his back away from her and crying. Nurses said that John was a typical case.

Robertson learned through follow-up visits that John continued to show signs of insecurity and anger for months. He threw tantrums and was "destructive and aggressive in his play." Three years after his stay, he was fearful of his mother leaving and was upset when she was not where he expected her to be, but he would also go through phases of marked aggression toward her lasting several days. Robertson feared that he had been damaged irreparably—after only nine days.

Despite the fact that children like John had always expressed a range of negative emotions while being hospitalized without their parents or living in large residential nurseries, the professional establishments were strangely unmoved by the suffering of children in these situations. Some felt that the child's difficulty was only temporary and would have no real impact. Some thought the trauma of separation couldn't possibly make an impression on someone so young. Another view was that a child's fussiness was an inborn temperament that couldn't be changed, and therefore, the child's sensitivity would present itself no matter the circumstance.

"Regardless of what theories people adhered to in order to maintain this emotional distance, it seems plain now that the distance was needed because the suffering of children, especially when it is great, is terrible to witness," writes Robert Karen in his comprehensive and illuminating history of attachment theory, *Becoming Attached: First Relationships and How They Shape Our Capacity to Love*. "Even to see a little baby not have his spontaneous gestures responded to is heartrending; and the decline that follows is much worse."

As Karen points out, a child-care worker exposed to such circumstances on a daily basis builds a callous. "To have to experience for forty hours a week the agony of a child who is too depressed to eat is a great deal to endure," Karen explains. "Some way must be found to defend oneself from empathizing with such pain or life will not seem livable." Over time, workers are overwhelmed with the task of caring for more children than they are able to manage. Over time, they become what Robertson calls occupationally blind—and, one could add, deaf.

And so John's cries go unheard, and Jacob's cries go unheard, and eventually, if they are left long enough, the cries will cease.

By the time Robertson's film appeared in 1969, certain child psychologists and doctors ahead of their time had amassed decades of empirical research and writing about the damages done to children in institutional settings. Sadly, the inertia of old ideas and modes of operation were powerful. Any effort to make institutional child care more attentive, individual, loving, and constant would require radical paradigm shifts, including expensive increases in labor, uncomfortable changes in routine, and new ways of seeing children. Because of this, children's advocates faced a long trek, one that was uneven and uphill. While they had made some progress, much of their work was highly contested and contributed more to debate than to true reform.

Ironically, films like Robertson's had the most impact. Only after seeing the contorted faces of suffering children projected on a screen in a room where no child was present, with the child's cries muted by the silent film stock, were doctors and nurses able to truly see and hear the children's pain. Only then were governments willing to institute changes, to admit that children were sensitive, sentient beings who suffered just like their parents. Somehow, *John* struck that chord. "Horrifying," said a reviewer in the *British Journal of Psychiatric Social Work*: "What is so frightening is that the behaviour of the young nurses is kindly, but the system results in total failure to meet John's need of a stable substitute mother." *Child Care* magazine reviewed the film similarly. "John is an individual who is defeated by a system which fails to recognize or meet his needs," the reviewer says. "The nursery can be seen as a microcosm of many other caring institutions, and perhaps of a society itself and the many thousands who are damaged." The film pierced so many defenses and disturbed the psychiatric community to such an extent that within a few years, social service departments in

Britain began closing residential nurseries, and fostering became the officially approved form of care.

John was something of a turning point in policy, and an important one, but the fight had begun much earlier. In 1951, a British psychoanalyst named John Bowlby had taken up the banner of deprived children and marched into the fray with a report for the World Health Organization called *Maternal Care and Mental Health*. After finishing his training as a Freudian psychoanalyst, Bowlby began working at a child guidance center in London in 1936, where he noticed that disruptions in the mother-child bond were seriously debilitating to children. Over the next fifteen years, Bowlby spotted problems throughout the system, and the 1951 report was a compilation of findings he'd gathered from social workers and child psychiatrists in Europe and America. Detailing the damage done to children raised in institutions or traumatically separated from their primary caregivers, "Bowlby admonished governments, social agencies and the public for their failure to appreciate the central value of maternal care," explains Karen, "as important for mental health in infancy and childhood 'as are vitamins and proteins for physical health.'"

Bowlby was an unconventional candidate to lead the charge for change, since his professional training in Freudian psychoanalysis would insist that the root of psychological disturbance lay in the unconscious, internal life, rather than in external experience. But early in his career, Bowlby had been influenced by Nobel laureates Konrad Lorenz and Niko Tinbergen, natural scientists who, after studying the bonding of birds, had moved away from the idea of instinct, which implied behavior that was hardwired and inevitable, toward the concept of "species-specific behavior," a trait that is instinctive but not a *fait accompli*. "In order to come into being it must encounter certain responses in the environment," Karen explains. "Thus, the song a chaffinch will sing is limited to a certain range and quality by its genetic predisposition. But it must hear the song of an adult chaffinch if its song is to develop at all."

Straddling a controversial line between behaviorists, who saw human development as conditioned by the environment, and biological determinists, who saw things like temperament and intelligence as inborn, Bowlby realized that "people, too, must have bonding behaviors and intergenerational cues, that they, too, must be prewired for some sort of relational experience, and that with them, too, nature's intentions could go awry if the environment failed them," writes Karen. Bowlby began to argue that species-specific behavior in humans involved the attachment between a child and the primary caregiver, usually the mother. Because it is biologically necessary for survival, the baby finds a relationship with a primary caregiver intensely satisfying; therefore, obtaining love and security from a caregiver is something a child desperately needs. But if a child misses the opportunity to attach to another human being in its first few years, the child will have serious difficulty building healthy, fulfilling relationships later in life. Children with abusive or incompetent parents are at risk for poor attachment and may face other psychological traumas or illnesses. But children raised in institutional settings are the most vulnerable to missing the opportunity for attachment altogether, and, as Bowlby sought to prove in his later work, in some cases they become emotionally disturbed, even exhibiting psychopathic behavior.

When Bowlby's report was issued, the predominant practices and policies in hospitals and nurseries couldn't have been less concerned with the child's emotional life. In the West, the discovery of germs in the mid-nineteenth century was instrumental in combating the spread of disease, which affected all infants but especially those in institutions. "The frustrating, impossible, terrible thing about orphanages could be summarized like this: They were baby killers," writes Deborah Blum in *Love at Goon Park*, her biography of Harry Harlow and his experiments with rhesus monkeys. The centuries-long problem of infant mortality in orphanages across Western Europe and America was harrowing, with rates of 50 and 70 percent reported into the late nineteenth century, and "yet babies, toddlers, elementary school children, and even adolescents kept coming to foundling homes, like a ragged, endless, stubbornly hopeful parade," writes Blum. For doctors and child-care workers, the mortality rate was a baffling prospect—until Pasteur and company explained the presence of microscopic pathogens that could be passed from person to person, causing illness and death.

But by the early twentieth century, child-care authorities had reached what could be called an overcorrection. Medical experts advised parents to touch their children as little as possible. "Sterility and isolation became the gods of hospital practice," writes Blum, especially in pediatric wards. According to Karen, it was common practice at New York's Bellevue Hospital for nurses and doctors to be masked and scrubbed and to wear a white lab coat specifically assigned for each child to prevent the spread of bacteria. Like Jacob, babies were prop fed in many residential facilities, which reduced potential bacterial transmission but also saved labor.

In 1942, pediatrician Harry Bakwin published a paper entitled *Loneliness in*

Infants, a shocking assertion at a time when few professionals believed that infants could experience such emotions as loneliness, sadness, or grief. In it, Bakwin describes how procedures increasingly isolated the child from others, how staff used "a box equipped with inlet and outlet valves and sleeve arrangements for the attendants. The infant is placed in the box and can be taken care of almost untouched by human hands." Bakwin contended that children were suffering under such sterile, isolated conditions, but to most experts, who believed handling a child jeopardized its health, this sterile treatment seemed to be a true advance.

Despite the fact that these new standards seemed to contradict child-rearing practices over the course of millennia, such drastic isolation was not at odds with the advice of behaviorists, who oversaw the academic establishment of psychology. At the forefront of this movement was John B. Watson, who warned parents, especially mothers, of ruining their children through indulgent affection. In 1928 he published his best-selling *The Psychological Care of the Child and Infant,* endorsed by popular and wide-reaching platforms like the *New York Times* and *Parents* magazine. Watson insisted that instead of coddling children, it was the parents' responsibility to train their children the way they might train their pets, and the best thing was to push them toward independence from the day of their birth. Physicians were happily agreed, and government pamphlets advised the same.

Dovetailing with Watson's dispassionate advice was the widely accepted psychoanalytic theory that the child only preferred the mother because the mother provided food. The connection was simply a means to an end, a conditioned response, not a mystical bond between mother and child nor evidence that children needed love or security. In fact, the word "love" wasn't even in the vocabulary of psychology. (And it wouldn't be until Harry Harlow published his groundbreaking study in 1958, where infant monkeys spent sixteen to eighteen hours a day clinging to a terrycloth surrogate mother with no food, when a wire-mesh mother with milk sat just a few feet away.) "Medicine reinforced psychology; psychology supported medicine," Blum explains. Fears of poor hygiene, a growing belief that science could cure the world's ills, and the prevalence of behaviorist theory "all came together to create one of the chilliest possible periods in child-rearing."

In some ways, pediatricians and orphanage directors were accomplishing their goals. Through improved hygiene, the rates of infant mortality in institutions were dropping, from near 100 or 70 or 50 percent to 30. But many of the youngest and most fragile children were still dying, and it was perplexing why, in such sterile, hygienic environments, infant mortality hadn't been eradicated. Some assumed the babies were suffering from chronic infections, malnutrition, or the term used when the babies simply failed to thrive: hospitalism. But it was only when child psychologists began observing children separated from any affectionate care that they began making a connection between that and the downward spiral. At Bellevue, Harry Bakwin and his colleagues watched babies who were listless, unsmiling, sickly, and skinny in an institutional setting change within days of being placed into the hands of one affectionate caregiver in the hospital or in a good home. Fevers would disappear; the babies would become more animated and gain weight and develop better color in their faces.

Around the same time, Bill Goldfarb, a psychologist working with Jewish Family Services in New York City, began measuring the intellectual and psychosocial consequences of rearing children in institutions. He found that "institutionalized children at almost three years of age not only suffered from major deficits in their ability to form relationships and function maturely, but also had a mean IQ of 68, which is mildly retarded, while the mean IQ of a matched group of children in foster care was 96, which is average," writes Karen. Goldfarb followed two groups of children whose mothers had chosen not to parent the babies in infancy: "One group was raised in an institution until approximately three and a half, when they were placed in foster care. Babies in the other group were placed in foster homes as soon as their mothers gave them up. On each test of development—general intelligence, visual memory, concept formation, language ability, school adjustment—the figures revealed the damage done to institutionalized children and the benefits of foster care." The relationships of the institutionalized children were affected as well; thirteen of the fifteen were unable to form deep or lasting connections, a problem not found in the children who had been fostered.

As the number of studies grew, the pernicious effects of neglect, deprivation, and institutionalization continued to surface. Psychiatrists noticed a range of problems, from inadequate toilet training and indiscriminate affection—even to strangers in the street—to alarming aggression. There were various reports of language deficits. One was from Anna Freud, who observed delayed development of language in her home for children during World War II. Many parents sent their children to her home to protect them after their lives had been disrupted by the Blitz, but the children would visit their mothers periodically. "When the children are home on visits," Freud and her colleague Dorothy Burlington reported, "they sometimes gain in speech in one or two weeks what would have taken three months to gain in the nursery." There was nothing she and her colleagues could do to prevent the deterioration of the children, Freud told Bowlby. They believed the situation so grave, she concluded, that "It would be preferred to arrange for each helper to take a couple of children home with her and close the nursery." Yet this wouldn't happen on a large scale for another thirty years.

Bowlby's theory of attachment was highly contested for various reasons: by the psychoanalytic community for prioritizing reality over fantasy, by the feminist camp who felt his work shackled women to the home and demonized working mothers, and by the behaviorists and biological determinists who insisted on nurture *or* nature and not the interaction of the two. There were definitely blind spots in his theory, the most glaring of which was that he failed to note the role that fathers could play as primary or even secondary caregivers. But Bowlby's findings were a much-needed corrective. According to one analyst cited by Robert Karen, they were "refreshingly straightforward and tend, perhaps rather boringly, to be precisely what warm-hearted but naïve nonintellectuals have always thought."

Bowlby argued that children needed secure and affectionate care, and he advised mothers and fathers to do what mothers and fathers had been doing for thousands upon thousands of years: pick the child up when he cries; talk to the child in soft, endearing tones; soothe the child when she is tired, fearful, or distressed; and be a steady, safe refuge as the child comes to learn his place in the world.

❧ ❧ ❧

For Jacob, things could have been much different. What-ifs abound: what if he'd been born in a place where his birth defect had been accepted, to parents who were capable of staying by his side and nurturing him through his sickness, which might not have persisted so violently in the presence of love? What if Hong Kong had disbanded large institutions earlier, and he'd been fostered earlier and adopted earlier? What if that meant he'd learned to speak, to read Braille, and to develop the skills necessary to live independently as an adult? To hold a job and marry and have children of his own? But none of those things occurred. Instead, a young boy suffered tremendous deprivation, followed by tremendous struggles for him and everyone around him attempting to rectify the failure.

Jacob's story is utilitarian in its message. It benefits society in every way to care for its children, to help them learn and grow into healthy, well-adjusted adults who will participate in the workforce, contribute their individual gifts to the common good, have productive, fulfilling relationships, and raise children to do the same. But at the same time, the story is rooted in the ethical model of intrinsic virtue found in the Geneva Convention of the Rights of the Child, that the child has worth and deserves a high quality of life, that caring for a child has value in and of itself, that to discard a child—as unwanted or beyond hope—compromises the global human family and the inherent dignity of the individual, which is the foundation of any attempt at peace and justice.

CHAPTER 2

FIRST MOVEMENTS

❧

Peace is not a question of stopping this or that catastrophe, but of rediscovering a vision, a path of hope for all of humanity.

JEAN VANIER, *FINDING PEACE*

Grand Junction—Lausanne—The Middle East—
South Asia—Munich—Dallas—Grand Junction—Hong Kong

Gary Stephens met Helen Blackinton in late December of 1970 on a staircase leading to the basement kitchen of the Hotel du Golf, a small chalet seated on a hilltop and surrounded by the forests of Lausanne, Switzerland. Only twenty minutes after his arrival, on an introductory tour of what would be his home for the next eight months, they paused three steps from the top and were introduced by Gary's guide as fellow students. "Now I can't describe what she was wearing, but that's where I met her for the first time," Gary says. "She had long, light brown hair, and the same blue eyes." Then the brief hello was over, as she continued up and he headed down to the rooms beneath.

Their separate paths met at that pause on a stairway, and together, they would accomplish extraordinary things through hard work and sacrifice. But that day in Lausanne, Gary and Helen were young—just twenty-one and twenty-three—and unknown to one another. They were participating in a training school run by Youth With a Mission, a missionary organization similarly structured to the Peace Corps. Gary had joined somewhat suddenly, his older brother Don a huge influence to that end. Don and his wife Deyon had joined Youth With a Mission after Don graduated from Bethany University in Southern California in 1969. They spent the next year in Europe, studying foreign languages and spiritual formation. In the fall of 1970, they came back to the States to visit family and to share their experiences.

By then, Gary was attending the University of Colorado at Boulder. After high school, he had stayed closer to home, studying business at Mesa College in Grand Junction. His first foray away from Colorado was a semester he spent in California, living with Don and Deyon and attending Bethany, but when they went overseas, Gary returned to his mountain roots, finished his associate's degree at Mesa, and then transferred to Colorado with a four-year degree in mind.

Don and Deyon were different when they visited him that October. Gary distinguished a subtle change in character from when he'd lived with them just a year earlier—a noticeable difference in purpose and perspective. "They were more others conscious and less worried about themselves," Gary says. "I think they were softer as people, but more engaging, and that selflessness was a very positive, desirable characteristic for me." When he heard Don was speaking at a small country church near Boulder, hoping to recruit young people to the next training he and Deyon would help lead, Gary decided to attend. Maybe Don would describe the forces that had contributed to this transformation, Gary thought, and he was eager to listen.

So he went, and that night Don's message invoked the sixth chapter of Isaiah, where the Old Testament prophet has a vision of God surrounded by seraphim, the flaming birdlike creatures with six wings that encircle the throne of God. At the same time, the temple quakes and fills with smoke, as when God appeared in clouds to the exiled Israelites on Mount Sinai. Then one seraphim flies to Isaiah holding an ember and touches it to his lips, and it is in this moment that he is purified for his calling as a prophet. As God appeals for someone to be his messenger and move among his people, Isaiah is compelled to answer, "Here I am, Lord. Send me."

Gary calls this a "typical missionary text," and after hearing it again and again as a child, predictably repeated by each missionary who came to speak at his family church like a crier with his news, he was surprised at his response. "That night," he says, "I felt a tugging at my heart." The feeling was unexpected yet not unwelcome, and as they shared a meal the next day and he listened to Don and Deyon speak about their time in Europe and the Middle East, Gary felt an opening. He called his mother and father, who said they'd support him if he wanted to go. Gary thought they might not understand, so he added that he would withdraw from school immediately and get a job before departing. And they said, "Fine."

"Now, my folks are saying 'fine' to me withdrawing from college, which seems like a contradiction of Parenting 101," Gary says. "But Don and Deyon had already been in Grand Junction with Mom and Dad and they would have seen the same things that I had seen, and they understood." Gary went to the registrar the next day to withdraw from his classes, found someone to sublease his apartment, then packed all his belongings and drove west to earn money before he began the long trek east.

When Gary and Helen met three steps from the top of the staircase, it was only several weeks later, and Gary had just arrived for an eight-month training. Helen had joined a longer training; for the previous six months, she had been studying Spanish in Madrid. They became acquainted quickly. In the mornings they had classes together, at midday they were on the same lunch prep duty, and because they were the weekend cooks, they were together every Saturday and Sunday.

"We spent probably eighteen hours a day together for twelve weeks," Gary says, "even on the weekends." When they weren't in class or working, they played ping-pong, and she taught him to play chess. The quantity of time was great and easy to come by, but almost never were they alone. Separating themselves from the group was a challenge, not only because pairing off was discouraged by the leaders to avoid the temptation of sexual activity, but also because the community valued an atmosphere of inclusion. Everybody lived and worked and studied and prayed and socialized together. This type of community has its benefits: rarely are you lonely, rarely do you feel far from a friend willing to listen or console or advise. But downfalls exist as well. A budding relationship can feel crowded by so many eyes, as the community, with nothing but the best intentions, observes every interaction.

At the time, Don and Deyon's eldest child, Heidi, was about eighteen months old, and on afternoons when he had free time, Gary would place a bundled Heidi in a sling on his chest, wrap an overcoat around the both of them, and take walks through the snowy forests—a chilly but refreshing respite from community life. After several days, he asked Helen if she'd like to join them on the country lanes through forests of towering linden trees and the snug firs beneath. "My rationale was that there were going to be three of us and it was daylight," Gary says, laughing. "The fact that Heidi went to sleep within a hundred yards didn't matter." During this time alone, Gary began to see that Helen was, in his words, "a pretty phenomenal woman."

"She was very sincere in seeking God," Gary recalls. "I hadn't been around other women so sincere in their devotion to their faith."

Over the course of three months, they spent as much time together, Gary argues, as most couples who date for a couple of years but see each other only on the weekends. To observe the spiritual development of an individual, to witness the ideas and concepts impacting a person's heart and mind over a short period of time, was revelatory and provided an opportunity for deep and lasting intimacy. So it was that in March of 1971, while they were walking down forest trails with Heidi, Gary asked Helen how she'd feel about becoming the mother of his children. Unaware that the role would entail four biological children, a blind Chinese son, and thousands of others who would pass through the doors of the homes they would open for orphans and children with special needs, Helen answered, "Yes. Absolutely."

One Friday night soon after, Gary and Helen decided to sneak away the next morning to Lausanne's town center to look for rings. They were sufficiently young and eager, but as they were living on savings and meager support from friends and family, they had no plans to buy. Still, they awoke on Saturday and met downstairs in the hallway close to the mailboxes. They grabbed their coats from the hallway closet, and though Gary had checked his mail on Friday and had not received anything, he looked again. In the box was a white envelope with his name on it, though Stephens was misspelled, with a v instead of a ph. Inside there was no letter or note, only cash.

Gary and Helen read this as a sign. After the twenty-minute bus ride in, they found the jewelry shop, where they didn't look for diamonds, but abiding by the European custom instead, picked out a pair of simple gold rings with a delicate Florentine finish. They purchased the rings on the spot, and on the way home, despite the biting cold of early March in Switzerland, Helen took off her left glove and slid the band over her finger. As they walked up the street and caught the bus back to their chalet in the woods, Helen held his gloved hand with her bare one. Later, they would have one another's initials engraved inside the bands: HAS, for Helen Arlene Stephens, in his; GWS, for Gary Wayne Stephens, in hers.

And then, only two weeks into their engagement, they loaded into crowded vans and headed east from Lausanne, on the north shore of Lake Geneva, through Italy and the Balkans, Greece and Turkey, and then south to Israel, where they spent two weeks. They couldn't make specific arrangements while they were away, but they were able to set a date. "I think it was from Haifa in Israel that I called her parents and asked for their permission," Gary recalls. "And we told them our plan was to be married on June 6 in Lausanne." Because they'd be home fewer than the ten days needed to get a marriage license, they visited the Swiss consulate in Athens to fill out the necessary paperwork, which would be filed in Athens and then forwarded to Lausanne.

They arrived in Lausanne on a Tuesday, the first of June. Wednesday, they picked up Helen's parents, her two sisters, and her brother from the airport in Geneva. Thursday, they went to the registrar's office to see if their marriage had been authorized. "I said to the woman behind the desk, in my perfect French, 'Excuse me, do you speak English?'" Gary recalls, laughing. "And the woman said, 'You must be Mr. Stephens, and you must be Miss Blackinton. Your paperwork was finished this morning. You are free to get married.'"

On Sunday, June 6, they were married on the front lawn of the hotel. The wedding was simple and communal, allowing others to show their support for the marriage in concrete ways. Two of their fellow students arranged wildflowers they had gathered from the countryside around the chalet. One, who was a talented amateur photographer, took photos and gave them as a wedding gift. Another friend volunteered to bake the wedding cake, which was served in old-style silver champagne goblets from the hotel's wares, layered with whipped cream and strawberries. "That was our single largest expense—buying fresh strawberries for the cake," Gary says.

What Gary remembers most from that day is how graceful and blessed the union felt. Even the weather, which had been disagreeable all morning in the form of steady showers, relented. The rain cleared thirty minutes before the ceremony, and the clouds parted briefly as the sun came out. After the ceremony, the clouds closed up, and the rain continued.

But inevitably, the worries of the world intruded. "I remember having tea with Helen's very pragmatic father at the hotel," Gary says, "and he asked me, 'What's your education? Do you intend to go back to university and finish? How are you going to provide for my daughter?' In my heart I was saying, 'Come on— I love her!'" But answering was difficult. Gary had spent three years at college, which had earned him a two-year degree. Helen also had an associate's degree, but one that guaranteed her a profession as a nurse. "I was a registered jack-of-all-trades, master of none," Gary says.

Gary told Helen's father he wasn't sure how things would work out because he didn't know *how;* he was simply confident that they *would.* Devoted to one another and to their shared faith, he and Helen were beginning a journey, the end of which they could not begin to foresee, the breadth of which they had not the hubris to imagine, and the depth of which they could only reach with unshakable commitment and resolve. Over the next months and years and even decades, they would see what Paul Auster, the absurdist and existentialist writer, calls "rhyming events," moments where the sheer mathematical improbability of a circumstance is too great to comprehend how it actually occurred. The world repeats itself, or an unlikely pathway opens up, and that, perhaps, reveals a larger intention at work—called by some fate, by others divine providence, by the rest given no name and instead handled with a shrug of the shoulders and a steady gaze forward.

❧ ❧ ❧

Gary and Helen have never been idlers. They fill their days with work, their evenings with family, their vacations with friends. This constant motion was especially apparent in the first five years of their married life, which were a blur of movement back and forth across the Northern Hemisphere. They spent several months traveling from Lausanne to India and Afghanistan in 1971, and afterward they moved to Southern Germany in preparation for a large outreach during the 1972 Munich Olympics. There, Youth With a Mission bought a sixteenth-century castle, and Gary and Helen were responsible for setting up accommodations and stocking the larders with food for over one thousand people. The Olympics arrived with the usual fanfare, yet on September 5, they watched with the rest of the world as eleven Israeli athletes were taken hostage by eight members of the Black September group. Gary even found himself among the Munich sharpshooters, looking into the windows of the apartments in the Olympic Village. After the eleven hostages were killed, as well as five of the Palestinians and one Munich police officer, "We got permission to hold a peace march through the downtown streets of Munich carrying flowers," Gary says, "to try to speak peace into a volatile situation." Witnessing this conflict strengthened their resolve to lead lives of service, to do what they could to meet the many needs they saw in a suffering world.

Their next project took them back to the States. In December of 1972, they moved to Dallas, Texas, as directors of a Youth With a Mission program that sent groups to universities to help local Christian groups share their faith on campuses. These were their first months as a couple in their home country, but soon, they added a third member to the family: their eldest daughter, Shawna, was born in December of 1973. Eight months later they moved again, taking a sabbatical from full-time missionary life and returning to Gary's home state of Colorado. For the first time, their lives were conventional—Helen worked at St. Mary's Hospital in

Grand Junction as a nurse, and Gary found a job as a field engineer for an oil and gas company.

But conventional didn't last long. Near the end of 1975, Loren Cunningham, the founder of Youth With a Mission, asked Gary to rejoin the organization and work as his personal assistant. The decision to accept came easily. "Here was a man who had become a statesman in the faith world, inviting me to work with him," Gary says, "and it was an opportunity for mentorship." They moved from Colorado to Hawaii, where Youth With a Mission had a large base on the big island of Hawaii, in the Kona district. Gary helped run training schools like the one he had participated in several years earlier in Lausanne, and Helen managed the facilities at Kona. In the meantime, their family continued to grow. In February of 1978, Helen gave birth to their second daughter, Amy.

During this time, Gary began traveling extensively; for the next twenty years, he would be gone up to seventy percent of the time, leading schools on three-month outreaches or traveling to sites under consideration for new satellite locations or service opportunities. Gary's absence from home was something both he and Helen accepted as a matter of course, a necessary sacrifice for the work they had chosen. "We were in this together," Gary says. "Helen has always said, 'If you feel like this is something you feel truly called to do, I'm with you 100 percent,' even if she knew that it was going to mean more responsibility for her. She knows I'd do the same for her."

But even with that commitment, Gary's departure for Hong Kong in December of 1979, ten days after the birth of his son, Andrew, is difficult to comprehend. Just a few months earlier, in August of 1979, Loren Cunningham and Gary's brother Don had traveled to Southeast Asia after hearing about camps of Vietnamese and Cambodian refugees popping up across the region. Afterward Don headed back to Germany, where he was working, and Loren to Hawaii, both to share with their communities the desperate situations they had witnessed.

"The night Loren returned, he spoke with so much passion and emotion, was so moved to recount what he had seen firsthand," Gary recalls. "He showed us pictures of the conditions of people in the refugee camps—of little ones, older ones, in crowded, filthy conditions—and these people were fleeing for their lives. If you watched those slides and heard his words and it did not impact you deeply, there was something wrong with you."

Gary was leading the current training school, and he gathered his staff immediately. Unanimously they felt that for their twelve-week outreach, they should take their students to work in one of the refugee camps. From dry and rugged Western Colorado, the oft-repeated, traditional wisdom of Gary's father, unsurprisingly terse and sensibly efficient, was apropos. "My dad would say, 'Don't just stand there; do something.' It's a great old close-to-the-soil comment from parents to kids, and that's been in me for a long time now," Gary explains. "Another: 'Talk is cheap.' I've got friends around the world who talk about issues all over the world. But all they do is talk about issues. And that's not the bolt of cloth I'm cut from. We saw the conditions of those refugees, and we thought, 'We're here, we've got all these people. Why don't we figure out how we can help?'"

After consulting with Loren and other leaders, Gary and his team decided they would go to Hong Kong. Four days later, Gary and a colleague flew to Hong Kong for a three-day assessment. They met a man named Bill Mortson, who was working for the International Rescue Committee, a worldwide nonprofit managing a refugee camp called Jubilee in Kowloon, part of peninsular Hong Kong, and he took them through the facilities. "In person, it was worse than what Loren showed us," Gary says. Mortson lamented the horrid conditions of the camp, where almost nine thousand refugees were living in two condemned apartment buildings built for three hundred, but he was shorthanded and short of funds. "We'd love your help, but we can't pay," Mortson said. Gary explained that the group he had were volunteers and wouldn't cost them anything. "Then we can use as many as you can bring," Mortson said.

They returned to Hawaii and shared what they had seen, which confirmed for everyone the decision to serve in Hong Kong. The group would leave in mid-December. They planned an initial three-month outreach with the current school, and another team would join them in April of 1980.

Then, on the ninth of December, Andrew was born. "I tried not to think about it too much," Gary says, "but saying good-bye to your wife, your six-year-old, your two-year-old, and your ten-day-old baby was challenging. But I knew I had to lead these people because I had been training them. I couldn't send them if I was not willing to go." They bought tickets on Braniff International Airways nonstop from Honolulu to Hong Kong, leaving on December 19, 1979.

❀ ❀ ❀

By December of 1979, over half a dozen refugee camps had been established in Hong Kong, and a dozen more stretched down through Thailand, Malaysia, Singapore, and up to the Philippines. People had been fleeing Vietnam since before the fall of Saigon on April 30, 1975, the first wave being those associated directly with the South Vietnamese and American governments. Many of these refugees were quickly resettled in the United States. Then a deceptive calm spread out for several months. It wasn't until over a year later, in July of 1976, that the government in Hanoi began instituting in earnest more repressive political and economic policies: stripping South Vietnam of any residual autonomy, placing citizens in reeducation camps, forcing people to relocate from urban areas into the new economic zones in the countryside, and seizing private businesses.

In *Voices from the Camps,* James M. Freeman and Nguyen Dinh Huu argue that these policies resulted directly in "unemployment and poverty, massive food shortages, and numerous healthcare crises, including extensive malnutrition." So the massive exodus continued. Some went north overland to China, but the majority boarded boats, from large steel freighters that packed over two thousand people in a single journey to slow-moving wooden junks overloaded with human cargo. The refugees were extremely vulnerable once on the water, and during their perilous journey, they would be forced to endure the dangerous storms and swirling tides of the South China Sea, to elude shore guards and coastal patrols who might send them back, and to evade pirates who would rape and murder and steal any valuables on board. Most often there was not much to take; after scraping together everything they could to pay the fares and bribes necessary to secure a place on a boat—an amount ranging from $2400 to $3000—many of the boat people had only the clothes on their backs. If a boat made it past all of these obstacles, there was still no guarantee that they would find refuge. Sometimes a boat would near a shore—say Singapore or Malaysia—and a government vessel would approach; only, instead of offering aid or asylum, the ship would tow them farther out to sea, to be carried away to another shore, to be someone else's problem.

The harbors of Hong Kong were soon inundated. On June 25, 1977, an article in the *South China Morning Post,* an English-language newspaper in Hong Kong, warned of a "Vietnamese armada" composed of more than five thousand refugees "in vessels of all shapes and sizes sailing toward Hong-kong." Many of these refugees had heard they'd be given safe haven for at least three months and be cared for by Hong Kong's social welfare establishment, which had a much better track record than those of Thailand or Malaysia. By July 31, 1979, the number of Vietnamese who fled by boat had reached almost three hundred thousand. By

1995, that number would reach nearly eight hundred thousand, one-quarter of whom landed on the shores of craggy, crowded, cosmopolitan Hong Kong.

Many of the refugees to Hong Kong were ethnic Chinese whose ancestors had settled in Vietnam in the late eighteenth and early nineteenth centuries. Their reasons for fleeing were twofold. First, economic policy came into play: their history as merchants and businesspeople drew the ire of Ho Chi Minh's anticapitalist regime. Second, their ancestry became a problem: after a month-long border conflict between Vietnam and China at the beginning of 1979, Chinese residents of Vietnam left to avoid reprisals. They bought and bribed their way onto boats, and after days or weeks on open water, overcrowded, without proper food, water, or sanitation, the people who actually made it ashore found themselves in refugee camps where conditions were not much better. Though the Hong Kong camps had the reputation of being the most humane, allowing the refugees to come and go freely and to find work outside the camp, the facilities were entirely substandard, like all the others across the region.

Jubilee Refugee Camp was made up of two identical four-story buildings, sitting back-to-back and separated by a ten-foot-wide alley. Built for British police cadets and their families in the early 1900s, the buildings had been condemned by the Hong Kong government and had been in disuse for many years. Like most camps in Hong Kong, the area was surrounded by wire fences, with guards checking identification upon entrance and exit and locking the gates at evening curfew. Inside, the overcrowding was unimaginable. In the two buildings, there were a total of forty-eight apartments, each with high ceilings and three bedrooms and bathrooms. "That meant 144 bedrooms and 144 bathrooms for 8,800 people," Gary explains. "Each bedroom had three or four triple-decker bunks, approximately three feet wide. Each level had a different family assigned it, which meant there were about thirty-six families per apartment—a space meant for a single family."

On their first day at Jubilee, Mortson, the camp administrator, reaffirmed that he couldn't pay but said he could provide the volunteers with rubber boots and rubber gloves. "I remember thinking, *Why in the world would we want rubber boots and gloves?*" Gary says. The answer was almost immediately apparent. Soon after they arrived, they began surveying the grounds to determine their first task, then tried to cut through the alley between the two buildings. They found it impassable. "There was water six or eight inches deep with raw human waste floating in it," Gary said. "Soon we discovered that the sewer lines underground were plugged." They also noticed standing water on the floors of the outdoor kitchen areas, where the refugees were using 220-volt rice cookers to prepare their staple food. The cookers sat on solid cement blocks the size of small tables, and the women used these as surfaces upon which to prepare meals.

These might have been the only surfaces available, but they were a miserable substitute for even a clean patch of dirt. The cement blocks were a base for cast-iron sewer pipes which ran down the side of the building from three stories above, through the cement blocks, and into the sewer system below. These pipes were eighty years old, revealed by the letters cast in capitals: ERI, for *Eduardus Rex et Imperatur,* Edward VII, king of England and its empire from 1901–1910. After eight decades weathering warm and cool, sunshine and monsoon, the pipes had cracked, and raw sewage ran down the sides and gathered in fetid pools on the cement blocks.

"This was an accident waiting to happen," Gary says. "Someone was going to get electrocuted. People were going to die from infection." So they looked around and discovered manholes beneath the raw sewage in the alley. One team member went to a nearby local market and bought long coiled bamboo about three feet in diameter. "We started running that bamboo up and down the buried sewer line like a pushrod until we broke through whatever was blocking it," Gary explains. "After a couple of days, we got this unblocked. By the time we got to the last few, we had some refugees working with us because they saw that we were trying to help."

All the standing liquid was now able to drain, but it didn't stop the cracked cast-iron pipes from leaking sewage down the pipes and the sides of the building or stop the sewage from pooling on the blocks where people prepared their food. But as would often happen in the coming years when there was a need with no apparent solution, someone stepped forward with an idea. One of the team members, a man named Joe who hailed from a town in Montana almost on the Canadian border, had once worked in a body shop where they used Bondo, a plastic putty, to build a solid surface in metal. He believed he could use a similar tactic on the pipes if they lowered him from a rope down the side of the building. "So we put a sling together, lowered him off the roof, and he used a grinder to make the cast-iron pipe smooth," Gary recalls. "Then he used putty to fill the cracks."

Once they stopped the blocked and leaking sewage, the grounds dried and conditions were much improved. They then began sanitizing everything: people scrubbed walls, pipes, and surrounding cement with steel-bristled brushes and buckets of bleach. The work was difficult and exhausting, but Gary and his team knew that the filthy conditions were inhumane and only exacerbated the trauma and hopelessness that the refugees were suffering.

Believing they could use their hands to show God's love in the world, they continued to travel to the camp each day from where they were staying on Nathan Road in the vicarage at St. Andrew's Anglican Church. Emptied after the vicar had moved to a more fashionable high-rise, the two-story red-brick house with an arcaded verandah was normally a calm place, set back and secluded from bustling Nathan Road. Yet they stuffed it to the brim: with over thirty people in the four bedrooms and living rooms, many had to sleep on floors. But they were there to work, not for a vacation with luxury accommodations, and their time at Jubilee was a constant reminder to be ever grateful, even in difficult circumstances.

At Jubilee, the disrepair of the buildings was a continuing problem, mostly because the broken-down facilities simply could not accommodate the number of people packed inside. Often the work that was necessary to establish humane standards was difficult beyond imagining. "When we would go up on the roofs of the buildings, we would often find clumps of human waste up there," Gary recalls. "I remember one day in the camp in early 1980, being up on the roof of one of the buildings, and I actually completely shut down. I knew I couldn't feel or think right then—I just had to *do*. I remember cleaning feces ungloved, and in the back of my mind wondering if I'd even do this for my kids. And then I told myself to shut up."

Gary discovered the reason for the unsanitary rooftop conditions soon after. One day in the first few weeks of work, he left one building and walked into the equivalent hallway in the other, where he noticed an open door to a bathroom. Yet in the building he had just left, the door had been bound with wire to keep it closed. "Remember, the two buildings were identical—each floor, each hallway, each apartment, each door," Gary says. "So we got some wire cutters and forced the closed doors opened, and yes, they were bathrooms too, but they were filled with human waste piled two to three feet deep." A thorough assessment of the bathrooms in both buildings revealed there were only nine toilets working—only nine out of the total of 144 were functional for 8,800 people. Quickly, they acquired bamboo baskets lined with plastic bags and rubber gloves and shovels and emptied the rooms, but the floors and walls were covered with miniature tiles—little one-inch-square tiles, with the spaces between filled with grout.

"So once we got all the waste out of there, it was hands and knees scouring the walls and the floors," Gary recalls. "I walked into one of the bathrooms one day in early January, and I was talking to one of our team leaders, a woman from Richmond, Virginia, named Janet. Janet had her nose buried in the left elbow of her flannel shirt and was scouring with her right hand. Then after a few minutes, she switched and scoured with her left hand and buried her nose in her right elbow. Suddenly the man next to her said, 'Janet, I need your elbow.' And he buried his nose in the crook of her arm, inhaled deeply, then left. I said, 'Janet, what's going on with your elbow?' She told me that every morning before she left where we were staying, she would sprinkle a few drops of perfume on the inside sleeve of each elbow, and that's how she made it through the day."

At a certain point, they were able to move their focus away from sanitizing the facilities, and people on their team began employing their own skill sets for the benefit of the refugees. One couple on the team—the husband was a doctor and the wife a nurse—opened and staffed a makeshift medical clinic. A dentist set up a chair to examine and work on the refugees' teeth. One of their team members was a social worker from Canada who started offered counseling. "Anybody who had a skill set like this, we put immediately to work," Gary says. "People who didn't have an immediately useful skill set, like me, they were manual laborers."

Another major addition to the camp was a preschool that some team members with backgrounds in early childhood education created in an abandoned double-decker bus. With no seats, motor, or wheels, the red frame sat on the ground ready to be transformed, and using it to serve young children seemed most appropriate.

Many of the adult refugees were moving in and out of the camp daily. "At the time, the unemployment rate in Hong Kong was virtually zero," Gary recalls, "and because the camp was an open camp, it was quite possible for the refugees to go out and find work, doing menial jobs or maybe even putting their specific skill set to work—whatever it was they did in Vietnam." But the children of the camp had few options for how to spend each day. According to the United Nations High Commissioner for Refugees, these most vulnerable of all refugees are guaranteed certain rights: the right to adequate food, housing, health care, and conditions that promote mental health. Providing educational opportunities for children is therefore the responsibility of the country of asylum, yet this does not always happen. With the preschool, Gary's team was filling another void in the camp. The team members behind the effort took pains to make it comfortable and pleasant; they carpeted the bus and painted the inside with the letters of the Roman alphabet, with different fruits and plants and animals. For the children, the preschool was a cheerful and productive break from the poverty and chaos that surrounded them.

❧ ❧ ❧

In mid-February of 1980, halfway through that first three-month service, Gary got a free flight from a refugee service back to Hawaii to see Helen, his daughters, and his son, Andrew. "Here's my little baby boy who I haven't seen in seven weeks," Gary recalls with tenderness. "He's changed enormously from a little infant into a chubby, two-month old baby." The reunion was sweet, but his time at home was short and stressful. He was in Hawaii for only two weeks; then he would return to Hong Kong in early March for another six months. Because of the continuing need and the effectiveness of their work, the original team had decided to stay on, and another group—called the Far East Evangelism Team, with twenty-six members—would arrive in April. They would have twice the manpower, but Gary would also have twice as many people to lead.

This time he would not leave Helen and the kids in Hawaii. They would be joining him in Hong Kong in a matter of weeks, so while he was home, they made arrangements for the move. They pared their belongings down to the clothes that would fit inside their two matching suitcases and a stereo (their prize possession). They gave their Mazda station wagon to the principal of the Youth With a Mission school. Then Gary departed, taking six-year-old Shawna with him.

They flew back to Hong Kong three weeks ahead of Helen, Amy, and Andrew. Shawna moved into the vicarage with the rest of the original team of thirty, and each day, Shawna went to the refugee camp and stuck close by Gary's side. For a little girl whose experience had been defined by the stability and security of life ringed by the blue Pacific and a mother's steady arms, Shawna was understandably uncertain. The vicarage was full of unfamiliar faces, and the camp was chaotic compared to her previous surroundings. "I remember one day, she and I were painting silver oxide paint on the corrugated tin that was covering the trash receptacles," Gary says, "and these refugees would come up and pinch her cheeks. And she asked me, 'Dad, what should I do?' I said, 'Pinch their cheeks back—play with them.'" Over thirty years later, Shawna feels gratitude for this exposure to the myriad cultures in Hong Kong and their diverse religious faiths. Attending an international school in one of the most international cities in the world was a chance to explore the complexities of culture and belief in nuanced and profound ways. "I don't think I could have had a better childhood," Shawna says.

❀ ❀ ❀

A few weeks after Gary and Shawna returned to Hong Kong, Helen and the rest of the family arrived with the new team—but the vicarage was already beyond capacity with thirty people. Now that there were sixty, it was untenable to stay there. They began looking for permanent accommodation for the group, including Gary and Helen and their three young children. Temporarily, they were given shelter on Hong Kong Island, in a Catholic retreat center run by Salesian monks. For two weeks, they could rely on floor space for sleeping bags and a roof over their heads while they continued looking for something more permanent, yet with such a large group and limited funds, finding themselves homeless was a looming prospect.

It was during this time that Amy, who was two-and-a-half, fell and injured her front teeth on some concrete steps, an event incidental in itself but the impetus for an important discovery. Worried about long-term damage to Amy's teeth, Gary and Helen jumped in a taxi and rushed her to a dentist, who examined her and said all was well, that her baby teeth would fall out but her permanent teeth were uninjured. On the way back from the dentist, they drove past an unfamiliar part of town—one which would soon become very familiar—and noticed a large building midway up the mountain. Not only by its size but also by its visibility at the top of a hill did it distinguish itself, and they asked the driver to wind his way up there.

It was the old British Military Hospital at 10 Borrett Road; the actual medical center had moved to Kowloon in 1967, leaving the facility vacant. They surveyed the complex: three stories of solid red brick with arcaded verandahs, with two long wings and a two-story building in the middle. At the promontory to the far left, the former home of the commodore of the British navy sat a few feet below the level of the hospital. Gary and Helen took down the address, then loaded back up in the taxi. They wound back down Borrett Road, which spilled onto Kennedy Road, and after a few minutes, they noticed other colonial-era buildings also sitting empty. These were smaller: they were two-story brick-and-mortar buildings painted white, containing four apartments, all constructed in the late nineteenth century as a part of the Victoria Barracks to house the British army. Again, they took down the address, 7A Kennedy Road, and returned to the taxi.

Gary called the Government Property Association the next morning, a Friday, and spoke to the director's assistant, a man named John Gilbert. He explained who they were, what they were doing, and that they only had accommodations until the following Saturday. He asked if the government would give them use of the vacant apartments so they could continue their work. Gilbert answered, "Let me check." He followed that with, "Don't call me. I'll call you." So Gary let it rest and continued pursuing any facility they could find to house sixty people. "On Thursday, only two days before we were without shelter, we still had nothing, and I was seriously sweating it," Gary says, "and I was asking myself, 'What am I going to do with all these people? We have nowhere to stay!'" He had no connections to fall back on, so that afternoon, as others ate lunch and returned to work, Gary secluded himself for a few hours to fast and pray.

Somehow he fell asleep, and his next memory is of Helen coming in to wake him. "Someone called from this number," she said. "I think it's John Gilbert." Gary hurriedly returned the call.

"It's yours," was Gilbert's answer. He said they could stay in the vacant buildings free of charge and told Gary where to get the keys. Immediately, Gary put on his seersucker leisure suit and raced to the designated office. On Saturday morning they moved in at 7A Kennedy Road, where they would stay until the end of 1980. The entire group was a hive of activity, as some moved luggage, some went shopping for chopsticks and soupspoons, some headed to the grocery.

On Kennedy Road, Gary and Helen found themselves in a city where the language and customs were unfamiliar. They planned to work hard for a season, meeting the needs of thousands of people in crisis, then return to Hawaii. Yet Hong Kong would soon become home. And though they would move from one colonial structure to another, and though some spaces were spacious and others very, very small, Helen, Gary, and their children would soon understand the meaning of provision. Beginning in 1980, their entire family lived rent free in Hong Kong, one of the most expensive cities in the world. That continued for twenty-three years.

CHAPTER 3

HOME

❖

People who are powerless and vulnerable attract what is most beautiful and luminous in those who are stronger: they call them to be compassionate, to love intelligently, and not only in a sentimental way. Those who are weak help those who are capable discover their own humanity and to leave the world of competition in order to put their energies at the service of love, justice, and peace.

JEAN VANIER, *THE SCANDAL OF SERVICE: JESUS WASHES OUR FEET*

Western Colorado

In the southwest corner of Colorado, Telluride's Ute Park stretches high up the mountainside, with gentle, broad ski runs and stunning views of the surrounding peaks. When the sun is out, the sky is cobalt against the brilliant whitecaps of the San Juan Mountains, some of the most rugged of the Rockies. But on a Friday in mid-February, the peaks are veiled by a curtain of snowfall. At the edges of the run, a line of tall, thin evergreens, a combination of Engelmann spruces and Rocky Mountain firs, forms a fence. Dense and unbroken, the sky is pale gray, only shades darker than the ground, and in the diffuse light, most objects are colorless. The deep greens and browns of the trees are muted, almost black, and the few people out are simply dark silhouettes ahead of them.

Jacob can't see these details, but he can feel the snow as it falls steadily and is driven sideways by the constant wind. He turns his head slightly to the left to keep the flakes from his face and begins humming softly. Side by side, Jacob and Gary glide easily from left to right down the slope. With Gary on his right, Jacob's carriage stands tall, his left hand raised from the elbow and his gloved fingers working themselves one over the other. As they near the left edge, Gary says calmly, "Right hand turn, right hand turn."

So Jacob knows he is beside him, Gary holds Jacob gently by his right elbow. Gary guides him toward the middle, and as they straighten out, Jacob's left hand drops. He is relaxed and steady as they pick up speed down the middle of the slope, then coast to the right. It has been a week since Telluride has seen snowfall, and because the snow is packed and icy, they're moving fast, approaching twenty miles an hour down the steeper inclines. The run opens up and flattens out as they reach the bottom, where they make their way to the lift. Jacob knows the routine. He sits when he feels the chair hit the back of his legs, and when they reach the top, Gary holds his arm and counts to three as the chair nears the dismount. They stand and glide down, and Jacob is impatient to begin again.

✿ ✿ ✿

Several years ago, Gary and Helen couldn't have imagined such a day. But Jacob's is a story of growth and reconciliation. Because Jacob doesn't speak, it's difficult to know how hard the journey has been; whether he ever felt secure or comforted as he moved between hospitals and child-care facilities, or if his whole existence, from waking to erratic and fitful sleep, was fearful, stressed, and uncertain. From the day he came into their care, they have had to imagine what it's like for him, to observe and intuit what might set him off. Sixteen years after leaving the child-care facility for mentally disabled children, an area about the size of a palm on the back of his head is still flat from lying on his back in the crib, and various problems—physical and psychosocial, but more than anything, neurological—have presented themselves over time, some that have eased and others that have persisted. For years he was sick with chronic chest infections and pneumonia three weeks out of a month. Situations that normal children would take in stride—like eating outside the home or walking up a flight of stairs—would leave him physically and emotionally exhausted. He was anxious, had trouble sleeping, and threw tantrums to try the patience of a saint.

As his primary caregiver, Helen struggled with seeing him this distressed and pursued anything that might bring Jacob comfort and repose, with varying results. After a blood test showed he would be better without dairy, she changed his diet, and his illnesses decreased significantly. She met with counselors who observed Jacob's tantrums and told Helen that it was okay to let him release his frustration and rage, and over time, as she instituted strict routines, they decreased. Because he resisted change, she introduced him to new situations slowly. When they moved from a log cabin on a hilltop outside of Montrose to their current home, they introduced the new house gradually over the course of a week, bringing him to the new house for a meal, then a meal and a bath, and finally to stay. Because he struggled with sleep and moods, Helen contacted two naturopathic physicians, one of whom enrolled him in a research study that monitored his serotonin and dopamine levels and prescribed supplements for him to take five times a day. For six years, Helen opened nineteen capsules a day and mixed the contents with water so that Jacob, who couldn't swallow pills, could take the supplements. She was relieved when the study ended; it had been a valiant attempt, but not nearly as effective as they had hoped. Jacob was still anxious, still high-strung, still a poor sleeper. Currently he has an array of regular therapists—a psychiatrist, a psychotherapist, a speech therapist, an occupational therapist, and a mobility expert—as well a devoted team of special-education teachers and aides who all are looking for solutions. Often they are stymied by the many factors in Jacob's equation, and his inability to communicate only adds a layer of complexity.

Jacob's verbal skills are something Gary and Helen hoped to develop for many years after Jacob came to live with them, and in 2004, they had Jacob's brain mapped to determine if some sort of biofeedback therapy could help improve his brain function. The reading found a slowing over Broca's area, the part of the brain responsible for expressive language. Since Jacob is nonverbal, this was more of a confirmation than news. He has always understood what others said—at two years old, he'd make feeble attempts to stand up when his physical therapist in Hong Kong said *"Hei sun"* and helped him to his feet—but the way that Gary and Helen understand Jacob is by observing him, watching closely for signs of distress or delight, and through the few words he utters: *Mom, Dad, yeah, no,* and several that have appeared unexpectedly over time, like "to the bank," the number eleven, and "Becca," the name of his occupational therapist. He has a few other phonemes, mainly *dih* and *dah,* which he uses to mimic the rhythm and pitch of human speech. Like many children who develop institutionalized autism after neglect in orphanages, his language is esoteric; only the people closest to him can make out what he means. Some phrases are distinctive, and strangers can be coached to understand Jacob's "How are you today?"—"Dah dah *dih* dih dah?"—as he extends his hand to shake. Yet it's hard to tell the difference between "Walmart" and "Starbucks," even for his parents.

There is technology he can use, mostly at school for the staff who can't under-stand him. He wears a device the size of a remote control with about eight buttons hooked to his belt loop. Each button is programmed with a recording of Gary's voice, saying things like "I want to see Kevin" (his mobility expert) or "I had a good weekend," followed by a brief retelling of the weekend's events, maybe skiing at Telluride or running errands with Dad. There's another speech augmenter with much more in-depth communication that his therapists are training him to use, but whether he'll be able to master it is uncertain.

While the barriers for Jacob to express himself are real, he truly yearns to converse. As he sits at his chair eating breakfast, he hears Gary walk into the room. Immediately Jacob says, "Dah dah *dah* dah dah *dah,*" meaning "Take a bath, go to bed." It's his routine every evening after dinner: Gary helps him wash his hands and face at the sink, then helps Helen prepare Jacob for his bath. Gary answers him, "Yes, we will. Tonight after dinner." But Jacob's repetitive phrases are insufficient for the connections he wishes to make, and this inability to communicate leads to frustration for everyone, especially Jacob. He can't express any nuance or explain why something bothers him.

This difficulty intensified with the onset of puberty. Jacob grew more anxious, and the ritualistic behaviors he had displayed since childhood became more unmanageable. Given the neglect he experienced during his first two years, this anxiety is unsurprising. What he experienced all those hours, crying for someone who never came, waiting for the reassuring arms of a caregiver who seldom appeared, was toxic stress, according to Dr. Anna Reisman, and that has very real, even physical consequences. She even compares it to a hurricane that can permanently damage vital structures.

"Toxic stress enlarges the amygdala, a brain structure that activates the stress response, triggering excessive release of stress hormones and bumping the risk for uncontrolled fear and anxiety," Dr. Reisman explains in her article "Tender Young Brains" in *Slate* magazine. At the same time, toxic stress can cause damage to the prefrontal cortex, the part of the brain that helps moderate social behavior, determines cause and effect, and shapes personality. But the prefrontal cortex also plays another pivotal role: keeping the amygdala and its stress reflex from getting out of control. If the prefrontal cortex is damaged by toxic stress, however, it can't regulate the amygdala as effectively, the stress response increases, and the child has difficulty handling this high level of stress throughout childhood and adolescence and often into adulthood. For Jacob, there were several manifestations of this anxiety. He would point at his left shoe or put it in his mouth, repeat the same phrases dozens of times, chew on the end of his belt in church, and most disturbingly, lick the ground, the wall at school, the asphalt of a parking lot, or the tile floor at Vitamin Cottage, a local health food store. Helen began to worry about electrical outlets. At the same time, his demeanor grew more nervous and high-strung.

Just after Jacob's seventeenth birthday in May of 2011, Helen had him see his pediatrician, Dr. Wiard, for a checkup. Jacob was physically healthy, even breaking one hundred pounds for the first time, but his behavior—incessantly rubbing the back of his hand on his ear and face—caught Dr. Wiard's attention within the first ten minutes. Compulsive behaviors can be extremely painful and stressful for the child, so Dr. Wiard started him immediately on a safe and conservative treatment, prescribing clonidine to lower Jacob's blood pressure and help calm him and provide him a better quality of life, and then called the Children's Hospital of Colorado in Denver, the closest location for the type of attention Jacob needs, to see if they could get him a full neurological and psychiatric assessment.

In mid-July Gary, Helen, and Jacob loaded up in Gary's truck at dawn and began the three-hundred-mile trek to Denver. They buckled Jacob in the backseat and covered him with the heavy quilt from his bed, which he immediately pulled over his face in one of his self-soothing tactics. Because they had to wean him off all medications before the appointment, Jacob was humming with anxiety. To help pacify him during the five-hour drive, they named each town they drove through to help him map the trip in his head. After a little while, he asked again to name the towns they'd driven through. "First was Montrose," they said, "and then what was next?"

"Dah-*dah*-dah," he answered. O-*lath*-ah.

"What's next?" they asked.

"*Del*-dah." He can almost say Delta.

"Then after that?"

"*Duh*-dah." Hotchkiss.

Then the next town, where his mobility expert, Kevin O'Brien, lives.

"Dah-*dah*-duh." Paonia—Pa-*own*-ya.

Afterward, Helen began counting, and Jacob counted with her, following the intonation and pitch rather than the proper sound, getting up to fifty or sixty before he would lie down on the seat. After a few minutes of rest, he would sit up and say, "Ma!" It was his signal, *Let's start over again.*

Around 11 a.m., they reached the Children's Hospital of Colorado and were sent to the psych unit. Helen went through Jacob's medical records and history with their medical social worker, who was so impacted by Jacob's story that she was in tears when they finished. After five-and-a-half hours of observation, the clinicians diagnosed him with anxiety and compulsions. Gary and Helen had hoped Jacob would be admitted that day, but because Jacob wasn't in danger of harming himself or others, the doctors told them they wouldn't be scheduling anything else for several weeks. So at 6 p.m., Gary gave Jacob two clonidine, and they loaded back up and started home.

Again they counted, but this time, he made it to 150, then 170. "When he gets to one hundred, dah-*dah*-duh," Gary says, "you can tell by his intonation and his inflection that he's got the right number, and between that and the medicine, we could hear in his voice that he was calming down." They pulled into their driveway at 11:22 p.m. and headed straight for bed.

The next day his occupational therapist visited and noted Jacob was more hyper than usual. He spent a few hours in the swimming pool, twisting his body sideways and somersaulting underwater. Three feet below the surface of the water, he would remain suspended, releasing a long stream of bubbles before coming back up for a breath, only to sink down again. Like being under his quilt, the water is a refuge, a place that's quiet, providing even pressure against his skin, maintaining predictable boundaries. He knows the pool's dimensions, Gary says, and exactly where he is at all times. It's soothing balm after the long day in Denver.

"In the short term, we know that the process of getting him tested and finding the right treatment is going to cause some discomfort for Jacob," Gary says. "But he needs it for himself, for his family, and for his teachers at school, for everyone he has social interaction with." The treatments are expensive and the paperwork is highly complex, requiring extensive communication between Jacob's doctors in Western Colorado and those in Denver, three hundred miles to the east. And because Jacob is approved for government assistance, Medicaid adds a whole extra layer of red tape. The bureaucracy is maddening to Gary, who sees the frustration in his son and wants a prompt and ready solution more than anything.

On a second trip to the Children's Hospital of Colorado in late September, Jacob met with a developmental-behavioral pediatrician, Dr. William Campbell, for a three-hour consultation. "Jacob accommodated nicely—perhaps with his foot in his mouth twenty-five times during our visit and much belt-licking behavior—so that Dr. Campbell could see what the situation was," Helen wrote afterward in an e-mail to one of Jacob's therapists, a woman named Julia. Soon after the first trip to Denver in July, Jacob's psychiatrist had started him on an atypical antipsychotic called risperidone, a more aggressive treatment for conditions ranging from autism and obsessive-compulsive disorder to schizophrenia, and Jacob's ritualistic behaviors had decreased. Dr. Campbell believed that Jacob's improvement on the risperidone was simply a secondary effect of his lessened anxiety, however, and that the behaviors were not compulsive tics. Instead he described them as "voluntary stereotypical movements."

"The origin of these behaviors may well have started earlier, when he was in the orphanage," Dr. Campbell wrote in his report. "In that setting, he lacked social and environmental stimulation, and he spent a lot of time on his back, possibly putting his feet in his mouth."

Helen had not made the connection to his toddler days, but suddenly it made sense. "When Jacob was young and spent the first three years in his crib, his favorite 'toys' were his fingers and toes, and he would often have one or the other in his mouth while lying on his back," Helen confirmed in the e-mail to Julia.

Dr. Campbell administered tests for autism and found Jacob's repetitive behaviors and his preoccupation with following schedules "atypical," but because of his responsiveness and sociability, Dr. Campbell refrained from a hard and fast diagnosis of autism spectrum disorder. The assessments also revealed that Jacob was in the range of severe intellectual disability. Dr. Campbell confirmed the first diagnosis of general anxiety, exacerbated by illness or by changes in schedule or routine. For Jacob's licking and chewing, Dr. Campbell recommended outpatient behavior modification therapy. (Inpatient treatment, where he'd be separated from both his parents for all but thirty minutes a day, is not really an option for a child with Jacob's history.) Gary and Helen would have to find a place to stay in Denver and bring Jacob to the hospital each day for two weeks, hoping that the loss of his familiar environments would not prove too much for him.

The constant evaluations and appointments and therapies are a hardship, but they are nothing compared to the sorrow Gary and Helen feel when they don't know what is upsetting Jacob, when they can't find solutions for his problems. And though it has not been an easy path, they know that adopting him was the right decision. In the sixteen years that he has lived with Gary and Helen, Jacob has learned to be a part of their family and to trust Helen and Gary as stable and loving parents. "He loves habit, he loves structure, but he also is able to segregate in his mind—these are the things I do with Dad, these are the things I do with Mom," Gary explains. During the week, he gets ready for school with Mom, then runs errands with Dad on Saturdays. He skis with Dad and rides ATVs in the mountains with Dad. But swimming is something he does with Mom. Gary might get him dressed in his swimsuit and bring him out to the pool, but as soon as he's in, he's calling "Ma! Ma!"—hurrying her into the water with him. To them, these preferences demonstrate his connection with each of them, connections that were slow to form but have deepened and strengthened over time, fruits of the hard work they have done to provide the right treatments, the necessary routines, and the stable home he didn't have.

Jacob has brought about a shift in their whole outlook on parenting. "Most people think of their children in terms of what they will become—that they'll go to Harvard and make a lot of money, or whatever," Helen says. "Jacob has just changed our family so much in that way." He has taught them to appreciate who he is, not who he will become. Reading the work of Jean Vanier, a man who has founded communities for people with intellectual disabilities all over the world, helped her discover that truth.

"Our society is geared to growth, development, progress," Vanier writes in *Becoming Human,* a meditation on love, service, brokenness, and humanity. "Life, for most of us, is a race to be won. Families are about evolution: at a certain stage, children are encouraged to leave home, get married, have children of their own, move on with their lives. But people with disabilities have no such future." But Vanier discerns in the people he has dedicated his life to a subversive power, one that does not clothe itself in power's typical symbols. Instead, their weakness is a shroud for the peace they hold, a peace free from the competition of the modern world; a shroud for their pure and whole trust, born out of vulnerability; a shroud for their love, which responds to love from those who accept them, who understand them, who tell them they matter. "Weakness carries with it a secret power," Vanier says. "They cry, and the trust that flows from weakness can open up hearts. The one who is weaker will call forth powers of love in the one who is stronger."

Jacob has wrought this change in Gary and Helen, and over the years, he has taught them to delight in him just as he is. "I love his sense of humor," Gary says. "I love his courage. And I love that he loves to engage with us." Gary recalls a simple story of how one day, Jacob came out of his room and found Helen and grabbed her hand. He walked to the back door leading to the porch and said, "*Dah*-dah," and pointed at his head. *Hair*cut.

Before, Helen had always been the one to pull *him* by the hand to the back porch, where she'd crop his hair close in an all-over buzz. But on a whim, she had decided to let it grow, to see how he looked with longer hair but also to keep Jacob's head warm from the winter cold.

It's hard to explain why Gary was so moved as he watched this event transpire, when all that happened was that his son initiated a haircut for the very first time. Except it was just that: the first time he'd expressed his will regarding his hair, evidence that he had the confidence and the ability to ask for what he wanted.

So Helen cut his hair, and when she finished a few minutes later, Jacob grabbed her hand again and pulled her to the porch swing, where they sat together in the sun.

❦ ❦ ❦

Though Gary and Helen have spent many years abroad, in Europe and Asia and different parts of the United States, Western Colorado has always been home. The eldest of five, Helen grew up in the sprawling city of Los Angeles, the daughter of a hardworking mechanic and a devoted homemaker, but she doesn't miss the coast a bit. She loves the mountains, though it's hard to say if she loves them as much as Gary does. There is still awe in his voice when he talks about spending mornings out hunting elk and afternoons in the foothills building fence. He is proud of his home, proud of the view and the spaciousness, proud when all five children and their husbands, wives, and children, who are spread across the world from Australia to England to the United States, make it home for Christmas.

Montrose is a small town ringed by national forests—Grand Mesa to the north, Uncompahgre to the west, San Juan to the south, and Gunnison to the east—and some of the nation's most rugged peaks. Like many of the Rockies, the foothills and mountains in the vicinity have names that surprise and delight: to the east, there's Waterdog Peak, Sheep Knob, Poverty Mesa, and Coffee Pot Hill, and across the Gunnison River, a tributary of the mighty Colorado, Poison Spring Hill rises toward Cathedral Peak. Past Horsefly Peak to the south, the elevation climbs from ten thousand to almost fourteen thousand feet at the summit of Ulysses S. Grant Peak, just past the town of Telluride, where settlers once pulled ores from the mountains but now, along with thousands of frequent visitors, use the slopes for skiing.

The mountains are in Gary's blood. He's so natural trundling down ranch roads behind the wheel of his white Ford F-250 that it's hard to imagine him living on crowded Hong Kong Island, where each building touches the next and the sky, and where the population density is one of the highest in the world. Gary is the youngest of three children in a family that equally valued hard work and generosity. His father, Paul, owned a grocery store and ran the family farm in Olathe, Colorado, and his mother, Jean, the daughter of Norwegian immigrants, was a homemaker with a steady and heartfelt Christian faith. Gary grew up milking cows and doing other farmwork, and the family practiced traditional American charity. "Dad taught us about extending credit—you could also call it grace—to people who didn't have the means," Gary says. "He would carry families through the winter, giving them beans or produce to keep them from going hungry. And Mom would make care packages and distribute them to people in the community who were in need."

All three of Paul and Jean's children adopted hard work and generosity, but they extended their boundaries, and from these simple, local roots, up sprang a surprising global consciousness. In 1978, the oldest son, Don, founded Mercy Ships, an international charity that operates the world's largest nongovernmental hospital ship, providing medical care to the world's forgotten poor. For twenty years, daughter Joan worked as a fund-raiser for academic medicine and community hospitals before being named senior vice president for advancement for Boston's Museum of Science. And with his work in Hong Kong and China, Gary has pursued the true religion described in the book of James: to care for widows and orphans in their distress. They may have grown up in Olathe, a tiny farm town with a population of one thousand, but the Stephens children have devoted themselves to being global forces for change.

Gary and Helen have served others and sacrificed more than most people could even comprehend, yet they see their sacrifice very simply: as the work they had before them, as the next thing they had to do. Over the years, they have tackled so many projects in so many different places that it's sometimes hard to keep things straight. Through Europe, Asia, and the United States, as sometime construction workers, missionaries, social workers, and parents, they were, and still are, constantly evolving, and their adaptability seems to be one of their key strengths. Gary and Helen do not define themselves by what they do, or, despite their love for Western Colorado, even by where they live. "It's a great source of frustration to have your identity tied to something that can change in a minute," Gary says, "and I prefer to live without frustration."

But one's perspective matters as well. Gary and Helen have faced tremendous challenges in the work they have done, but Helen is determined and unwilling to give up even in the most difficult situations. A thin and young-looking sixty-five, Helen is constantly doing: making herself a cup of tea, wiping counters, preparing a sandwich for Jacob's lunch the next day, or cutting up grapefruit for an old friend visiting from Hong Kong—but always quietly. After a lifetime of managing a family and dozens of workers and services for hundreds of babies, Helen has developed a system. She hones in on details, shifting and changing them until she gets them right, and then as things fall into place, she steps back and lets go. By contrast, Gary's strengths rest in his ideas, in the way he sees the future in terms of possibility instead of likelihood, in the way he retells mainly the successes and joys of the past instead of the difficulties. The way they view the world keeps them grounded and effective, and that perspective is integral to their story.

Seated on a low ridge south of town and overlooking a small valley called Duckett Draw, where a few heavy-coated cattle graze, Gary and Helen's house seems a place apart. The peaks of the San Juan Mountains stand in the distance, and as clouds move across the valley, the subtle gray shadows on the near land are contrasted by the striking gradations of white and gold where the sun cuts through and glances off the snowcaps. The windows spanning the back of the house were designed for admiring those views, from Gary's office where he works from home, through the open kitchen and living room, and across to the bedrooms on the other side. Sometimes the line of sight stretches for miles; other times, snowy clouds roll through the valley very suddenly, and the windows display only a thick gray curtain. Outside, flurries blow their way across windshields and highways, rooftops and slopes, then clear to show fences and fir trees cloaked in a blanket of white. But the house is a warm and quiet retreat from it all.

Because Jacob has trouble in high-stimulus environments, their current home is deliberately calm and soothing. Classical music or instrumental versions of old hymns play throughout the day. The ground floor is centered around the great room, an open kitchen and living room with a fireplace and plush chairs and couches. The basement below, with its maze of bedrooms and living areas thickly carpeted, seems cavernous, private, a place to be quiet and recharge. There Jacob's therapeutic swing—a virtual cocoon of heavy elastic fabric he can wrap himself in and rest, bounce, and turn—hangs from the low ceiling. In the afternoons after school, he often feels his way down the stairs and burrows into his swing to recuperate from the long day.

Jacob eats dinner around five, seated at a stool at the end of the kitchen counter. On a cold Colorado afternoon, snow moves in across the mountains from the east, and half the sky is a gray slate hovering over ridges just a few hundred yards away. Gary has made stew with elk meat—from his own hunting exploits—and celery, onions, carrots, and potatoes in a thin beefy broth. Jacob eats a full bowl, but he also loves homemade rolls, drizzled with olive oil and honey. He asks for more and more, and since Helen and Gary want him to gain weight, they indulge. After that, it's banana cake, which he devours, and a banana, which he tosses aside.

During dinner, he says a few words that he's learning with his occupational therapist. "Dah-*dah*-dah." Va-*nil*-la. He says cinnamon and strawberry too. Cinnamon is rapid-fire and his favorite, a quick staccato with a very slight emphasis on the first syllable—"*dih*-dih-dih." *Straw* is smooth and long; *berry* follows hurriedly—"*daaah*-dah-dah." Helen leaves him as he eats. She used to stay by his side for every minute of every meal, but at some point she realized that he'd never quite gotten the social aspect of a meal, and it was not as important to him as it was to her. So just a few yards away, she sits in her office and checks e-mail, and every few minutes, he'll blurt out, "Ma. *Dah*-dih *dah* dah." *Mon*-trose *High* School. "Yes, Jacob, Mom will take you tomorrow," she answers, and continues typing.

After he's finished, Gary stands behind him at the sink and washes the cake from his hands and face, asking him jokingly why he put bread and honey in his hair. "Go ahead to your bathroom, Jacob," Gary says. But Jacob pauses, and Gary quickly understands. "You want to walk with Dad? Okay." Jacob slips his arm around Gary's back, and together they move down the darkened hallway toward Jacob's bathroom. On the way, he says it again: "*Dah*-dih *dah* dah"—*Mon*-trose *High* School, then "Ma." He wants Helen to take him, which she will, and Gary answers, "Tomorrow morning."

Jacob loves going to school and asks about it several times each evening, and even more frequently on weekends. It's a typical American high school, a two-story brick building spanning two city blocks, with the sprawling grounds—for baseball, football, tennis—encompassing another ten. It backs up to Townsend Avenue, the main thoroughfare in Montrose, but the front entrance is on the opposite side, in a quiet residential neighborhood at the intersection of South 5th and Selig. Inside, the walls are cinder blocks painted white, accented with red for school spirit, and there's a glass trophy case lining the main hallway. The floors are tiled, so the echoes of lockers slamming, of teenagers chattering between classes, and of footfalls hurrying to make it to class before the bell rings are amplified. On the walls are posters reminding students that Spirit Day costumes have to follow dress code, and that if a hat is involved, it has to be part of the ensemble.

What's not typical is Jacob's enthusiasm: he loves Montrose High School. He knows the morning routine by heart: get up, eat breakfast with Mom—a bowl of oatmeal and a fried egg with steamed greens on the side. Then he leaves the kitchen to get dressed and heads to the laundry room beside the garage. His prosthetic eyes are there in a drawer, and Helen takes them out and rinses them with warm water. She places a few drops of aloe vera on the concave backs, then slips the left eye under his top lid and in past the bottom. She does the same with the right, and he blinks a few times. "They feel okay?" Helen asks. "Yeah," he answers and nods his head. The routine continues efficiently as Helen slips one sock halfway up his right foot, and Jacob reaches for the top to pull it up the rest of the way with a quick and somewhat jerky motion. They take the second foot, then there's a debate about outerwear. The day is too cold for a sweatshirt, so Helen slips a navy blue jacket on him, but he resists. She doesn't insist but quickly pulls that jacket off, hangs it on a hook, and grabs a bright red one, heavier, with silky rayon lining. "Yeah," Jacob answers. "Yeah." She opens the drawer for a hat, pulls it over his head, and they are out the door.

As they take Highway 550 into town, it turns into Townsend Avenue. They pass the City Market on the right and the Home Depot on the left, crossing numbered streets, South 12th, South 11th, and Helen chatters the whole way, marking the route with her voice, narrating the landmarks and the turns, and Jacob takes part. When she says, "We're now passing Home Depot," Jacob says, "Da," because it's "Dad" who takes him there. He's excited to get to school and see his teachers and Kevin. But he's always happy to get home, where he can rest and relax, and where his parents are in the next room, ready to answer at the slightest call.

✸ ✸ ✸

The snow continues to fall throughout their Friday on the slopes. Gary and Jacob stop for lunch at a picnic area halfway down the mountain, and Jacob swallows half of the sandwich Helen packed for him and drinks half a thermos of water. Before Gary can finish, Jacob is up and pulling his arm eagerly—let's get back to the lift, back up the mountain, back into the wind and the smoothness of skis on snow. On the lift, he's happy and wants to talk, and he begins by retelling what he had for breakfast. He starts with oatmeal, but Gary laughs and says, "You didn't have oatmeal this morning! You had eggs!" Jacob quickly changes the subject. "*Dah*-duh-duh," he says. "Yes, we're at Telluride," Gary replies. "We're skiing." And immediately Jacob goes right back to oatmeal, and Gary laughs. They dismount the lift, and run after run, Jacob stands straight and allows Gary to guide him down the mountain.

"Who would have ever thought that I could take my blind son skiing, much less by myself?" Gary says. "I didn't know it would have been possible." Jacob gets stronger all the time, he improves as a skier, and his confidence increases. Over the past three years, others have noticed his growth as well. Once a man followed them to the adaptive ski program facilities, where they were returning their gear after a day on the slopes. "He found us," Gary recalls, "and he said to me, 'I just wanted to come and say that I saw you skiing last year, and now I see you this year. Your son is making such progress, and he is an inspiration.'" Gary, whose primary means of motivating others is through storytelling, is awed by how Jacob does it. "He doesn't really have any English words at all, yet he just inspires people."

Helen never imagined he'd do so well either, that after years of obstacles in his path, after precipitous setbacks followed by slow and meager headway, he'd excel in such a fashion. "I still remember the first day he went," she says. "I thought, 'This is crazy.' He hates cold, and for a blind person to have something slippery under his feet is terrifying."

The snow can also be disorienting in other ways for someone who is blind. John Hull, a professor at the University of Birmingham in England, was born sighted but had vision problems beginning at the age of thirteen. By forty-five, he was completely blind. One morning, three years into blindness, Hull went out though snow was predicted. "I left the house," Hull writes in his memoir *Touching the Rock,* "but had only gone a hundred yards when I became aware of a growing feeling of doubt. I became intensely aware of the fact that I was walking through nothing. It was a very interesting, cold nothing. I worked my way along the lines of the fences, wanting to take my gloves off so I could feel them better, but knowing it would be too cold. The feeling that I was going nowhere grew stronger. I was alone, entering the night of an endless tunnel of intense cold. I knew that once I went in I would not be able to come back." The sounds he used to locate himself in space were silenced by the snow on the ground, in the branches of the trees, and in the air. His hands, one of the most important tools a blind person uses to understand his world, were virtually bound. At a certain point, he could not go on; instead, he turned around and went home.

But Jacob doesn't fear the snowy day on the mountainside. As Helen says, "He has to display the ultimate trust in Gary to lead him." To Gary, that's the most precious and rewarding part of the whole experience: that this young boy who was left without parents, without a home, without a future, has learned that Gary will protect him and provide security and comfort.

When Jacob falls a few times in the course of the day, he gets up and Gary helps him back onto his skis. Jacob is unfazed, unscathed, ready to reach the bottom only to head back up to the top. When they go faster than he wants, he might grab for Gary's arm or simply sit down on his skis, but mostly he chatters to his dad with excitement or sings to himself, a sign that he's at peace. Gary and Jacob make twenty-three runs down the mountain, then call it quits after almost five hours. Gary notices on the drive back to Montrose that Jacob is as happy as a clam. When they reach the house, Helen meets them at the back door and says cheerfully, "Is that my Jacob Lok Chi?" She helps Jacob take out his prosthetic eyes, then puts them in a case.

Helen comments that they must have had a phenomenal time. She knows it from his smile, from the way Jacob backs into Gary and grabs him as if to say, "I'm not ready for this day to end," from how his attempts to speak are heightened and intensified, from his request for the hot tub—"*dah* dah"—to soothe his tired legs.

CHAPTER 4

IN THE MID-LEVELS

❦

Learn to do right; seek justice.
Defend the oppressed.
Take up the cause of the fatherless;
plead the case of the widow.

ISAIAH 1:17

Hong Kong

By the end of 1980, Youth With a Mission had found permanent facilities at the former British Military Hospital on Borrett Road, high above Victoria Harbor. Shortly after that, Gary and Helen became the directors of the work there. "Somewhere in the summer of 1981, Loren and I were speaking at a conference in Indonesia, and I explained what was happening in Hong Kong," Gary recalls. "Loren said to me, 'Gary, there's no way you can come back to Hawaii. It's obvious that doors have opened for you in Hong Kong. You just need to accept that's where you should be.'" Loren's response surprised Gary, but it also helped reframe his and Helen's ideas about their work and gave them permission to put down roots. Helen became the manager of the Youth With a Mission facilities in Hong Kong, which involved overseeing a staff of twenty people in food services, housekeeping, and hospitality for the base. Gary assumed the role of director of East Asia, overseeing the work in thirteen countries stretching from Japan to Singapore, and traveled regularly throughout the region.

At the government's suggestion, Youth With a Mission had moved into the British Military Hospital, the hilltop complex of red brick buildings at 10 Borrett Road, when the barracks at 7A Kennedy Road were sold at private auction for US $93 million, then torn down and replaced by a high-rise. Opened in 1907, the Borrett Road hospital had served the British garrison for sixty years when the government closed the hospital and relocated to Kowloon. At that point, the building had passed into civilian usage. Other nongovernmental organizations occupied the building as well, so Youth With a Mission had only one-and-a-half floors in the western wing as well as the central administrative wing. Even so, it was considerably more space than they'd had at 7A Kennedy Road.

The six years in Hong Kong had passed quickly. During that time, they continued their mission to serve refugees in Jubilee and other camps, at Kai Tak and at Whitehead. They taught English language classes, counseled the refugees, and also worked in camp maintenance projects. But when the numbers arriving in Hong Kong's harbors dropped off in 1982, Youth With a Mission's emphasis began expanding into serving the homeless in the area and holding training schools in Hong Kong, as well as facilitating outreaches to other parts of Asia. Regularly, they had one hundred people living on the base at Borrett Road as part of short-term teams, training schools, or long-term staff. The leaders also spent time looking for new needs to which their teams might minister. One way they found these needs was through their weekly communication meetings, where different teams would brief one another on the work they were doing and could raise concerns, either relating to work within the organization or to a larger social issue they felt needed attention.

On Monday, June 9, 1986, two staff members shared a front-page article from the *South China Morning Post* with the headline: "Hongkong women fuel border abortion boom." In the article, reporter Ophelia Suen described how young women from Hong Kong were "heading across the border in increasing numbers to take advantage of cheap, no-questions-asked abortions services", and "also taking advantage of the fact that Chinese doctors perform these simple operations with no regard to how advanced the pregnancy is or how old the patient is." Shenzhen People's Hospital, the largest hospital in the Shenzhen area, was routinely carrying out terminations "even in the ninth month of pregnancy and on women as young as 13 or 14." In this special economic zone, where the Chinese government had recently relaxed regulations to encourage business, abortion proved to be lucrative, with as many as one hundred cases a day on weekends and holidays. Gary and Helen and the rest of their group were affected by how young the girls were, how difficult it was to abstract such late-term abortions, how many of the fetuses were viable outside the womb, and how commercialized, industrialized, and routinized the whole process had become.

Suen's main source of information was Dr. Chan Ayshian, the head of the Shenzhen hospital's gynecology and obstetrics department, who said that half of the abortions happening in Shenzhen were taking place either in her hospital or in their new six-story abortion clinic, located only a fifteen-minute walk from the train station. With dispassion, Dr. Chan described the process: a drug, which she refused to name, was injected into the amniotic fluid that "usually" killed the baby within forty-eight to seventy-two hours. "The mother is not affected by the drug," Dr. Chan explained. "She goes through the simple, natural birth process. The only difference is that the baby is dead by the time it is born. In very rare cases, the baby is still alive, but its central nervous system has already been affected. Its liver and kidneys will never be able to function normally. No one wants it—a mentally-retarded baby—anyway."

In a photo three columns wide and half the page long, Dr. Chan stood smiling behind a piece of medical equipment, apparently the apparatus used for the procedure. Given that unplanned births were illegal in China, her quote reads like a propaganda slogan for the one-child policy: "Pregnancy that comes before the directed time calls for abortion."

Dr. Chan's attitude is unsurprising in context. Worldwide, fears of population booms and overcrowding surfaced in the early and mid-1970s, and by the end of that decade, the leaders of the Chinese Communist Party had determined that their huge population was the single issue preventing China from becoming modern and prosperous. The numbers—nearly one billion at the end of 1978—had been a source of pride under Mao Zedong, but were recast by the new leadership as backward and humiliating. Leaders felt the situation must be remedied immediately to improve China's status as a cooperative member of the global community. Very quickly, reproduction became a state-planned domain, first through suggestions like "later-longer-fewer," where people were encouraged to marry later and have fewer children with longer spacing between births; then through "one is best, two at most"; and finally through the strict one-child policy. Yet as anthropologist Susan Greenhalgh points out in her book *Just One Child*, planning reproduction in the same manner as planning the production of food and steel "carried the worrying potential to dehumanize the objects of population planning," the Chinese people. In the succeeding decades, credible reports of forced abortions and sterilizations and the abandonment of baby girls across China seem to support Greenhalgh's claim.

Yet as Suen pointed out, the abortion boom had other "disturbing implications." Just below the main article, a second headline read, "Scientists look for live fetuses." In it, Suen reported that scientists in China were "working on a theory that live fetuses from late-term abortions might help in the body's natural production of insulin, thus helping the treatment of diabetes." One researcher traveled to the Shenzhen hospital from Beijing "to pursue further studies"; however, Dr. Chan denied having enough live fetuses to supply their study.

"As we read these articles, we became very burdened, first for the babies," Gary recalls. But then they realized that these girls were very young, and many were completely alone in dealing with the incredible stress of an unplanned pregnancy and the decision to terminate it. "We began praying for these teenage pregnant girls, that somehow there would be people—professional, compassionate people—who would be made available to them. We knew there would be some emotional and psychological scars, and we hoped social workers would be able to help them heal." Busy with their own mission work, as well as raising four children, they had no plans for further involvement, but they continued praying for a period of a few weeks.

"Every time we would gather for prayer," Gary says, "it seemed that this was the thing that our hearts and our minds were drawn to."

❦ ❦ ❦

By the summer of 1986, Gary and Helen had been involved with Youth With a Mission for almost fifteen years and had acquired substantial responsibilities. Yet that did not translate into material wealth, and besides the frequent flier miles that Gary racked up with his frequent travel, there were very few perks attached to being the directors of the base. The family of six lived in a tiny corner apartment in the hospital, only 225 square feet, which had been quite bare when they moved in. A year later, some friends had helped them loft one side and a corner of the high-ceilinged room, brick in the verandah for more square footage, and build fold-down bunks for Amy and Andrew. They had also added a small bathroom, which eliminated the need to bathe the kids in buckets in the communal showers down the hall.

"Shawna had a room that was about seven feet long by six feet wide," Gary recalls. "Our youngest daughter Katie was born on the bed in the loft and slept on a New Zealand sheepskin on the floor beside our bed, which became a sore subject when Helen read her *Goldilocks and the Three Bears*." The older kids were in school during the day as Helen worked and Gary traveled, and three-year-old Katie spent the days at Small World Kindergarten, the Youth With a Mission preschool just down the corridor from their apartment.

Working with Youth With a Mission and living on the base provided a built-in community, but they also began forming external ties. Bill Mortson, the International Rescue Committee administrator they had worked with at Jubilee, invited the Stephens family to attend church with him at a place called Repulse Bay Baptist Church—"neither in Repulse Bay nor Baptist," Gary laughs. They joined the church in early 1986, though for the first three weeks Helen attended, Gary was in Indonesia, on a tiny island next to Bali, and Helen went without him. She was taken by the dynamic, lay-led congregation of 250 individuals, and she felt embraced by the diverse community, made up of many families, many with children. As soon as Gary returned, the family attended a Sunday morning service together. That particular Sunday, Ranjan Marwah, an Indian businessman in the Hong Kong community, was the greeter at the door.

Gary lapses into present tense, as he often does when telling a story: "Ranjan shakes my hand and then he says, 'Helen, it's nice to finally meet him, because I thought he was a figment of your imagination.'" Gary, always up for banter, laughed and asked where Ranjan imagined Helen had gotten her four kids.

One Sunday in late June, after the Stephens family had been attending Repulse Bay Baptist for a few months, Ranjan and his wife Phyllis asked their family to lunch. "Several of our kids were the same ages," Gary explains, "and we had a wonderful Indian meal together at their home on the south side of Hong Kong Island." After lunch, the adults remained at the table talking as the children played together. Soon the conversation turned to origins. Gary and Helen explained how they had come to Hong Kong to serve the Vietnamese boat people in their crisis, and how that work continued but had evolved and expanded. They explained the beginnings of a ministry serving street sleepers: how one summer a few years earlier, a short-term team of two hundred people had come to Hong Kong and one group had rented an apartment in Wan Chai, and how, as they were walking through the neighborhood, they noticed close to eighty homeless people in an area comprising twenty square blocks. So the team began preparing their main meal, but instead of eating it, they fasted and gave the food to the street sleepers. Several years later, the ministry continued. This was how the work in Hong Kong operated: the Youth With a Mission community would see a need, then do their best to gather the people and the resources to serve it. They had a firm belief that when they responded to people who were hungry or naked or thirsty or lost, whatever they needed to do the work would be provided.

The Marwahs were interested in hearing more, and they asked what would be next.

"That's when we shared about the articles we'd read a few weeks previously and how we were praying for the babies and these pregnant girls," Gary says. "We talked about it for a few minutes and that was it."

But that wasn't it, because several days later, Gary received a telephone call from Ranjan, who—after a very brief hello—got to the point. "So what are you doing about the pregnant girls?" Ranjan asked.

Gary was surprised, but he had nothing new to report. "We're praying about the pregnant girls," he said.

Again, Ranjan asked, "What are you doing about the pregnant girls?"

Gary replied, "We're praying about the pregnant girls."

And a third time, he asked, "What are you doing about the pregnant girls?"

"I may be slow," Gary says, laughing, "but I'm not completely stupid. Finally I asked him, 'What do you suggest?'"

"Let's get a group together," Ranjan answered, "and discuss what can be done."

A few days later, they arranged for a meeting of eight or ten mutual friends and acquaintances at the Hong Kong Country Club, where Ranjan and Phyllis were members. In a private dining room, they gathered around a round wooden table, and Ranjan introduced the subject. "We are here to talk about these young girls going into Shenzhen," Ranjan said, and he turned to Gary and Helen. "You've been giving some thought to this. In your minds, what is needed?"

So Gary and Helen explained the services they felt were necessary to respond to this need. They imagined an organization made up of social workers and counselors to provide advice and support to these young women, to their families, and even to the boyfriends and their families. They could provide a home for the girls while they were pregnant; then the organization would provide child care for the babies if the girls opted against terminating their pregnancies and would coordinate with the Social Welfare Department to see these children adopted, either locally or overseas. They felt the organization should be broad enough in its scope that it could do all of these things—"and anything in between that we can't think of right now."

Ranjan looked around the table, asking people, "Are you willing to lead this new endeavor?" But the concept was huge, and with the responsibilities of work and family and community, it seemed that no one was willing to volunteer.

Then Ranjan turned to Helen, and he said, "Helen, are you willing to lead this work?"

Although Ranjan didn't know it, that was a moment of tremendous weight, when a tragic history met Helen in the present moment. Years before, when Helen was twenty-one, her eighteen-year-old sister had become pregnant. It was the early 1970s in America, and though being pregnant and unmarried wasn't unspeakable, as it had been a few decades earlier, it was stigmatized and kept very quiet. Young women like Helen's sister had two options: they could marry, or they could leave their homes and families to live in a girls' home in a secluded location or with a merciful relative until the baby was born and then adopted.

In a personal essay called "Shunned," Meredith Hall describes such an experience, when, in 1965, she became pregnant at sixteen. After hiding her secret for five months, her body betrayed the truth, and she was expelled from school. "You can't stay here" was her mother's reaction, and the scared teenager was sent to live with her estranged father and his new wife. Hall spent the gray winter in an upstairs bedroom, "isolated from any life, from any belief, from any sense that I belonged to anyone. I was alone," she says. "My fear and grief burned like wildfires on a silent and distant horizon." After four decades of reflection, Hall came to understand, if not completely heal from, her trauma. She argues that sending young pregnant girls away aims to prevent such transgressions, to issue a warning to other young girls that they must at all costs avoid such a fate. It also removes the shame from the family and the community, "as precise as a scalpel, an absolute excision," Hall writes, scarring only the girl, who carries the pain of the shunning for the rest of her life.

True to the times, Helen's sister left the family home in Los Angeles and went to live with family friends one hundred miles away, where she gave birth to a healthy baby girl whom she never held. Though the family had decided on this course of action with the best of intentions, she was never able to recover from the trauma, from the sudden loss of innocence, from a total loss of former self. Helen knew that her sister wasn't the only one affected by the crisis pregnancy. "It affects the whole family," Helen says. "The whole family grieves, the whole family suffers and is worried about what her future will be."

Though times had changed in the fifteen years since her sister's pregnancy, Helen knew that young women in Hong Kong still faced tremendous scrutiny and judgment. In the 1980s, the social stigma of teenage pregnancy in Hong Kong was similar to two decades earlier in the United States. Gary says that there were almost no single-parent families in Hong Kong. "We did quite a bit of research," he explains, "and we could only find one single parent, a Cantonese woman, who was studying and then working abroad. During that time, she became pregnant, then came back to Hong Kong with her child." Sex itself was a taboo topic in Hong Kong, with its Victorian influences and Chinese decorum; recent studies show that sexual education is still severely lacking in Hong Kong, with parents leaving it to television and movies and schools to teach their kids about sex, and schools shirking the responsibility of such an awkward topic. But young people have never abstained from sexual activity because they were uninformed; they simply make bad decisions. "Then when a young woman became pregnant, it was an embarrassment to the family," Gary explains. "Often the family didn't want anything to do with her."

Perhaps only subconsciously, Helen felt motivated to respond to these young women because of her own sister's struggles, as a way to honor her sister. But the decision wasn't less than fraught. "There was a part of me that thought, I'm already stretched too thin," Helen recalls. Between raising four young children and her Youth With a Mission duties, it didn't seem there was space or time for new commitments. "But I just remember thinking that God was asking me, 'Helen, are you willing to get your hands dirty?' And I knew that what God gave me the strength and courage to do, I could do."

When Helen finally answered Ranjan, it was with her characteristic honesty and humility.

"I don't know if I have the right skill set," Helen said, "but yes. I'll give it my best shot."

The others left that day having claimed different responsibilities. Ranjan would contact Baker & McKenzie, one of Hong Kong's largest law firms, to set up a charter for the organization, pro bono, so that legally they could do the work they felt called to do. In the meantime, Gary was to find a facility that would serve several purposes—administrative offices, a hostel for pregnant girls, and a child-care facility for the babies who would be born on their watch.

CHAPTER 5

A MOTHER'S CHOICE

❧

I could feel his small heel or an elbow pressing hard against the inside of my belly as he rolled. I spent the days doing nothing but thinking, learning to live in my head, my arms wrapped under my belly, my baby absorbing my stunned sadness. He had hiccups in the night. I lay in the deep, cold emptiness of the house, the night shared with another living being. My blood flowed through him. Tenacious threads joined us outside the world. I could not feel loved by him, ever. But we were one life, small and scared and alone.

MEREDITH HALL, "SHUNNED"
A STORY OF TEENAGE PREGNANCY IN AMERICA, 1965

Hong Kong

Within days of that initial meeting, Helen's responsibilities of managing the facilities and accommodations at the British Military Hospital were delegated to other staff members, and she began making the transition to managing director of this new organization that would minister to the physical and psychological needs of pregnant teenagers and their families in Hong Kong. She and another member of the Youth With a Mission staff, a midwife from Great Britain named Sally Quinton, began taking classes in Cantonese and sketching out the parameters for their new project.

Though Gary and Helen had been involved with a nonprofit organization for many years, they had never attempted to establish one from the ground up, and the first consideration they had was whether or not to work under Youth With a Mission's umbrella. Ultimately, and wisely, they decided that the organization would be a stand-alone entity, a social service organization meeting an obvious social need in Hong Kong. In a decade, Hong Kong would be transferred from British to Chinese authority. Though the People's Republic had agreed to retain the laws, customs, and social systems of Hong Kong, including free speech, freedom of the press, and even a clause allowing welfare institutions run by religious organizations to continue, people suspected that the Chinese government was unlikely to follow through on their promises. They believed instead that the Chinese government was saying what people wanted to hear so Britain wouldn't have qualms about the transfer. On top of that, the leaders of this new organization were aware of the Communist Party's track record with religious organizations inside China, and they were not interested in undergoing a similar ordeal. But their decision also reflected their desire for their services to transcend religious or cultural affiliation. "We wanted girls of any kind of faith, any kind of background to feel comfortable," Helen says. "Some of us felt that girls would not be so comfortable coming to a Christian organization if they themselves weren't Christians." They wanted the doors to be open to all people, regardless of race or creed, and there would be no requirement for the women to profess a Christian faith before they came to stay or while they were there.

With the help of Baker & McKenzie, Helen and Gary and the Marwahs drew up a charter that was as broad as possible: from caring for pregnant girls all the way through to facilitating adoption. They didn't know the conditions of the child-care institutions in Hong Kong because they had not, to this point, had occasion to visit them. "All we knew then was that if we were going to help the girl," Gary says, "we certainly weren't going to relinquish the care of the baby." With Sally trained as a midwife and in neonatal care, and with Helen trained as a nurse herself, they felt they could even deliver the babies themselves if they had to. Sally had actually delivered Gary and Helen's youngest daughter, Katie, in 1983, in their apartment in the old British Military Hospital, so they knew her skill level firsthand.

But years of experience in missions work had taught them that going it alone wasn't the most efficient or effective way to do a job. They began looking for other groups skilled in the fields of crisis pregnancy and adoption with whom they could partner and receive advice. They contacted John Williams, the president of Holt International Children's Services, a leader in the field of international adoption, to see if he would consult with them on their program. He stopped by for a week as he was traveling between Hanoi and Seoul, where Holt had begun international adoptions after the Korean War left thousands of children orphans. His first suggestion was to research the services available to young women in Hong Kong to ensure there truly was a need for the facility they were planning.

So they spent some time looking at the options available for young women facing crisis pregnancy. In their research, they found out that two shelters existed. One had strict rules about admission; they wouldn't accept a girl who was six months pregnant or more, and their services were available to ethnic Chinese women only, leaving out many groups in Hong Kong's multiracial population. The second facility was Po Leung Kok, the Society for the Protection of Women and Children, which had been established in 1882 to prevent women and children from being sold into prostitution. Later it evolved into an alternative legal system for the colony's Chinese residents, who were not subject to the British legal system. The holdover from Po Leung Kok's legal role was still evident; at the time, the young girls were kept behind tall fences and basically under lock and key. "They couldn't even go outside the facility without a staff member from that organization going with them," Helen says. "It was very secretive, very hush-hush."

After visiting both places, John Williams and Helen agreed that there was a need in Hong Kong for a home that would help young women through crisis pregnancy and bring healing; that, instead of criminalizing or shunning them, would provide acceptance and stability. "We wanted there to be an open atmosphere so the girls could come and go as they wanted," Gary says. "We also wanted the atmosphere of the home to be such that the girl's extended family felt welcome to visit her, that the boyfriend and his family felt welcome to visit. We were not going to be a secret in the Mid-levels of Hong Kong Island, where Hong Kong pregnant girls came but were never heard from again."

After much deliberation, they had formed the framework for the organization, but they were not sure of what to call it. Appropriately, it was Ranjan, an advertising executive, who found the name. On a trip to the Philippines, he saw a sign for a group called Mother's Choice. He shared the name with Helen and Gary, and immediately, it resonated.

"The name Mother's Choice struck something deeply within us," Gary says, "because that's what we were talking about. We wanted to give these young girls a shelter, a retreat, a haven, and a choice, and to help advise on the many choices they had to make, between terminating the pregnancy or carrying the baby to term, between choosing adoption for their child or parenting the child with support from us or other organizations. So the name Mother's Choice really fit, and we were thrilled to have a name that truly mirrored our mission."

❋ ❋ ❋

Mother's Choice incorporated in the fall of 1987. Soon after, Helen, as newly appointed managing director, began speaking with Ranjan at Rotary Clubs and giving interviews with various media outlets around Hong Kong to raise awareness of the issues and to gather support for the work. In these meetings, they struggled against centuries-long prejudices leveled at young women who were sexually active. "We had people refer to the pregnant girls as 'those naughty girls,'" Gary recalls, "which revealed a cultural paradigm that didn't recognize that it took two to tango—that he couldn't be a 'naughty boy' because he couldn't get pregnant." The leaders of Mother's Choice, along with other supporters over the years, would point to the narrow-mindedness in such a statement as a major part of the problem, since it prevented frank discussions about sex that could help young people make better choices to begin with.

There were also cultural and racial boundaries that people believed might come into play. At some of those early service club meetings where Helen and Ranjan were speaking, one of the early questions often raised was, "You're a bunch of foreigners. How do you know one of these girls will even want to come?" There was a historical element to this reluctance; for more than a century after the British entrance to Hong Kong, British and Chinese people mixed very little. There was a British legal system and a Chinese legal system, British medicine and Chinese medicine, British sections of the island and Chinese sections of the island. Institutionalized discrimination was evident in social clubs and the civil service, and residential segregation of British and Asian communities was codified as official policy until 1946. And although the Westerners held "irritating assumptions of superiority which were deeply resented," writes Frank Welsh in his *History of Hong Kong,* the Chinese populace preferred to maintain their own enclaves. Unlike other British colonies, the Chinese in Hong Kong were initially uninterested in socializing with Westerners and rarely assimilated British habits or practices. The city did integrate after World War II, and today, there is a distinctly British paradigm that persists, even after the transfer to Chinese rule. But when Mother's Choice was opening, Western and Chinese camps were still somewhat wary of each other. Over time, Helen and Ranjan grew to expect the question, and they admitted to their audiences that they couldn't be sure. Then Helen, always determined and resolute, would add, "But we are going to give them the opportunity."

Undoubtedly the most controversial question they faced early on was their stance on abortion. "When we were establishing Mother's Choice, it was in an atmosphere of pro-life, pro-choice dialogue all over America," Gary explains. "People tried to engage us in that discussion in Hong Kong, and early on, we said we weren't here to comment on that issue. In the name of Mother's Choice, the emphasis was on the young women making the choice. We were trying to empower them to make the very best choice for themselves, and we were there to provide a safe, nurturing environment for children who needed it."

Despite prejudices such as these, Gary says the community's response to the idea of Mother's Choice was overwhelmingly positive. "There was something about Mother's Choice that resonated in the hearts of the people of Hong Kong," Gary says, and many people offered support in the form of money, labor, and gifts in kind, all of which continue to the present day. Yet in the first days, Mother's Choice found themselves struggling against an unlikely institution: the Social Welfare Department of Hong Kong, the division of the government their work would benefit the most.

Gary had maintained close ties with the Government Property Agency during the years they had been in Hong Kong. Given the agency's generosity with housing in the past, Gary felt assured in requesting another empty colonial-era building for Mother's Choice. Montgomery Block was located at 42 Kennedy Road, and like the apartments at 7A Kennedy Road where they had lived in 1980, it was part of the Victoria Barracks. Built in the 1880s, the three-story, six-flat complex was just over a hundred yards from the former British Military Hospital where they lived. With classical white columns supporting the open verandahs on the façade, Montgomery Block had a gorgeous view of Victoria Harbor and the central business district of Hong Kong from its perch halfway up the mountainside. Though abandoned, the foundation was solid and the walls, made of brick eighteen inches thick, were sound. For years it had withstood typhoon after typhoon. But because it was neither modern nor convenient—it sat 150 steps above Kennedy Road and about the same number of steps below Borrett Road, with no vehicular access—it had been empty for about a decade.

Gary filed the necessary paperwork with the Government Property Agency and was confident they'd be approved. They had continued to track the issues related to teen pregnancy in the newspaper, and recent reports gave statistics that in the last twelve months, the Family Planning Association had turned away around two thousand young women because they were past the first trimester, which was when an abortion could be obtained with no questions asked. But after a few weeks, Gary got a call from a friend at the property agency. He informed Gary that the Social Welfare Department was denying the need for such a program, and therefore they were recommending denying the request for the facilities.

"I don't know what all of their reasons were for denying the need," Gary says, "but I know they were wrong. I think part of the resistance was because this was a shameful matter. Another thing was that if you don't admit it's a need, you don't have to deal with it. But they were denying reality of a true social issue, one that was becoming a larger issue in Hong Kong life."

Gary thanked him for the heads-up and immediately called Ranjan at his office. Unwilling to risk the time and effort they had invested in the project or to see such an obvious need overlooked, Ranjan acted promptly. With Gary still on the line, Ranjan picked up another phone on his desk. "He called directly to Libby Wong, the director of Social Welfare," Gary says, "got her office, got her on the phone. He reminded her of the articles in the *South China Morning Post,* and I quoted statistics from the follow-ups about how many girls were being turned away by the Family Planning Association. He asked her why anyone in the Social Welfare Department would say that there was no need in Hong Kong for the types of services that we wanted to supply."

"Well, that's incorrect," Wong answered. "Obviously there is a need." She told Ranjan that the Social Welfare Department would appreciate any cooperation from a nongovernmental organization willing to provide such a service.

A few weeks later, the Government Property Agency contacted the new leadership of Mother's Choice with an answer. The director of Social Welfare had affirmed the need for their services, and the Government Property Agency was granting them use of Montgomery Block. Thus began an alliance between Mother's Choice and the Social Welfare Department of Hong Kong to respond to the needs of young women and children all across the city, a productive partnership that continues today.

❀ ❀ ❀

Mother's Choice was thrilled to find a home at 42 Kennedy Road, but the disrepair in Montgomery Block was significant, and making it livable for the young women and babies required substantial upgrades, repairs, and additions. Gary recalls leaks in the roof where water from the typhoons and rainstorms had entered and damaged the ceilings and walls. High humidity in Hong Kong requires constant maintenance of painted surfaces, but after being open to the elements for so long, the paint had blistered, cracked, and fallen off the walls. Before those surfaces were attended to, they had to rewire, replumb, and reroof the entire building, and even the windows needed to be replaced.

Yet the disrepair of Montgomery Block provided an opportunity for the Hong Kong community to show support and generosity in ways the leaders of Mother's Choice had never expected. "Out of the woodwork, people began stepping forward," Gary says, "some associated with service organizations, some with our church, some who had just heard about Mother's Choice and appreciated what we were doing." A woman named Sharon Tin, one of Hong Kong's top interior decorators, obtained bids from the contractors she used when working on private residences, asking for their services at cost. Another friend was an instructor for the police academy in Hong Kong, and he sent two hundred police cadets to trim the overgrown vines and trees and clear the undergrowth that had proliferated over the years. Bankers and attorneys for international corporations showed up to help. "They'd say things like, 'I was working my way through university and did some bricklaying,'" Gary recalls. "'I could lay some bricks on these verandahs to make them more secure'—or they'd offer to paint." Phyllis Marwah and her older children joined Helen and hers to form a painting crew for the administrative offices and the bedrooms where the pregnant girls would stay. That early involvement would have lasting effects on many of the Stephens and Marwah children, most notably Alia Marwah Eyres, the eldest daughter of Phyllis and Ranjan. Alia now works as the managing director of Mother's Choice and lives with her husband and young son on the third floor of Montgomery Block, in the same apartment Gary and Helen would call home for fifteen years.

People continued to give. During the renovation of Montgomery Block, a man walked through and commented that the rooms would be hot in summer. As the owner of a company that manufactured ceiling fans, it was a detail he would be likely to note. "Decide if you want fans fitted with light fixtures or without, and the type of finish you prefer, and I'll have them delivered," he said. The owner of a flooring company supplied ceramic tile for the floors.

Toward the end of the renovation, a member of the newly formed board of directors for Mother's Choice, Mike Ullman, toured the facilities and commented that soon they would need to furnish them. As a manager of three five-star hotels in Hong Kong, along with over a dozen other businesses, he gave what he could. One of his hotels was renovating and refurbishing two floors of executive suites, and Mother's Choice could take their pick from the furnishings. "So we went one day and we had twelve hours to get all of the furniture out of that hotel, into trucks, and delivered to Mother's Choice," Gary says. "We chose beds, rattan writing desks with glass tops, rattan couches and chairs, televisions, brass and silver floor lamps and wall lamps, pictures off the wall—everything that we could imagine we could use, and all of it less than two years old." Seven truckloads of furnishings were transported to Mother's Choice that day, and a friend who worked for St. Stephen's Society, helping addicts get clean, asked some of her people in recovery to come and carry furniture down. They filled the bedrooms for the pregnant girls, the administrative offices, and some staff living spaces as well.

"As these people were coming forward one by one, we thought, 'This is a good sign,'" Gary says. "This wasn't just something that we were interested in. People were seeing our vision and feeling passionately about what we were doing."

As the opening of Mother's Choice drew closer, the board of directors decided to begin promoting the organization in an official, public way. In February of 1988, they arranged a press conference to announce the opening. Montgomery Block was still a few months from completion, so they set up for the conference at the British Military Hospital in what was being used as a dining room. The room was long with French doors opening onto the covered verandahs along the sides. They placed a podium in the middle of one of the long walls, then arranged several rows of chairs in semicircles around it. Hugging the podium in this democratic arrangement, the chairs were soon filled with people from the Social Welfare Department, from radio and television, and from both English- and Chinese-language newspapers. Mother's Choice had invited administrators and medical staff from the local hospitals, both private and government-run, to spread the word among medical professionals. The program was simple: first Helen would speak, then they would offer to take people on a walking tour through the facilities at Montgomery Block.

Always an unwilling public speaker, Helen presented her statement about the services Mother's Choice was looking to provide in less than five minutes. Then she opened the floor for questions. A reporter who worked for a Chinese-language paper raised his hand and asked the familiar question: "A lot of you are from overseas. How do you know that Hong Kong pregnant girls will even want to come to this place?"

This time, Helen had more than simple hope as an answer. "Thank you so much for that question," she said. "Let me tell you about two phone calls we received this morning. One of them was from an English-speaking young lady who is pregnant and seventeen years old. A second call was in Cantonese, and it was a young lady asking, 'Can I come and please see you tomorrow? I'm pregnant.'"

Before any official announcement or advertisement, Mother's Choice had found its way to the young women it was seeking to serve.

"The next day, there were newspaper articles in all of the major Chinese newspapers and news reports on TV and coverage on the radio," Gary says. One newspaper devoted almost a full page to their article on Mother's Choice and Helen, with a photo of her standing in front of Montgomery Block. "And the phone started ringing off the hook."

Despite all of the media attention they received and the statistics and stories of young women in need, Gary and Helen were stunned by the immediate response. The first young lady who had called the morning of the press conference was on the steps of the British Military Hospital at 8:30 the morning after. Her name was Jessica, and she was five months into her pregnancy. She asked if she could move in, but the remodel at Montgomery Block wouldn't be finished until May. Always willing to improvise, they shuffled some staff members around, and one of the men's dormitory rooms at the British Military Hospital became a temporary refuge for teenage girls like Jessica. They would be able to house six young women, albeit in close quarters, until Montgomery Block was ready for occupancy.

The two phone lines for Mother's Choice continued ringing throughout the day. They fielded calls from young women needing advice and from people asking how they could get involved. They were encouraged by the community's support and by the young ladies' willingness to call on them for help, but because Mother's Choice hadn't yet hired a full staff, they didn't have a bilingual receptionist to handle the two phone lines. With many of the calls from Cantonese speakers, they turned to Jessica, fluent in both English and Cantonese, for help. She became a lynchpin. "Twenty minutes after arriving, she was in a flurry taking down names and numbers," Gary says. "Essentially she became one of our Mother's Choice volunteers herself, as our first bilingual receptionist."

Things continued to move quickly. At about four o'clock that afternoon, the second young girl who had called the previous day arrived with her two sisters. She spoke only Cantonese, and she was visibly advanced in her pregnancy. Sally Quinton sat down with the young girl and a translator to fill out paperwork and establish the girl's medical history, and one of the first questions she asked was when the girl had last seen a physician. Sally listened expectantly as the translator conveyed the question in Cantonese, then gave the girl's answer in English.

"Two and a half months ago," the woman said.

"And how far along in her pregnancy did the doctor say she was?" Sally asked.

Again, the question was relayed in Cantonese, then the young woman's response echoed back in English. "Seven months," the translator said.

"We did the math," Gary says, "then called the private hospital the woman at the press conference had volunteered the day before and made an appointment for the following morning. But the girl didn't even make it through the night." She went into labor, and instead of the twenty-five-minute drive to the top of Victoria Peak, they took her in a taxi to the nearest government hospital, about five minutes away, where the girl made it through the delivery without a complication. "We hadn't even been open for twenty-four hours," Gary says, "and we had our first baby boy."

❧ ❧ ❧

In May of 1988, Mother's Choice moved into a remodeled and fully furnished Montgomery Block, and young women began filling the eighteen spaces available in the hostel. Their rooms were located on the second floor of the building, and Maria Brinkman, a young, dark-haired Dutch woman who spoke Cantonese, became the first housemother. Maria was a mentor, guardian, and translator for them, and she moved into one of the third-floor flats with several other full-time staff members, which made her available around the clock.

The young women were able to come and go freely. After a few trips to local street markets with Maria, where she gave them lessons in haggling for fruits, vegetables, and meats, they would go on their own and buy the necessary items for a meal. Then Maria would hold a cooking class. "She had all the girls working with her in the kitchen, and you would hear so much laughter coming out of the room as they were preparing meals and then eating together," Gary says. "We were really trying to establish the Mother's Choice hostel as a home, and the way Maria just loved these girls and was like a big sister to them really helped create that atmosphere."

The young women followed a scheduled daily program to give them some structure; it involved group and individual counseling sessions, prenatal classes, and certain duties around the house. People in the community began volunteering to give lessons in English, typing, or computer skills, hoping to equip the girls with an employable skill set in case they didn't make it back to school. Other classes, like art therapy, music appreciation, and aerobics, were a way to engage the girls' minds and bodies and keep them healthy. "These girls were not going to school and didn't have jobs, and they would've had a lot of time on their hands," Gary says. "We didn't want them just sitting in front of the television or constantly thinking about their situations—that wouldn't be good for them physically or psychologically."

Sally and Helen worked together closely to coordinate the services for the young women. As the midwife, Sally was involved with accompanying them to doctor's visits and overseeing their prenatal care. As a nurse and a mother of four children herself, Helen also knew what to expect in different seasons of pregnancy, and together they were able to give solid advice and support to the young women in their care. They also helped develop the counseling services for young women who didn't come until it was time to give birth and those who never even moved into the facility. The Mother's Choice twenty-four-hour hotline fielded hundreds and then thousands of calls from young girls in need, or sometimes from their boyfriends or parents.

So that Helen could keep up both with her responsibilities at Mother's Choice and her family, she and Gary had moved their family into a flat on the third floor of Montgomery Block. The design of the building was such that a central staircase connected the offices on the first floor with the girls' rooms on the second floor and the staff quarters on the third; it was a main thoroughfare for all the workers and residents of the building. One day, Gary was headed up to the family apartment from the offices down below, and he crossed three young women on these stairs. In his head, he knew the circumstances they were facing and the facts of teenage pregnancy. But when he passed them, heavy and holding the handrail tightly as they headed down, with swollen bellies belying their ages, Gary was struck by how incongruous their teenage lives were with the very adult responsibilities of having a child.

"I went upstairs to Helen and I said, 'Helen, I just met three young girls on the stairs,'" Gary recalls. "I described them, and she said, 'Gary, one of those girls was only thirteen.' I was thinking, 'How is this possible?'" They were younger than his seventeen-year-old daughter Shawna, than his fourteen-year-old daughter Amy, and they were facing realities difficult for women twice their age. "One of the girls had gotten pregnant the very first time she ovulated. She didn't know she was pregnant because she had never even known the natural monthly cycle."

Teenage years aren't usually a time of great perspective. A typical teenager's whole world is contained in the daily dramas at school, navigating a social space of trivialities that the teen imagines having disastrous consequences. Yet these young women's situations were the opposite, and their actions had consequences far beyond themselves.

An early annual report to supporters of Mother's Choice featured several pregnant girls answering the question, "What would have happened if you had not come to Mother's Choice?" The first answered, "I would have had an abortion, or I would have delivered the baby and thrown it out on the street." A second: "I kept my pregnancy a secret from my parents, my friends, and my relatives. I hid it from my teachers and my classmates, and I had to withdraw from school. At that time, I really wished that I would die. It seemed I had lost everything." The third felt hopeless: "I don't think I could have faced the future."

The responses affirmed the aims of Mother's Choice to be a refuge, a comfort, a support, and a home. "Girls wrote letters and said things like, 'This is the very first place I ever knew family in my life,'" Gary recalls. "'This is the very first place I really understood what love and acceptance are all about.' So when you get that kind of feedback, you know that you are filling a void, answering a need."

In the first few years, the average age of the girls in the hostel was between fifteen and sixteen. This fact compounded the responsibility of Mother's Choice to provide them with the best support and information so that they could make the right decisions for themselves and the babies, especially if they decided against terminating pregnancy.

"There were many questions for the girls to answer," Gary explains. "They had to decide, 'Will I parent? What will I need to be a successful parent? Will my family participate in this? Will they accept me and my child? Will I choose adoption? How will the child live in an adoptive family?' A lot of those questions are very real and very deep questions, and as they saw and met adoptive families, and they saw how these children were really loved, for some of them it became an easier decision. They knew at fourteen or fifteen years old, they weren't equipped or ready to be full-time parents."

Mother's Choice also continued to serve young women after they left the hostel and were forced into the realities and challenges that they had been insulated from while at Montgomery Block. "One of our social workers would stay in contact with them until they felt like the girl was back and reestablished in her community or support system," Gary says. "We had ongoing support for those who chose parenthood so that we could help bridge the gap and be part of that support system that they needed."

But the leaders of Mother's Choice also realized that the trauma the young women were facing, the mature decisions they were having to make at such a young age, could be avoided. The best solution for the problem of unplanned pregnancy would be to prevent the pregnancy in the first place. An article in the *South China Morning Post* appeared at the third anniversary of Mother's Choice. "When teenagers are left holding the baby" argued that the cultural inability to talk about sex combined with the stigma of teenage pregnancy made it impossible for young girls to get information that could help prevent pregnancy or to ask for help when they found themselves in crisis. In a statement in 1992, Ranjan, serving as the chairman of the board of directors, told supporters, "Much still needs to be done to lessen the number of unplanned pregnancies amongst the very young in our society. The counseling and support given by Mother's Choice to young pregnant girls, their boyfriends, and their families reveals an urgent need for more resources to be focused in this area."

By that time, Mother's Choice was already sending social workers to schools to conduct workshops about sex and relationships, to educate young people and dispel myths and ignorance about sexual activity. Though they started small, with just a few workshops in local schools, they began increasing the number of school presentations, media interviews, and visits from community groups to remove the stigma associated with sex and open the discussion. In the first ten years of Mother's Choice, their presentations grew from half a dozen in the early 1990s to one hundred in 1999, when they reached almost twenty thousand school-aged kids.

In 2001, Mother's Choice began a major sex education campaign targeted toward combating not only teenage pregnancies and late-term abortions, but also the rise in sexually transmitted diseases. With the support of the Hong Kong Jockey Club and some generous web designers, they launched the Mother's Choice website, a bilingual resource that provided frank, comprehensive information on sexuality, from determining when one was ready for sex, to contraception, pregnancy, and adoption. There were message boards for teenagers to ask questions or have discussions regarding relationships or sexual health, and there were ways to contact a social worker for a private conversation. In the first year, they had almost two million hits, which would grow to fifteen, twenty-four, and almost forty million in the following decade. At the same time, media interviews and school talks continued, and advertising firms began offering to design advertisements to help get the word out for Mother's Choice.

In 2002, Mother's Choice enlisted the help of Fruit Chan, an acclaimed Hong Kong film director, to make three television ads which would coincide with print and poster campaigns. With an eye on both the current and future generations of Hong Kong, Chan hoped to open a discussion between teenagers, parents, and schools on a topic that, according to him, the people of Hong Kong weren't willing to talk about. Casting proved difficult, illustrating Chan's point. Finding teenagers who wanted to get involved with a topic as taboo as unwanted pregnancy was tough, but it was even more of a challenge to get their parents to sign off on their kids' participation. In the end, they produced three public service announcements that encouraged young people to pause, to think, and to make good choices, because in the end, "the person most affected is yourself."

In the years that followed, Mother's Choice continued these efforts, but they also shifted the focus from teenage girls to the other parties involved. The message in 2003 was targeted toward young men, asking them to think before they act, and Fruit Chan directed two more public service announcements for television, again with real teenagers, but this time with boys playing the role of the girls. "I wanted the boys to feel what the girls feel—to go through all the emotions, the pain, the shame, the rejection—when they are left to deal with a crisis pregnancy alone," Chan explains. "Too often the boys get away with taking no responsibility." In 2006, Mother's Choice launched a campaign emphasizing that sex education begins with parents, warning them that if they didn't talk to their children about sex, someone else would.

By 2008, Mother's Choice was holding almost three hundred seminars a year in schools and even at local shopping malls, where they could reach teenagers, parents, and other members of the community, including teachers. The sex education programs reached sixty-one thousand people, and exponentially more were addressed through the television spots and billboards in busy shopping areas and in the Hong Kong metro. Between the ad campaigns, the education programs, and the website, Mother's Choice was broaching the taboo topics of sex, unplanned pregnancy, and sexually transmitted diseases in ways the Hong Kong public found harder and harder to ignore.

CHAPTER 6

HOMES FOR CHILDREN

❋

Early the next morning, Abraham took some food and a skin of water and gave
them to Hagar. He set them on her shoulders and then sent her off with Ishmael.
She went on her way and wandered in the Desert of Beersheba.

When the water in the skin was gone, she put the boy under one of the
bushes. Then she went off and sat down about a bowshot away, for she thought,
"I cannot watch the boy die." And as she sat there, she began to sob.

God heard the boy crying, and the angel of God called to Hagar from
heaven and said to her, "What is the matter, Hagar? Do not be afraid; God has
heard the boy crying as he lies there. Lift the boy up and take him by the hand,
for I will make him into a great nation."

Then God opened her eyes and she saw a well of water. So she went and
filled the skin with water and gave the boy a drink.

God was with the boy as he grew up.

GENESIS 21:14–20

Rural China—Hong Kong

Late at night in a provincial city in China, three young men entered a public bathroom, a necessary stop in the middle of a night out on the town. The cement building was rudimentary and small, divided in the middle into men's and women's sections. They'd been inside only a few moments when one turned to the others and said, "Listen!" They became quiet, and after a moment, the other two heard, very clearly, the sound of a baby's cry. They looked around, on the floors and behind the partitions that divided the urinals from the holes in the ground that constitute toilets in many parts of Asia. They saw nothing.

But the cries continued. Finally one of the young men looked down through one of the holes, and below, in the circle of light that fell through the opening, he could see the legs of an infant, kicking weakly, wriggling in the mess. Instinctively, he reached down and grabbed the baby by her legs. He pulled it out. Another young man ripped off his shirt and wrapped it around the infant, and all three ran outside. On the street, taxis were lined up, the drivers milling about, chatting with one another. The young men shouted to them, "Where can we take this baby?"

One taxi driver shot his hand up in the air. "I know a place," he said. "I'll take you."

The young men loaded into the taxi and were soon leaving the middle of the city behind and moving over rough and pocked roads toward the outskirts. The driver pulled up in front of a white building that was home to a privately run orphanage called Mother's Care, a satellite of Mother's Choice, which he'd only learned about earlier that day when he was hired by a few staff members for a ride home. He stopped, then pointed at the front door. "Go knock," he said. "They'll come help you."

Though it was nearly midnight, a woman soon answered the door. Immediately she took the child from the boys' arms and brought her upstairs to bathe her. She washed the baby's skin and shampooed her full head of hair three times. She used a suction bulb on the baby's nose and mouth and ears, then wrapped the baby tightly in warm and clean clothes and fed her a bottle of formula. After the baby had finished eating, she took the child into her own room and kept her beside her for the next three days.

The workers at the orphanage gave the baby girl a Chinese name that means "Celebrating Grace." There was no knowing how long she'd been abandoned, but she recovered quickly and thrived in the hands of the child-care workers. Within a few weeks she was placed in a foster family, who provided stable and nurturing care for almost a year.

On one of Gary's trips into China to consult with the leaders of this orphanage, Gary visited her. He arrived at the foster family's small home, a haphazardly constructed brick house with a corrugated tin roof and dirt floors, like many others in the neighborhood. They had taught her two or three words of English that they knew—*hello* and *thank you*—and how to shake hands, which she offered to Gary when he entered the house and squatted next to her. Gary had heard of this little girl so many times over the course of almost a year, and he was so moved by her story, that he asked the foster family if he could spend a few moments alone with her, carrying her in his arms. They said, "Of course you may."

"So I walked outside with this precious girl in my arms," Gary recalls, "and I was thinking of a verse in the Psalms of the Old Testament, that God listens to their cry and he hears their desire. I was saying 'Thank you,' and I was, in my own way, just trying to breathe quietly a blessing on this little girl. The next week, she was leaving China for an adoptive home in the United States."

On schedule, the adoptive family arrived and met her, and as they were getting ready to depart, the director of the orphanage opened her desk drawer and retrieved a small scrap of paper with a telephone number scrawled across it. She called the number, and soon after, the three young men who had saved the baby girl drove down to the airport to say good-bye as she departed for her new home in America.

❀ ❀ ❀

When the leaders of Mother's Choice first wrote their charter, they had no idea that they'd soon be crossing international borders to help children. At the time, they imagined having just a handful of babies in Hong Kong, the ones born to the pregnant girls in their care, and they would work unofficially—caring for fewer than six babies did not require a license in Hong Kong. They set up two small rooms across from the offices on the ground floor of Montgomery Block with a pastel palette and cribs and mobiles, then recruited staff to care for the babies. Most would be adopted locally through the Social Welfare Department. But the legal process was slow and convoluted, and by the end of their first year, so many girls were choosing adoption for their babies that the child-care home was full, and with another due date fast approaching, they were in a bind.

"When the next child was born, legally we could not bring that child out of the hospital," Helen says. But instead of placing the child in another facility, Helen treated this as a moment for Mother's Choice to grow. With Sally's help, she took up the challenge to get Mother's Choice licensed as a child-care facility through the Social Welfare Department.

The licensing process was involved, with applications and regulations and inspections, and very early they had a meeting with the chief of Fire Services. He outlined the requirements that a building must meet to become licensed, and one rule stipulated that any child-care facility had to have a direct access road in case of fire. It was a practical regulation, but it was a true obstruction for Mother's Choice. Montgomery Block had no access road, and it was a five-minute walk to reach either of the roads it was situated between.

"So we looked into everything," Helen says. "We even asked a civil engineer from our church to come and take a look, and we asked him, 'How much would it cost to build a road to Montgomery Block?' And he said, 'It'd cost millions of dollars.' Literally, it was a roadblock. It felt like there was no way."

Some might have given up at this point, but Helen continued praying for guidance on where to go next. She had an impression that they needed to keep trying, that God was saying to them through the words of the prophet Isaiah, "Behold, I am about to do something new. I am making a roadway in the wilderness."

They persisted with the same goal, and after several unsuccessful meetings with the chief of Fire Services, they decided to change their approach, deploying a strategy that made use of their familiarity with the inner workings of the bureaucratic machine. "In Hong Kong, there are always the rules," Helen explains, "but the best question to ask is, 'How can you help us achieve our goal? What do we have to do to get a waiver on the rule?'"

Unfortunately, they were battling precedent. Before Mother's Choice had Montgomery Block, the chief of Fire Services had turned down a group wanting to use the building as a kindergarten, and he was therefore reluctant. "He said to us, 'Tell me, how can I be just and fair?'" Helen recalls. "'I said they could not because there is no access road. What can you do to show me that it will be safe for the children?'"

"I told him, 'We just want to have six to twelve babies,'" Helen explains, "'just a few babies, not two or three hundred kids. We're willing to have a stricter ratio of caregivers to children. We have staff members sleeping upstairs at night, which ensures there are plenty of hands in an emergency. We have a nice concrete area in the back that we can evacuate the children to. This would be our plan.'"

They left without an answer.

Several days later, Helen was at her desk when a staff member stuck her head in and said, "Helen, somebody is at the front gate." Helen got up, walked outside, and was surprised to see the chief of Fire Services standing there. He said to her, "I want to see your building. I want to see what you are asking for."

"I was astonished," Helen says, but she regrouped to show him around. She walked him out to the concrete patios outside which were far enough away from the building to be safe but close enough for quick evacuation. She showed him the rooms on the first floor and the very tiny babies in cribs there—no three-year-olds, four-year-olds, or five-year-olds, just little babies.

Finally, he answered, "Okay, you can have it. You'll get the document in the mail." Helen felt a flood of relief. The obstruction was gone; the path was clear.

A few days later, Helen was walking down the steps to Montgomery Block, returning from a meeting at the British Military Hospital. Sally had stayed behind to take care of the babies. Suddenly, they heard someone shouting "Hey! Hey!" from a distance, and they noticed Sally leaning out of an upper-story window, waving a white piece of paper. The mail had arrived, and the license had come.

"I think the next baby was born on Christmas Day," Helen says, "and we went to bring him home on December 31." For the next two years, they housed up to eighteen babies at a time in three small rooms across from the administrative offices as the infants waited for a home.

✿ ✿ ✿

Initially the infants at Baby Care, as the small home came to be called, were the babies of the pregnant girls. But after Mother's Choice was licensed and added more beds, babies were referred by hospitals across Hong Kong. "Someone from the hospital would call after a young mother had given birth," Gary explains, "and they would say, 'We've got an infant that the birth mother is not planning to parent.' A member of the Baby Care staff would take a taxi to the hospital and bring the newborn back to live at Montgomery Block." Later, they had more children come as referrals from the Social Welfare Department.

Knowing the limitations of a residential nursery to meet the needs of a developing child, the leadership and staff at Baby Care worked hard to overcome those and make a true home for the babies, to give each one individual attention, taking photographs and personalizing each child's crib with his or her name and recording milestones in a baby book. They wanted both the future adoptive parents and the child to know that from the beginning, this child was loved and valued. And the efforts were not wasted. Paul and Rose Kwa, the adoptive parents of a young boy named Simon who came to Baby Care when he was five days old, wrote a letter to Mother's Choice after Simon came to live with them. They thanked Mother's Choice for such attentions: "We are ever so grateful for all Simon's photos, which are priceless gifts to us."

Compared to Mother's Choice, no other child-care facility in Hong Kong provided such quality, individual care. Other facilities in the area were austere and institutional, followed the bare minimum of child-to-caregiver ratios, and had no volunteer support. Few were run by the state; instead, many were well-intentioned charities doing their best to meet the physical needs of the many children in their care, with little concern from society at large. This apathy from the greater society was in part due to a failure of leadership. In his 1994 *The History of Hong Kong,* historian Frank Welsh argues that Hong Kong community leaders had always been more concerned with business interests than the general good; modern attitudes in the territory displayed a "single-minded dedication to money-making which powered the engine of expansion, and an impatience with anything that smacked of the Welfare State," allowing only "sharply focused and minimal intervention on behalf of the most needy."

Children without parents certainly fit the description of the most needy, and "minimal" seemed an apt description for the intervention they were receiving. These children needed an advocate, and the more Mother's Choice learned about the plight of Hong Kong's orphans and abandoned children, the more they stepped in to fill that gap. Only a year after becoming a licensed child-care facility, their services were in such demand that Mother's Choice began exploring the idea of obtaining a larger facility for Baby Care. The small space at Montgomery Block was crowded for the eighteen babies already in their care and the necessary laundry and storage space for food and diapers; taking more was out of the question. "We were maxed out where we were," Gary says, "and it really wasn't the best to have the children we were caring for in the same building as the pregnant girls because of the angst it caused in the pregnant girls. It was a constant reminder that their babies would be one of these."

Through their network of supporters, Sir David Ford, the chief secretary of the Hong Kong government, heard of their need and asked if they would like another building. The board of directors of Mother's Choice acceded, and Gary and Helen toured the building offered. It was another colonial structure, at 5 Bowen Road, overlooking the tracks of the Victoria Peak Tram, which began in Central just above the harbor and trundled up to the highest point of the island. Like so many other colonial-era buildings, 5 Bowen Road was empty of inhabitants. "But it was full of canvas bags, and they were stacked higher than my height with Inland Revenue tax documents of Hong Kong citizenry," Gary recalls. "It was hard to even walk through the hallways or to judge how big the rooms were because they were so cluttered."

But the building was close to Montgomery Block and also three stories, also white with verandahs across the front. They imagined the possibilities: they could have their administrative offices on the bottom floor, rooms for babies on the second, and housing for staff members on the third. They presented the plan to the board of directors, who voted for expanding at 5 Bowen Road. Then an adviser and close friend named Barbara Rogers volunteered to raise the money for the renovation, and very soon, she came back with a check for HK $1 million.

Because of the donation, the remodel began immediately and was completed quickly. Baby Care moved to 5 Bowen Road on October 6, 1990. They were licensed to care for twenty-four babies, but the space was big enough for expanding. "We had an agreement with the Social Welfare Department, that we could train and license our own child-care workers using their curriculum," Gary explains. "So all of these people who came to work for Mother's Choice, both local and from overseas, went through the Social Welfare Department's curriculum to become a licensed child-care worker, and we were able to add more beds for babies." It was a significant increase: from April of 1990 to March of 1991, when they were licensed for twenty-four babies at a time, they cared for sixty-one babies, which led to forty-one adoptions, mostly local. By 1993, that had more than doubled to 136 babies cared for in a year and 88 adoptions. Eventually, they had capacity for sixty babies at a time.

Running a quality child-care establishment for so many infants can be a very expensive enterprise, and Mother's Choice depended on monetary donations from private individuals and social groups to support their work. But as with the Montgomery Block facilities, people were also forthcoming with gifts in kind, which significantly decreased their costs. One of their very first donations for the babies at Mother's Choice happened before they even opened the first facility in May of 1988. An American expatriate named Bill Jolly worked for Proctor & Gamble, owner of the diaper company Pampers. When he heard about Mother's Choice, he offered to supply diapers to the babies born to the young mothers free of charge, and before the Montgomery Block remodel was complete, they had closets full of diapers. An otherwise huge expense was erased, and Proctor & Gamble still provides Pampers to the babies at Mother's Choice to this day. In 2000, after ten years in operation, Gary estimated that the number of diapers Mother's Choice had used was nearly 1.2 million. In the ten years since, they've used at least that many over again.

There were other donations, things like milk and baby bottles, that also attended to the babies' physical needs, but the single most cost-saving measure for Mother's Choice was the full-time volunteer staff, which cut millions of dollars from their budgets each year. "In our child-care facilities, we had to maintain a strict ratio of full-time staff set by the Social Welfare Department," Gary explains.

"We had to have one full-time staff member for every eight children, twenty-four hours a day, seven days a week." For most nonprofit organizations, employee salaries make up the bulk of expenditures, but in the early years, almost all the staff members at Mother's Choice were overseas volunteers who lived on support from family and friends. As the different child-care programs at Mother's Choice expanded, and as they later began taking children with special needs and moving into foster care, they hired some salaried workers, but the staff at Mother's Choice was consistently made up of at least 50 percent volunteers. Gary and Helen were included among them; in their twenty-three years in Hong Kong, they never took a salary from Mother's Choice.

As the number of babies grew, part-time volunteers began coming in droves to hold, feed, and play with the infants. "We recognized upfront that the way to be successful was to give local people the opportunity to get involved and volunteer their services," Gary says. "And our part-time volunteers became our own advertising resource. It was by word of mouth that people heard about the babies at Baby Care and became involved with us." Otherwise, Mother's Choice did very little advertising in order to generate funds, though they did make themselves available to different media outlets, mostly to bring attention to the social problems of teenage pregnancy and children in need of loving care.

In 1991, 160 part-time volunteers were signed up. In 1992, the number grew to 280. By 1993, 350 volunteers were supporting the babies at Mother's Choice, and within a few years, they had to cap the number around 450 to keep the lists manageable. The level of involvement was unprecedented. Volunteerism was not a prominent aspect of Hong Kong society, yet when given the opportunity, people were more than willing to respond.

At Baby Care, the primary concern was establishing an affectionate, nurturing environment for the child to thrive, both physically and psychologically, and to give each child an opportunity to build an emotional connection and trust with a caregiver that could then be replicated within an adopted family. "The professionals we consulted were telling us any child who has attached to a caregiver has the capacity to attach to others later in life," Gary explains, "but if a child does not bond to a caregiver in those first few months, the challenges against that child attaching to others grow exponentially as the age increases." To minimize the turnover of caregivers and allow the infants better opportunities to attach, Mother's Choice instituted practices that would have made John Bowlby proud. First, the full-time child-care workers were assigned to be the primary caregivers of certain babies. "We would tell our full-time people not to just chat with the other volunteers or other staff members while they were feeding the babies," Gary explains. "Engage with the child, talk to the child, make eye contact with the child, even if the child is only three months old. That kind of interaction is enormously positive for the child. It really does begin to build their sense of self-worth." Then the part-time volunteers, who were given the same instructions, could supplement the attention the child was getting from staff members.

For some volunteers, such instruction was unnecessary. Long-time volunteer Purvis Shroff began visiting Baby Care regularly shortly after the loss of her adult son, and soon she was there five days a week to hold and pamper the babies, cooing at them with pet names as she held them. She was consistent and dependable, especially in times of crisis. During the summer, typhoons are common in Hong Kong, with the more severe storms bringing sustained winds above 75 miles per hour with gusts close to 140 and dropping several inches of rain per hour. The government would issue a numbered warning in proportion to the strength of the storm, and a typhoon signal eight or higher instructed people to stay at home, keep an ample supply of food and water, and have flashlights handy. Public transport would shut down as the typhoon neared Hong Kong, and soon the streets were blocked by fallen limbs. Roads became difficult to navigate; water would flow through the streets like rivers. "You would think you were living in the mountains of Colorado during the spring melt," Gary says, "just enormous amounts of water coming down." Many staff members and volunteers were simply unable to get to Baby Care under these conditions.

"But we still had all these babies," Gary recalls. "So on days when the weather was too bad for travel, Purvis would say to her driver, 'It's too dangerous for you to drive. I will drive myself, and I'll do a double or triple shift.' She was absolutely committed to those babies who needed care."

❋ ❋ ❋

One of the most distinctive characteristics of Mother's Choice was that they were never static, always changing, always setting new goals for their work and always open to new ways they could help. Early in 1991, Lady Ford, the patron of Mother's Choice and the wife of Chief Secretary Sir David Ford, approached Helen with a special request: she had visited a little boy in the Duchess of Kent Hospital several times. He was missing more than one limb and had heart issues as well as other health problems. She asked Helen if Mother's Choice could help find an adoptive family for this child in need. Helen immediately contacted Holt International Children's Services, with whom Mother's Choice had continued a relationship, to discuss the possibility of finding a home for this young boy. Very soon they had located an adoptive family in the United States, near a hospital renowned for its care of children with special needs. The Social Welfare Department approved the match, and soon, the young boy left Hong Kong for his new home in Portland, Oregon.

Lady Ford's request highlighted another service that Mother's Choice could provide, this time as a home and haven for children with special needs. Though this would require significant resources and a steep learning curve for the staff, in May of 1991, a four-year-old boy with Down syndrome came to live at 5 Bowen Road. His name was Ho Chi, and his arrival marked the beginning of Wee Care, a program designed for longer-term care of children aged two to six, both those who were typically developing and those with special needs. Wee Care admitted children from other institutions into a less formal, more homelike environment so they could adapt to the routines and surroundings of family life. The hope was that, as soon as possible, the child could be placed in foster care and then matched with an adoptive family. Ho Chi was the template: he lived at Wee Care for six months before moving into foster care with an expatriate family in Hong Kong. Less than a year later, an American couple—two doctors—adopted Ho Chi in October of 1992. He went to live on a ten-acre property in Mount Vernon, Iowa, where he met his four new siblings, one being a seven-year-old boy from Korea who also had Down syndrome.

Located on the first floor of 5 Bowen Road, Wee Care took in twenty-five children in its first year, thirteen of whom had physical disabilities or developmental delays. Two bedrooms housed six children each, and down the hall was a common room, the site of play, therapy, and education, with a door that led to an outside patio with swings and sunshine. The administrative offices for the social workers and directors of Baby Care were buried in the middle of it all, so there were always extra hands to help, and even there, the child was the central emphasis.

"Helen's office was right in the middle of a beehive of activity, with volunteers, social workers, nurses coming in and out," Gary recalls. "Often she had some of the Wee Care children in her office, and because it was such tight quarters, she used children's little plastic chairs for guests. I'd say, 'This doesn't work this way,

Helen! You can't ask people to come in and sit on those little children's chairs!' And she'd say, 'But we're here for the children!'"

Gary laughs with delight at Helen's insistence on principle, but the entire organization had a single-minded focus on the child's best interest, which is what made their work so effective. They were willing to go to great lengths for the kids, leading them by the hand down to the nearby Zoological Gardens and enrolling the Wee Care children in an adaptive riding program in Hong Kong, around the western side of the island near Pok Fu Lam. With indoor and outdoor arenas and riding trails, it was a nice break from the bustle of the city. Mother's Choice would bring six of the children from Wee Care for a horseback riding lesson; with a trainer leading the horse and walkers on either side attending to the child, they would ride for about an hour. "It was so therapeutic, some of our children would fall asleep in the saddle, just from the soothing motion of the ride," Gary recalls. The child would begin to slump to the side, and one of the walkers would support the child if she began to fall.

When Jacob was old enough and could handle the stimulation, they signed him up as well. "He was about four or five, and he just loved it," Gary says. "He'd lean over and put his face in the mane of the horse and pat the horse on the neck. Jacob really began to appreciate the outdoors by being on horseback, and I think he adapted to riding on ATVs up in the mountains here in Western Colorado because of those early riding lessons."

Though they made valiant efforts to promote the physical, emotional, and psychological growth of the children in their care, Mother's Choice was well aware of the limitations of a child-care facility. "We never thought we were getting into lifelong care for children," Gary says. "We never thought that was our mandate or our core competency. Our goal was to get children into permanently loving families."

For children who were not available for adoption or who would have to wait longer, Mother's Choice did begin a program of foster care, which greatly increased when the director of Social Welfare began disbanding Hong Kong's large institutions in the early '90s. At that point, the director also solicited several organizations to open small group homes. Mother's Choice opened three, where up to eight children lived together in an actual home, not an institution. But their main focus was still to find permanent solutions for as many children as they could.

To this end, they kept detailed and thorough notes of all the pertinent information that a family would want on all the children in their care, from simple medical histories to extensive notes on the child's personality and temperament. "We welcomed questions from the prospective adoptive family through their agency, so that they knew what they were getting into," Gary explains. "That's one of the things we believed at Mother's Choice—that the more detailed and specific your information is, the greater level of comfort and peace you're providing to the adoptive family, and the less chance that they'll feel blindsided by difficulties they didn't anticipate."

Mother's Choice also facilitated communication between reputable international adoption agencies and the Social Welfare Department. "We made a real concerted effort to keep those agencies informed of children who were available for adoption," Gary says, "so that the kids were not being forgotten."

That focus was truly able to effect change in the system. When Mother's Choice first started, the average age of a child going to an adoptive family was a year and a half. Tremendous growth of every kind happens in that period of a child's development, yet the stimulus for arguably the most important kinds of growth—neurological and relational—was absent in these situations. Mother's Choice knew of this crucial window, where children begin to discover whether the world is a safe, responsive place, where they develop the confidence to try their hand in that world. They began applying pressure for the Social Welfare Department to place children in permanent homes more quickly. In fact, Mother's Choice had a long-term goal of children going straight from the hospital to adoptive families that had been vetted by Social Welfare before the child was born, similar to the processes used in the United States. If those efforts succeeded, the child would begin life belonging to a family.

"We were asking questions and following up, and we were persistent," Gary says. The typical delay wasn't for the protection of the child, to vet the prospective parents, or to ensure the child was legally free for adoption. Without the knowledge of how important the first few months were to a child's ability to attach to a family, there was simply no urgency. "Mother's Choice was becoming a very public organization, and I think it was our gentle pressure that got the Social Welfare Department to examine why they were doing what they were doing. This helped them streamline their systems. Within a short window, the average age of a healthy, typically developing child entering a local adoptive family dropped from eighteen months to less than three months."

In the midst of this change, Gary had a meeting with Michael Cartland, who was the director of Social Welfare in Hong Kong from 1989–1992. Though they were scheduled to discuss a separate issue, he took the time to let Gary know the difference that Mother's Choice had made.

"He said, 'I want you to tell Helen and the staff at Mother's Choice that they have helped us change our policies and our practices,'" Gary recalls. Helen had been a great force in this endeavor, and her personal strengths seemed well fitted for such work. She was detailed, deliberate, and determined, and she paid close attention to make sure no children slipped through the cracks. She had a great ability to remember children's histories and specifics about them, mostly because she believed each life deserved such attention. The details also helped her see uncanny and seemingly miraculous matches.

"It was as if she was a silent observer," Gary says, "seeing adoptions take place, knowing both sides of the equation. And she marveled at how *that* child ended up in *that* family. She kept it all very confidential, and she never drew attention to these things. She just smiled and said, 'This is full of grace.'"

CHAPTER 7

QUIET INSTAR

❦

*The fundamental principle of peace is a belief that each person is important.
Even if you cannot speak, even if you cannot walk, even if you've been abandoned, you have a gift to give to the other.*

JEAN VANIER, ENCOUNTERING "THE OTHER"

Hong Kong

They imagined it was something like a cocoon. Jacob simply hadn't had a chance
to come forth, the social workers at Mother's Choice thought, but this little boy,
who couldn't see or speak, who didn't like to be touched, and who lay on his
back rocking ever so slightly, deserved the opportunity to emerge and thrive. They
would bring him to their small group home for children with special needs, a
new addition called Wee Care Extension, where two resident caregivers would
ensure stable, abundant, affectionate care. Hopefully that cocoon was soft and
translucent and easy for him to break through, and they could reflect in a few
months, *This boy has grown and gained weight and learned to laugh and play.* They
cleared the paperwork, waited for a vacancy in their home, and then, on the
morning of July 25, Jacob left the ward for mentally disabled children where he'd
lived for a year. They drove him across the harbor and up through the green and
gray Mid-levels.

Wee Care Extension was located at the ex-commodore's house beside the former British Military Hospital on Borrett Road and was devoted to older children,
who because of their specific needs would not be adopted as quickly and would
therefore need longer-term care. At the time, the five others in the home had conditions ranging from severe autism to Down syndrome and cerebral palsy, and
there was also another blind child in residence.

Like many institutionalized children, Jacob was undersized. Just over two
years old, he weighed only sixteen pounds (compared to the normal weight range
of a child of the same age, which is between twenty-three and thirty-five pounds),
and if a caregiver applied soft pressure to his skin, her fingers would go straight

to bone. He had no muscle tone and still could not sit up on his own or crawl, much less stand or walk, skills many children master in their first year. He was miserable outside of his crib. The other children were loud and playful and tumbled against one another often in the course of a day, but when they brushed up against him, when they sat on his leg or toppled him over, it caused Jacob incredible stress, and he cried for hours on end.

The new space was an enigma to him in its dimensions, noises, and textures, and he lacked the skills to learn it. Besides the sense of sound, the physical world of a blind person exists through touch, to the reach of hands, arms, legs, and feet, John Hull explains in his memoir *Touching the Rock*. To have an understanding of the spaces above and beyond the fleeting and intermittent sounds emanating from children and caretakers, Jacob needed to touch the corners, to discover walls, to fashion a map in his head. Yet he was weak and couldn't move himself, and even if he could have, he'd never been trained that exploring his space was something he should do. In hindsight, it's only reasonable that he screamed when placed on a blanket in the middle of the floor.

But the most crucial change, which no one realized had such an impact on Jacob until his later therapies with experts on blindness, was the change in language. In all of his previous placements, the workers spoke Cantonese. At his new home, he heard English and also Tagalog from the Filipina staff members. And so the words that swirled around him, one of the most important tools for a blind person in deciphering the world, were lost on him.

In a place that relied on routines and schedules, Jacob threw a wrench in the gears with his unpredictability. During the day, he might nap, sucking on two fingers and rocking himself from side to side in his crib, a tactic he had learned when there was no one to rock him to sleep. But then he would wake and scream again. If the staff let him stay up after the other children were asleep, he might find a few moments of peace, but soon he'd begin screaming, waking the other children and refusing the caregivers their much-needed rest. He wouldn't adhere to a schedule for anything—for sleeping, eating, or playing—and they couldn't determine what would set him off. It seemed anything might trigger a tantrum. After a month, his caregivers were at a loss.

Helen and Gary were in the States at that time, on their summer rest in Colorado. In 1987, Helen's parents had gifted them stock in American Express, and that summer, just before a major dip in the market, they cashed it in and used it to buy some land in Cimarron, Western Colorado. They built a log cabin there, and every summer, they spent several weeks resting and recuperating, a necessity for anyone working in relief and development to remain psychologically and emotionally healthy. When they returned at the end of August, Jacob had been there for over a month, and things weren't getting better.

Helen's office was in the same building as Wee Care Extension, just one floor down, though she was often between there, Montgomery Block, and Baby Care. "When we returned from Colorado, they told me what they'd been through with this little boy named Jacob, and I could see that their coping level was about to shift," Helen says. "Because I was responsible for them and for Baby Care, and for the decision of bringing him, I offered to take care of him while I was working in the office. I wanted to allow the child-care workers to care for the other children, but I also wanted to provide Jacob a smaller environment with fewer children to disturb him. And I had the sense that it would be good for him to have a consistent person and somewhat of a consistent schedule."

So Helen began carrying Jacob in a baby sling, like she had her biological children. Helen would turn his face toward her heart and tie him to her body for four or five hours a day, where he could hear her heart beat, and she would speak and sing to him gently. He had, by then, become more accustomed to touch, but his body was still as limp as a dishrag, his tiny limbs dangling as she carried on with her normal work responsibilities, walking between her office and Bowen Road, attending meetings, answering telephone calls, typing on the computer. In the afternoon she would bring him back, and he would have lunch and sleep and play in his crib. One child-care worker noted the difference in a short letter she wrote to him on his third birthday. "I think you liked that routine," wrote Elizabeth, his first caregiver at Wee Care Extension. "You were much more settled and happy."

Helen took him every morning and on the weekends as well. On Saturdays, she would pick him up, sling him, and from the quiet, arbored seclusion of the ex-commodore's perch just above the Mid-levels, she would make her way to the markets of Wan Chai, about a mile east down Kennedy Road and several hundred feet down the hillside terraced with high-rises. The sights and smells of Wan Chai are typical of a busy Chinese market. On a thoroughfare, the two-lane road is slow with car traffic, and the sidewalks are full of people and the attendant noises of chatter and car engines. Red signs with white Chinese characters, advertising massages, restaurants, groceries, and meat markets, cover the façades of buildings and stretch across the road like banners. On the narrow side lanes, produce stalls with their red and green awnings protrude above the shoulder-to-shoulder traffic, and the pungent odor of dried fish floats among fresh mounds of kale and cabbage and broccoli, lemongrass, scallions, and peppers. Here, Helen would bargain with fishmongers in white aprons, browsing the Styrofoam trays of silver fish for twenty Hong Kong dollars, then peruse tabletops of bananas and mandarin oranges and cartons of deep red apples. Next to her, a woman might be sitting on a stool beside a table of orchids and birds of paradise, and Helen might choose a bouquet of white freesia to place in a simple glass vase on the kitchen table.

All the while, Jacob lay against her with his face turned in, his forehead buried against her chest. When she was finished, Helen caught a minibus home, then climbed 180 steps with two hands full of vegetables for their family dinner. In the afternoon, she walked Jacob back up to Wee Care and returned him to his crib.

Seven days a week, Helen would carry him. For several weeks, Jacob was unresponsive and remained limp as she carried him and spoke to him softly, singing to him as she walked between her office building and her home at Montgomery Block.

Then one morning, as Helen walked the seven-minute trek between one Mother's Choice facility and another, her mind listing absently between things to do for work and family, she felt a light brush against her elbow. She looked around her for a person or a branch or an insect. And then she looked down. Jacob had raised a hand, and with his thin fingers, he was gently stroking her arm, grazing the skin lightly back and forth, back and forth. Helen was overcome with amazement and joy. "There was someone inside of this limp, small body who had been hearing me," she says. It was the first time they knew that someone was home.

Helen kept at it, pouching Jacob for several hours each day through the fall and into winter. Undoubtedly, Jacob's vulnerability and extreme dependence worked on Helen's heart as he lay in the carrier on her chest, and she was soon thinking that it might be good if she and Gary fostered him and he had even more of a home, more of a connection with people more like parents. "I know that Helen was there before me," Gary says, "and she was saying, 'Oh, God, you've gotta speak to my hard-hearted husband, because I know he won't listen to me.' We had been working with Mother's Choice for over ten years at this time, and raising our own four biological children, but never even really contemplated being foster parents. But in the back of my mind, I knew that you don't have a lot of authority to encourage other people to foster if you're not doing it."

They spent Christmas in Colorado that year, in the snow in the mountains. Earlier that fall, Gary had spoken at their church in Hong Kong about how he and Helen had met this young boy and felt like they needed to be open to fostering him. Perhaps he hadn't consciously come to terms with it. One evening a few days after Christmas, they visited some friends, Mike and Cathy Ullman, who had a second home in the mountains and were themselves adoptive parents. Though they had recently moved to Greenwich, Connecticut, the Ullmans had lived in Hong Kong for some time and been involved in the same church as Gary and Helen. They were also major supporters of Mother's Choice; Mike was a founding board member and had donated the furniture for Montgomery Block. Cathy had been at church the day Gary spoke about Jacob, and she asked how things were proceeding with regard to fostering this little boy. "I'd completely forgotten about it," Gary says, "but when she asked this, it was like my heart was pricked." Gary was leaving the next day to speak at a few conferences in Northern Europe. So that evening, they gathered as a family to see what their children thought about fostering. Their eldest daughter Shawna had left Hong Kong for college in the United States, but Amy, Andrew, and Katie had had the opportunity to meet Jacob and spend time with him. "Our children were unanimously positive about us fostering him," Gary explains. "So in January, we had a home study and became a licensed foster family." In February, Jacob became their foster son.

"You came to live with our family full-time on February 13, 1997," Helen wrote to Jacob on his third birthday in a small blue notebook where, over the next few years, she would record milestones and reflections on his life with them. "We were so excited that we got to bring you home. We tried to make the adjustment as easy for you as possible and were able to bring your old familiar crib with the same sheets and top." Initially they placed Jacob's crib in their son Andrew's old bedroom on the opposite end of the apartment, but soon they moved him to a small sitting area adjacent to their bedroom, where the only partition between them was a pair of French doors. He needed to be closer, they thought, so they could respond more readily when he cried at night, to let him know they were available, to facilitate bonding.

More than anything, the confined space of his crib was where Jacob preferred to be, to listen from that familiar and predictable space. "Any other child would love to be out of the crib," Helen says, "but that was a safe place for him. We had this theory that when he was in the crib at night, he would try to sit up and do the things we never saw him do during the day." A large part of it was that, though he had not been not diagnosed, Jacob showed symptoms of sensory integration disorder, meaning he had a difficult time organizing the information he encountered through his senses. To cope, he would braid his fingers, pulling the middle finger over the index finger, the ring finger over the middle finger, and the pinky finger over the ring again and again. This type of braiding is a common tactic for self-soothing in children with special needs and also for children who display symptoms of institutional autism—a way to focus one's mind and center oneself through that one sense.

Helen knew, however, that in order to learn to crawl, walk, and be socialized, to be acclimated to a higher-stimulus world that he could process and be a part of, Jacob had to leave that shelter. So Helen set a modest goal: to get him out of the crib without him screaming for twenty minutes, three times a day. She hoped to increase the amount of time he was out incrementally, but it was slow going. What was required was a completely different approach to mothering. This was a child who slept poorly, threw tantrums, and shied away from being touched. After raising four children who were typically developing, she had to make a paradigm shift, and she needed patience in abundance.

"In those first few months, there wasn't a lot of progress," Helen recalls. "There wasn't a lot of response. Sometimes he would like to eat, sometimes he wouldn't. It was unpredictable. I would have him in a pouch and take him to a staff lunch, and five minutes in, he would start screaming. I would have no option but to just walk out."

But progress was what they were most hoping for when Gary and Helen decided to foster him. The adoption professionals at Holt International had told them that a blind child who was nonverbal had almost no chance of being adopted, as most people were either unable or unwilling to take on such a challenge. But as studies showed, speech was unlikely if he stayed in a facility with ever-changing care. However, with Jacob in a fostering situation, maybe he'd learn to speak, and then maybe he'd be placed with a family in the United States, where potential adoptive parents were more willing to accept a child with special needs. Here was a chance to get him to that place, to do whatever they could to help him develop language and to find him a permanent family. It was a pivotal step, but they thought their place in Jacob's life was just an interim step, and someone else would take over sometime soon.

Others at Mother's Choice had the same wish. Many of them worked with Helen and so had shared their mornings with Jacob too. On his third birthday, they gathered in Helen and Gary's apartment for a birthday party. In a bright red polo shirt and denim shorts, Jacob squirmed in Helen's arms as they sang "Happy Birthday" and helped him blow out the three candles on a chocolate cake. Then they wrote notes in his blue notebook, and overwhelmingly, they delighted in him and hoped for his future. "You've added color to our office," wrote a social worker named Michelle, "and it's nice to hear you bubbling on the wooden horse." Another named Priscilla wrote, "You are a very smart, lovely boy. You have talent and courage to learn."

And Arthur combined tenderness and certainty, almost willing Jacob into a better life. "You have the most wonderful smile and laugh," he wrote. "It is a real treasure that comes from deep within you and can brighten up a whole room. Today we celebrate three years of your life, but mostly we are celebrating the time we have known you, joining together to celebrate what we know is going to be the best of times ahead."

❋ ❋ ❋

When Helen carried Jacob in the baby sling, she continued to carry him with his face in toward her so he wouldn't have to wear his prosthetic eyes, which weren't a perfect fit. Gary would face him outward, however, and they learned later that they were engaging in complementary roles: Helen provided him a secure base, and Gary gave him experience in facing the world.

Helen had learned that cause and effect were important to teach a child—especially a blind child—who had not been encouraged to act, but instead had only been acted upon. On a thin silver chain around her neck, she placed two charms with silver bells the size and shape of peppercorns. She would hold the charms in her fingers and rattle the bells, a delicate tinkling more whisper than song, so he could hear it. Then she'd place his hand on them. He must have liked the sound, because he reached for them often, and soon she had to buy a heavier chain. She was pleased that he was acting on the bells, that he knew he had the ability to make them ring.

Soon enough, they began to see small advances. By March, Jacob was able to sit up, and he began attending Small World Kindergarten's preschool program at the former British Military Hospital. Helen wrote to him again in the blue note-book, telling him that he seemed to enjoy meeting his teacher Miss Henrietta and touching her long black hair and her face and glasses. "You sat with your legs crossed today on your mat like all the other children," Helen wrote to him. Unlike the other children, he needed constant individual care, so Myrna, the woman who cared for him while Helen was at work, would take him and stay with him for however long he could last. Some days Jacob would throw a tantrum after fifteen minutes, some days after thirty, some days it would be after an hour or two.

"A big challenge in those days was to get him motivated to do anything," Helen recalls. "He was just so low energy, to try to get him to do anything was always a huge endeavor. And one day he would make some headway, and we'd think, 'Okay, yes, we're on the right track.' The next day, he'd do nothing."

Mealtime was one of those struggles. They had bought a wooden high chair before Jacob left Wee Care Extension and taken it there for him to use. That way, when he moved a week later, the details of mealtime would be more familiar. They stuck with the one menu item he would tolerate—rice, fish, and vegetables, cooked into a soup consistency, morning, midday, and evening, the same thing over and over—and they would spoon-feed him, often exhorting him to open his mouth. He would not feed himself. He would not eat anywhere except in that chair. And he would not eat anything except the fish and veggie and rice soup.

In mid-October, one of the children at Wee Care Extension turned five years old. They celebrated by loading all six children into a van and taking them to McDonald's. "You looked so handsome in your green, blue, and white-striped overall shorts, but I don't think you were feeling too well," Helen wrote. "As usual, you weren't too keen to eat anything, away from home and your familiar high chair—all you tasted was one French fry."

His insistence on eating at home and always the same meal imparted a rigidness and inflexibility to their schedule, but it was also a sign of Jacob's inability to adapt or process new experiences. Gary and Helen were looking for signs that he was growing, changing, and maturing into a typical little boy. They were hopeful—they wanted his life to be filled, as their other children's lives were, with exciting, new activities, to be open to the breadth of wonderment available. But he preferred a small, quiet existence, with few movements, few surprises.

It didn't help that Jacob was frequently sick, often with respiratory tract infections of varying intensities that caused him extreme stress and discomfort. In May of 1997, he battled a serious case of pneumonia. Though he was three years old, he was back down to twenty pounds, having lost much of the weight he had gained since the previous July. "You've not been able to eat, so you only weigh nine kilograms," Helen wrote. "Dr. Shraeder told me that if I worked really hard, we could keep you out of the hospital, but that I needed to know that it was going to be a hard journey ahead for the next few days." Helen stayed home from work for a week to tend him. He wouldn't eat, and he had always refused to drink from cups, which doctors guessed was due to high sensitivity around his mouth. To keep him hydrated, Helen resorted to bathing him three times a day, filling the tub quite full and encouraging him to lean his head forward and sip from the surface of the water.

Like most children, he resisted taking his medicine—probably because of the taste, though he didn't have the words to tell her why—and she had to use an oral syringe to administer it. "I would always try to give you a warning that it was coming and say, 'I'm sorry, Lok Chi, but it's time to take your medicine.' As soon as you would hear the word medicine, you would start to whimper," she wrote. But she saw a silver lining that indicated another small step forward: that he understood the word, that he knew what it meant, that he was acquiring vocabulary in a new language, that he might be nearing speech.

And there was another, very important milestone. They had been together almost every day since the previous September. It had been nine months, one quarter of Jacob's short life, yet he had never made a distinction between her embrace and that of any other child-care worker, between her words and those of others around him. After that week together, Jacob shifted slightly, from indifferent to everyone to showing a slight preference for Helen. He perked at her voice, and he was most comforted by her arms, and together, they had eluded hospital visit number seventeen.

❀ ❀ ❀

That fall, eight months into foster care, Jacob was showing marked signs of growth and glimpses of a distinct personality. A few months earlier, they had begun placing him in a baby walker so he could push himself around the apartment and build muscle mass, and that, combined with individual attention and increased nutrition, seemed to be working. "I am so excited because it seems like this week you are all of a sudden doing new things and feeling so confident," she wrote in Jacob's notebook on October 20. "I notice you like to pull yourself up to a standing position in your crib and spend lots of time on your feet, and you do the same on the couch in the TV area. Also, you make me so happy with how often you are saying 'ma-ma-ma-ma-ma-ma'—I love hearing you use your voice."

Less than a week later, Helen wrote again, "You are so clever, and you seem to love to be exploring now and are so much more adventurous. I love seeing you 'burrow' around—you crawl on your knees, with your forehead on the carpet, your hands also gliding carefully along the floor by your head like feelers. You keep going forward until you come to a wall, and then move backwards quite methodically, looking around. You seem to be giving much thought to it all."

Physically he was getting bigger and stronger. His face had grown so much that his prosthetic eyes had gotten too small, and he began an activity he would continue for years. "Now you can easily take out your eyeballs and throw them down," Helen wrote. "Next week I'll take you for your appointment to United Christian Hospital for new ones."

Just over a week later, Gary suggested they go have lunch at a Thai buffet to celebrate Helen's fiftieth birthday. It was a Sunday, the first of November, according to Helen's entry in the blue notebook, and Jacob had put on four pounds since his bout with pneumonia six months earlier. "Lok Chi, today you gave us such great joy," Helen wrote in her calm and gentle way. "While you were sitting on my lap at the table in the Thai restaurant, I tried to feed you a tiny piece of fish, from my finger to your mouth, and normally when you aren't at home in your high chair with your soft prepared food, you scream. But for some reason, today you gave us all such a special gift by getting so *excited* to eat that Gary had to go back to the buffet table to get you more. You ate three plates and then grinned and laughed while your fingers went open and closed so excitedly. What a special day." Helen cried—it was an overwhelmingly joyful gift, from this little boy, from God, from wherever it came, it was a joyful gift.

As time passed, it seemed he was slowly opening, that his brain and nervous system were beginning to tolerate and assimilate more stimuli. Besides the burrowing, he had developed another method of travel: a crab-like scooting across the floor. With his feet in front of him and his hands behind, Jacob would scoot himself forward until his feet brushed something in his path, which he could then maneuver himself around. "It's a pretty intelligent compensatory skill," says Kevin O'Brien, a teacher of the visually impaired who has worked with Jacob for nine years in Montrose schools. To feel confident moving, a blind person must feel safe, "and Jacob had learned that was the safest way to travel, to be on his backside with his feet in front of him." Maybe the hard way, he figured out his feet were less vulnerable than his head.

By February of 1998, one year after entering foster care with Gary and Helen, three months before his fourth birthday, Jacob had scooted and burrowed around enough to learn the apartment, and that month, he took his first steps. As Gary tells the story, he and Helen were at work, but Andrew was home and his friend Ben was there too. Andrew and Ben had spent enough time with Jacob that he was comfortable with them and trusted them, so much so that they could stand on either side of him, lift him by the arms, and run down a long corridor in the apartment. Jacob loved it. He would laugh and squeal, and they could do it again and again and he would squeal and laugh just the same. And then one day, Andrew called Helen at work and told her she needed to come home quickly, that in the master bedroom, Jacob had pulled himself up and toddled across the room.

"He translated immediately what he had memorized by scooting into an upright map," Gary says. "He could go anywhere in the house from that day on, walking."

Gary and Helen were, of course, elated. It was cause for celebration each time Jacob learned a new skill, each time he tried a new food or embraced a new activity, each time a space was illuminated where before there had been no light, an expansion where before there had only been a tiny, narrow crevice.

There were some areas, though, where things didn't unfold as they expected. Through it all, the most taxing part of the first years of living with Jacob was his irregular sleep. "There was no rhythm," Helen says. "He might sleep for three hours and be awake for two hours, and then he'd sleep for another hour and be awake." Human beings run on a twenty-four-hour clock based on the cycle of light and dark, called a circadian rhythm. A pathway from the retina leads to the hypothalamus, which regulates the production of melatonin, among other things. This neural circuit tells the brain that it's light outside, which means it's time to be awake and to suppress the production of melatonin, or that it's dark outside and time to sleep, so let the melatonin flow. Without retinas at all, Jacob's clock was unmoored, and he simply slept when he was tired and awoke when he was not.

An article about sleep disorders in blind children appeared in the *Journal of Visual Impairment and Blindness* around the time that Jacob went to live with Helen and Gary. The authors reported many subjects of their study who were blind from birth and drove their parents crazy with sleep habits like Jacob's. "Surprisingly little has been written about this problem in the medical literature," they write. "Perhaps pediatricians have discounted the problem as a variant of common childhood sleep difficulties or unfairly perceived it as a result of the lack of discipline by parents." The authors concluded that social interactions and rigid scheduling were less effective than one would think in training a child to have the same sleep patterns as a sighted person, and that sometimes the only solution was to allow the child to be awake at night in a safe environment, then sleep as needed during the day.

Jacob's free-running circadian rhythm was at odds with his sighted, very busy foster parents. They were sleep deprived but unaware of it, and even if they had been aware, there was little that could be done besides giving him melatonin at night and hoping, like parents with a newborn, for a few hours of undisturbed sleep. Jacob woke Helen and Gary up when he first moved in, when he became their adopted son, and on through his adolescent years. Into high school, Jacob would rouse them at three in the morning to ask if Mom would take him to Montrose High School.

During those first years of foster care, what they had hoped for most—that Jacob would learn to speak—was still elusive. They brought him to speech therapists at WatchDog, a nonprofit also located in the British Military Hospital that provided treatment for young children with special needs, and they worked with him at home as well. Still he remained nonverbal, except for the "*di*-dah" that signaled his assent that *yes*, he would like to eat or that he was excited to go outside and swing. His lack of speech was a puzzle with too many variables to be figured out easily. Was it the language change that had prevented him from gaining speech? Was there permanent damage from the early illness and neglect? Or would it just take time and determination? They continued to be cautiously hopeful, yet as the years passed, they wondered if there were some pieces that might never emerge from the cocoon.

CHAPTER 8

WHERE THEY BELONG

❧

Did He not find you an orphan and give [you] refuge?
And He found you lost and guided [you].

THE QUR'AN, SURAT AD-DUHAA, 93:6–7

Just the words themselves conjure worlds: orphan, abandoned, adoption.

The ancient stories are iconic, conveying volumes in simple images. Moses in a basket of papyrus reeds, pulled from the river by the daughter of the Pharaoh. Oedipus, a prince, left on a mountainside with his feet pinioned, rescued by a shepherd to fulfill a prophecy. Romulus and Remus, the mythic founders of Rome, exposed by their uncle to secure a crown, only to be found and suckled by a she-wolf. The prophet Muhammad, losing his father before birth and then his mother on a pilgrimage to visit his father's grave, tending sheep for his keep in his uncle's home.

These figures transcend their origins—in spite of, or maybe because of, their origins. They are figures set apart, rescued for a reason, saved for a specific purpose. The more modern orphans that emerge in literature are often no less heroic, but they are less idealized and feel their orphanhood acutely: Oliver Twist in the grimy, sordid streets of nineteenth-century London, Jane Eyre in the cold, unfeeling halls of the Lowood School, even a very contemporary Harry Potter living in a tiny bedroom under the stairs for the first eleven years of his life. The human imagination is full of this story, in varied shades of sorrow and triumph. Dissecting these tales across continents and centuries, scholars of culture and literature have noted the ways these luckless children reveal the human fear of isolation and the search for belonging, even if that belonging is to a group of wild animals, like Mowgli in Kipling's *The Jungle Book,* or to a tribe of lost boys in J.M. Barrie's *Peter Pan.*

Yet the history of adoption as a formal institution is less romantic than in folktales and fiction, and less compassionate as well. Most historical accounts of the institution begin by touching on a mythic figure like Moses, but quickly move on to reference the oldest adoption law on record, located in the Babylonian Code of Hammurabi of the eighteenth century BC. These accounts explain how in China and India, adoption was used to procure a son so that sonless families could participate in certain religious rites; how in Rome, a male heir was necessary to hold public office. Widely, the histories prove that adoption was a contingency, used to clarify inheritance or to continue family lines. "Two conclusions can be drawn from the early history of adoption," social workers Elizabeth Cole and Kathryn Donley write. "First, legal adoption was not a common but rather an exceptional experience. Second, the primary purpose of adoption was to serve adult interests rather than the child's interests." Throughout history, however, children without parents have been numerous, owing to the fact that many women died in childbirth; that in general, mortality was more imminent in eras past than in the present day. But instead of being adopted formally or legally, many children without parents or any means of support were placed with a family as additional labor in the house or on a farm. Others were placed in workhouses, where they earned their keep at the same time that they were trained for "useful-ness" later in life. Of course, the treatment at various homes and workhouses varied, but such solutions were pragmatic rather than ideal.

The year 1851 was a crucial moment in the history of child welfare because that was the year that the idea of "the best interest of the child" first appeared in adoption law—over 2600 years after the Code of Hammurabi, 1400 years after the fall of Rome, and 100 years after the Enlightenment. The Massachusetts Adoption of Children Act of 1851 was singular in this respect; unlike other laws in America at the time, which were meant to make a public record of adoption in the same way that they made public the selling of land or livestock, the primary purpose of the Massachusetts law was to provide children with homes where they would be nurtured and to provide a clear-cut set of responsibilities and rights for the adoptive parents. In the next twenty-five years, twenty-four other states followed suit, establishing a precedent that would shape modern adoption in America as well as the rest of the world.

The law was only the beginning of a child welfare reform movement that would last into the twentieth century, the most distinctive shift of which centered around what a child was in essence and how American society—and later the global society—viewed its smallest and most vulnerable members. Though it would be many years before child labor laws were passed in the United States and abroad, in the late 1800s and early 1900s people began valuing children in social terms rather than economic terms, and children were no longer thought of as smaller versions of adults. Instead, they were qualitatively different, more tender, more innocent, and by virtue of that difference, deserving of a separate quality of care. These ideas were formalized in the first Declaration of the Rights of the Child, written in 1923 by Eglantyne Jebb, founder of Save the Children. In her declaration, which was adopted by the United Nations in 1924, Jebb asserted that "mankind owes to the Child the best it has to give" and outlined food and shelter, appropriate protection, education, and medical care as rights to which the child was entitled. A second Declaration of the Rights of the Child, drafted and enacted by the United Nations in 1959, built on the idea that "the child, by reason of his physical and mental immaturity, needs special safeguards and care, including appropriate legal protection, before as well as after birth." In the course of a century, this was a striking transformation.

Between the time that "the best interest of the child" entered into the child welfare lexicon and the present day, a controversial debate has raged over how to achieve these special safeguards and appropriate legal protection for children without families: over the type and quality of care, over how and where to place orphaned and abandoned children, over the advantages and disadvantages of adoption and the methods for achieving it. Some of the elements have changed. In the 1850s, the major debate was whether a child should be placed with a family of the same religious background. In the 1970s, the argument shifted to whether a child should be placed in a family of the same race or cultural heritage. In the first half of the twentieth century, adoption workers advocated keeping children in institutions for their first few years, with the thought that only then could they see a child's personality and physical characteristics, including any "defects," which would allow for better matching with an adoptive family. Research in the mid-twentieth century by John Bowlby, Mary Ainsworth, and many others directly contradicted this and led to a move toward early placement to prevent the child from suffering the deleterious effects of institutions.

Similar to attitudes on early intervention, the economics of adoption have also entirely reversed—an unmarried woman used to pay a family to take her child, while contemporary adoption costs families thousands of dollars. However, the fact that adoption is shaped by economic factors at all, by the supply of children and the demand of adult adopters, or by the demand of willing homes for a supply of institutionalized children, has always raised ethical concerns about the buying and selling of children.

In this complex web, debate and opinions are fierce, yet the complicated nature of adoption and the many impressions it evokes make consensus difficult to attain. Some of the conflict relates to the nature of the institution itself, which is fraught with losses and gains for all participants of the adoption—the biological parents, the adopted child, and the adoptive parents. Research does little to help settle the disputes. Studies show that, in general, children fare better in adoptive homes than in foster homes and much better than children in institutions, but the research on adoption is piecemeal and sometimes contradictory. This is because, by and large, it's difficult to access and gather comprehensive information about adoption. Since the early twentieth century in the West, adoption has been shrouded in secrecy, and more recently in international adoption, marked by a dearth of information about the biological family and the child. Since 1975, the United States has kept no federal records of adoption, so that in America, the country that adopts more than any other in the world, information is almost completely absent. So who is adopting, who is adopted, and how they fare are largely unanswered questions.

In recent years, the debate over domestic adoption in the United States has cooled, and both in policy and public opinion, permanent placement with an adoptive family is seen as the most favorable option. At the same time, the debate over international adoption has grown more fierce. The phenomenon itself is relatively new, beginning in places where the United States had been involved in military conflicts to provide homes for children orphaned by war. After World War II, several hundred children were adopted to America from Western Europe, and even more from Asia, mainly Japan. A second wave came from Korea, mostly comprised of the children of American soldiers. International adoption became an ever more popular option as rates of infertility increased in the United States and the availability of healthy, white infants decreased, in large part due to access to contraception, a loosening of the stigma around single parenthood, and the Supreme Court ruling on *Roe v. Wade*. Between 1953 and 1962, American families adopted fifteen thousand children from abroad; between 1966 and 1976, that number had more than doubled, to thirty-two thousand, two-thirds of whom came from Korea. Then economic factors began to take effect, and areas of the world in financial crisis began sending children for adoption. In the 1970s and 1980s, Latin American countries became the most prominent sending countries. In the 1990s, after the fall of the Soviet Union, Russia and Romania began sending thousands of their institutionalized children for adoption. Around the same time,

China was overwhelmed with thousands of baby girls without homes and became another country with thousands of children available for adoption.

Since the practice began in earnest in the 1990s, the international adoption arena has become filled with loud voices. Some are concerned about cultural heritage, equating international adoption with cultural genocide or neocolonialism. In the 1990s, Georgian First Lady Schevardnadze opposed it as an issue of national identity. As Madelyn Freundlich explains in her series *Adoption and Ethics,* which attempts to provide a comprehensive guide to the voices and opinions on adoption, others have focused on how adoption might be exploiting women in difficult situations and people who are poor. Advocates, who are generally from the more developed countries that the children are being adopted to, have a different emphasis, believing that international adoption is a saving grace for children who otherwise would spend their most formative years in institutions or even die from their home country's conditions. Others look at the high numbers of babies who are adopted each year to the United States from other countries and lament the fact that tens of thousands of American children are stuck in a far-from-perfect foster-care system, with no permanent family anywhere on the horizon.

In this maelstrom, each voice asserts that what *we* are fighting for is the best interest of the child, that the child needs *this* most of all, or *that.* "Much of what is said about international adoption is shrouded in mystery, ideology, and innuendo," writes Sara Dillon, a Suffolk University law professor, in an essay on children's rights published in 2003 in the *Boston University International Law Journal.* "What is said to be best for children is often a function of the speaker's or organization's pre-existing viewpoint." With such widely divergent opinions and a dearth of comprehensive and compelling empirical evidence, middle ground is elusive.

And so the conflicts persist. With regard to the issue of culture and race in adoption, three stances have surfaced. The first group sees international adoption as wholly unacceptable and equates separating a child from her culture with separating a child from her family and environment. The opposite camp believes that international adoption is positive in every way, and that a child's race and culture weighs far below the child's need for a family. These wholehearted proponents of international adoption dismiss the opposition's argument as political correctness at the expense of a child's welfare. The third position in this argument rests between the two extremes. "From this perspective, there are significant benefits when children maintain their connections to their racial and cultural heritage within the family of origin or culture of origin and maintain their national identity by birth," says Madelyn Freundlich in *Adoption and Ethics: The Role of Race, Culture, and National Origin in Adoption*. Yet they also recognize that many children will not find a home in the country where they were born. This was true in China in the mid-1990s, where adoption law made it difficult to place abandoned children in families domestically; this was true in Korea throughout the second half of the twentieth century, when many abandoned children languished in institutions because the cultural value placed on blood ties was too high for domestic adoption to take hold. Pursuing international adoption under such circumstances would be, according to this third camp, the best option.

Given the history of institutions and the well-documented damage that institutional care does to children, it's hard to say that children are best served by being kept in institutions in their country of origin in order to protect their heritage. Many children in institutions do not know "their culture," but only the culture of the institution—meaning very basic, the *most* basic care, or even abuse and exploitation. The proof lies in studies decades old, with Bill Goldfarb noticing the IQs of institutionalized children were far below children reared in foster care, with stories that emerged from Russia, Eastern Europe, and China in the 1990s, as well as the story of Jacob's suffering. In light of these realities, complete insistence on preserving a child's heritage seems to fly in the face of history and fact. If a child does not receive the care she needs, care that is best guaranteed in families, the child cannot participate in that culture or heritage, and culture becomes less of a practical consideration and instead is only a theoretical one.

Less theoretical than heritage is the issue of baby trafficking, a very real crime and tragedy that occurs most frequently in countries that send large numbers of children for adoption when opportunists get wind of high demand for babies and seek their own interests instead of the child's. In August of 2011, an article appeared in the *New York Times* detailing how infants were seized and sold in Longhui County in central China, five hundred miles northwest of Hong Kong. "Just last week, the police announced that they had rescued 89 babies from child traffickers," writes *Times* reporter Sharon LaFraniere, "and the deputy director of the Public Security Ministry assailed what he called the practice of 'buying and selling children in this country.'" But even more disturbing were reports that local government officials had seized babies when the parents could not pay exorbitant fines for unsanctioned births, then put those babies up for adoption by foreigners.

"The practice in Longhui came to an end in 2006, parents said, only after an 8-month-old boy fell from the second-floor balcony of a local family planning office as officials tried to pluck him from his mother's arms."

Stories such as these are harrowing and criminal, attracting much media attention and condemnation from the public and politicians. Safeguards must be in place and followed in order to keep children from being stolen and adopted under false pretenses. But many experts in the field of international adoption insist that these stories are the exception rather than a widespread phenomenon, and that knee-jerk reactions to news of trafficking are not the most effective way to handle it. Dr. Jane Aronson, an adoption medicine specialist who has spent two decades promoting the cause of orphans, argues that child trafficking is rare. But when reports emerge, it is treated as an epidemic; countries often freeze their programs and leave children stranded in orphanages. In March of 2011, Dr. Aronson wrote an open letter to former President Bill Clinton, urging his intervention after a massive decrease in Ethiopia's adoption quotas. "The destruction of international adoption has become the cure for a misdiagnosed disease," Dr. Aronson wrote. "Uninspired, bureaucratic, desperate decision-makers in governments, including our own, and in large child welfare organizations, raise the cry of 'trafficking' and the rest is inevitable: to protect the children and stop the trafficking—stop adoption." The impassioned letter continues:

The real disease—the one not addressed—is much more complex. It involves developing nations, communities without social welfare systems or resources to help families living in extreme poverty, suffering from illness, depression and hopelessness. Without education, economic strengthening, and access to medical care, particularly HIV/AIDS care, families become desperate and relinquish their children to orphanages. And when the numbers are too large and the government is too embarrassed and when those who believe a child is better off rotting by the side of the road than living in a different culture, well, that's when we start hearing "trafficking," and that's when international adoption is slowed, then halted. All in the name of the children.

In my 20 years as an adoption medicine specialist, this scenario has been played out in Georgia, Romania, Cambodia, Vietnam, Guatemala, Kyrgyzstan, Kazakhstan, Nepal, and now Ethiopia...If you look historically at all the countries that halted international adoption, you will find thousands of children left to rot in institutions. The trafficking stories never come close to even a small percentage of the children left to suffer for the rest of their lives."

Another vocal supporter of international adoption, Harvard Law professor Elizabeth Bartholet, also decries the emphasis on trafficking as misplaced. "Opponents of international adoption always cite the risk of abuses," Bartholet writes in a *New York Times* blog discussion that appeared in February of 2011. "But it is hypocritical to delay or shut down such adoption in the name of protecting children. The real risk of abuses occurs when unparented children are *not* placed for adoption"—abuses like sex slavery or domestic servitude or neglect in an institution. In her *Boston University* article, Sara Dillon issues a critique similar to Dr. Aronson's and Bartholet's. "There is an obvious disproportion of concern," Dillon writes, "that is, far more concern over adoption profiteering than over the plight of children without families living in poor conditions."

As Dr. Aronson points out in her open letter to President Clinton, countries that have historically placed many orphaned or abandoned children have, under scrutiny from organizations like UNICEF, worked to significantly reduce the numbers of children being sent. According to Madelyn Freundlich of the Evan B. Donaldson Adoption Institute, between 1986 and 1998, Korean adoptions declined from 8,000 to 1,800 "at least partially in response to media criticisms of the Korean 'export' of abandoned children and a sense of national pride." Yet in many of these countries, domestic adoption has failed to take hold, either because people do not have the means to adopt, or because they are not interested in adopting. In Korea, despite laws allowing for the same rights of inheritance for adopted children, patriarchal bloodlines and family continuity hold more sway than providing permanent homes for children, and domestic adoption is still uncommon.

More recently, Guatemala has come under fire for the high number of children it was sending for adoption without appropriate safeguards. From 1996 to 2006, international adoption, mostly through private agencies and adoption lawyers, grew steadily, peaking at five thousand adoptions in 2006, making Guatemala the highest sending country in the world. Then in 2007, Guatemala froze all international adoptions, hoping instead to promote domestic adoptions for the thousands of children abandoned each year. In a short documentary film entitled *Abandoned in Guatemala: The Failure of International Adoption Policies*, Erick Rivas, the director of a Guatemalan state-run orphanage, notes how ineffective this attempt has been. "According to the National Adoption Council, there have been 35 adoptions in the past year," Rivas says. Not surprisingly, the number of children in his orphanage has doubled, from 350 to 700. In a time of global economic uncertainty, those numbers seem unlikely to decline; however, the number of children placed in families through international adoption has fallen by over half—from twenty-three thousand total international adoptions worldwide in 2005 to approximately eleven thousand in 2010.

In countries where domestic adoption is unpopular, or where high levels of poverty are widespread and most people cannot afford another mouth to feed, children are confined to child-care institutions. The practice goes back hundreds of years, but in an interesting and compelling argument that strives to make children's rights match general human rights, Sara Dillon insists that as a principle, children have a right to be free from institutions, as adults do. "It seems self-evident that it is inappropriate and damaging for the human child to grow up in an institution, without the benefit of his or her own family, whatever the longer-term benefits to the local culture of retaining 'possession' of its own," Dillon writes. She compares the right not to be institutionalized with the right not to be tortured, in that both are traumas with profound impacts on the human psyche and the ability to function as part of the human community. "Attachment disorders are psychological problems of the most fundamental kind; they make it all but impossible for an affected child to grow into a capable and well-adjusted human being," Dillon writes. "The suffering inflicted on institutionalized children is incalculable."

In light of this, she suggests that instead of a moratorium, countries should make strenuous efforts to eliminate abuses, to make the process as transparent, ethical, and efficient as possible. It's a balance, she writes, "between our concern for ethical procedures in adoption to avoid child trafficking, on the one hand, and the often overlooked fact of thousands of children without families waiting for a fair and humane international response to their isolation."

In truth, Gary and Helen have never considered themselves experts on human rights or international law. It was not in the nuanced arguments of experts that they found their position on what was in the best interests of the child. It was not in an anthropological study or a cultural treatise or a statistical report. It was firsthand that their opinions on international adoption were formed, while working with children in Hong Kong and later in mainland China, where the realities of institutional care for children far outweighed any of the political arguments they encountered. They saw how children flourished in their adoptive homes and how children like Jacob, left too long in an institution, suffered the consequences of impersonal, insufficient care, and a slow-moving, unfeeling bureaucratic machine. Any argument in favor of culture over family was undercut by what happened to their son: Jacob spent two-and-a-half years without sufficient care, at which point he was not capable of appreciating the unique culture of Hong Kong, or even in some cases, of tolerating it. "Saying it's an irreparable harm to separate a child from his or her cultural heritage is an argument by someone with no firsthand experience with children awaiting adoption," Gary says. "I think sometimes that people who hold that position feel there's something about their own culture that is better and must be preserved. But there is no better race or worse race, and there's no better culture or worse culture—culture is simply a man-made attempt at community. The primary weight for a child is for a loving, permanent family, and the child's cultural needs are secondary to a child's need for that family."

For his stance on adoption, Gary points to an incredibly simple measure. "The child should not wait for parents," he says. "The parents should wait for a child. That's the normal process, the natural process." There must be laws, Gary says, and safeguards to keep children from being exploited, to keep poor families from being exploited. But in Gary's opinion, it's a matter of enforcing those laws and making the process of finding a permanent family for a child as honest and efficient as possible, whether that is through domestic adoption or international.

"Theoretically, to have a child adopted within his or her culture is preferable," Gary says. "In places where that's not happening, it makes the discussion moot. And until such time that waiting parents outnumber waiting children, we need to keep working to get children into families."

❦ ❦ ❦

Many children from Mother's Choice were adopted locally in Hong Kong. At first, adoptive families were expatriates, mostly American and British families, but over time, the numbers of Hong Kong Chinese interested in both foster care and adoption began to grow. It was an exciting development, and yet, the children who were placed quickly were those whose files bore the marks of "healthy" and "typically developing." Children with special needs stayed at Wee Care for months and maybe even years before they were adopted, as is the case at many institutions, and the majority of children who found families were placed through inter-country adoption, mostly to the United States.

Adoption history is checkered with respect to children with special needs. Before World War II, American children with special needs were labeled "unadoptable" and confined to institutions, in part because social workers refused to place children with disabilities in families. It was as if a family that had passed inspection and been labeled fit to adopt, even labeled exemplary, deserved a child that had hit the same marks, and children with special needs did not fit that bill by the measure of the time. This remained the common attitude toward people with special needs or disabilities during Gary's childhood and even through high school.

"I was raised in an atmosphere where people with special needs lived at the state home, which was a place you didn't really visit," Gary says. "I remember one family in our community that would pick up a little girl with brittle bone disease from the state home and take her to church with them and then to Sunday lunch. She was very small, and her life expectancy was very short. That's the only family I ever saw reaching out to a child in that way, and it was once a week and only lasted a short period of time."

In the last fifty years, attitudes have changed, and more often than not, children with special needs are not immediately shuttled off to institutions or placed in special schools. Still, it's undeniable that people with physical and intellectual disabilities still face challenges in being accepted and embraced by their larger societies. After more than three decades of working with people with intellectual disabilities, Jean Vanier writes, "I have come to the conclusion that those with intellectual disabilities are some of the most oppressed and excluded people in the world." The first victims of mass extermination by the Nazis, people with intellectual disabilities across the globe still suffer from miserable conditions of abuse and neglect in institutions or as victims of indifferent communities. Today, the rejection of individuals with physical and intellectual disabilities is less extreme, or at least more covert, but attitudes toward people with disabilities register on the same spectrum.

"Our society is not set up to cope very well with people who are weaker or slower," writes Jean Vanier in his compassionate and compelling book *Becoming Human*. "A society that honours only the powerful, the clever, and the winners necessarily belittles the weak. It is as if to say: to be human is to be powerful." Yet these children with special needs hunger to be recognized as fully human; they hunger for belonging the same way typically developing children hunger for belonging, a hunger which originates in the same need that every child has: to feel secure and safe in a world where she is small, weak, and vulnerable.

Declarations by the United Nations claim that these children deserve care simply by their presence, by their birth into the human race. "Unfortunately, there is a very loud, consistent, and powerful message coming to us from our world that leads us to believe that we must prove our belovedness by how we look, by what we have, and by what we can accomplish," writes Henri Nouwen, a Catholic priest and theologian from the Netherlands.

Nouwen lived in one of Vanier's communities for people with physical and intellectual disabilities for ten years, and there he met a man named Adam. In a book called *Adam: God's Beloved*, Nouwen describes how Adam suffered a serious ear infection at three months old and had his first of many seizures. Adam was developmentally delayed—he never learned to speak or tell time—but he was able to run up and down the sidewalk in front of his house, and when sitting in the grocery cart at the store, he grabbed boxes and cans off the shelf that his mother didn't want, like any other child. Then when he was thirteen, he had a severe seizure, which led doctors to issue a new medication. Mistakenly, they forgot to cancel the old medication. After a few days, they recognized the overdose and canceled it, but Adam was never the same. He could no longer walk on his own, and he needed constant care. When he reached adulthood, Adam's parents could no longer care for him, and after a few years in a hospital, he found a home at L'Arche in Toronto.

Adam was the first person Henri Nouwen assisted when he arrived at L'Arche. In his book about Adam, Nouwen is honest about how difficult those first weeks and months were, an experience probably close to what most people would feel when faced with the same situation. "I began with fear and trembling," Nouwen writes. "I was afraid walking into Adam's room and waking up this stranger. His heavy breathing and his restless hand movements made me very self-conscious. I didn't know him. I didn't know what he expected of me. I didn't want to upset him. And in front of others, I didn't want to make a fool of myself." During the first few weeks, people told him how much he would come to love Adam, yet Henri was skeptical. "I had so much anxiety that I could not imagine what 'loving Adam' would mean."

But over time, Henri adjusted to life with Adam and came to cherish the few hours a day that he spent helping him bathe and dress. It reached the point where, even when he was away from Adam, caring for another person in the community or working on a book or paper, Henri's mind would wander back to Adam. He thought of him as an anchor and a place of peace. "Most people saw Adam as a disabled person who had little to give and who was a burden to his family, his community, and to society at large," Nouwen writes. "And as long as he was seen that way, his truth was hidden. What was not received was not given."

And what was it that someone who could not walk or speak or bathe himself give? "Adam was so completely dependent on us that he catapulted me to the essential, to the source," Nouwen writes. "What is community? What is care? What is love? What is life? And who am I, who are we, who is God? Adam was so fully alive to me, and he shed light on all these questions. This experience cannot be understood by a logical explanation but rather in and through the spiritual bonding of two very different people who discovered each other as completely equal in the heart of God. From my heart I could offer him the care he really needed, and from his heart he blessed me with a pure and lasting gift of himself." Through Adam, Nouwen heard "a radical call to accept the truth of our lives and to choose to give our love when we are strong and to receive the love of others when we are weak, always with tranquility and generosity."

Nouwen's understanding of Adam and his writings about people with intellectual and physical disabilities were a source of wisdom and comfort when Gary and Helen began their work with children with special needs in 1991. Nouwen's wisdom was also a presence when Gary met a different Adam, in China in 1999. Gary wasn't there the day the family arrived at Mother's Care, their satellite orphanage in China. But the director of Mother's Care described it, how the parents were dressed simply, in farm clothes that revealed their rural roots. They were carrying their son, who was several months old and hydrocephalic, his head enlarged from pent-up spinal fluid, comprising at least a third of his entire body weight.

"They asked one of our staff members what we did at this place," Gary says. "They already knew, or they wouldn't have traveled so far, but our staff gave them a tour and told them about our work, then showed them how we cared for the children, both in the baby room and the toddler room."

After the couple had seen the facilities, they turned to the staff member who was their guide and asked, "Would you ever care for someone like our son? Would you give him the same care you have given to all these other babies?"

"Absolutely," the staff member answered.

The mother was a very small woman, and they were very poor. "They didn't have the financial means to take care of him, or the knowledge about his health condition, or the physical stamina," Gary says. "He was already very difficult to carry because of the weight of his head."

The decision to relinquish a child is something most parents will never experience or understand, and the weight of such a decision has been explored in fiction and in psychology and in memoirs—the trauma, the loss, the reluctant resolve. These things were etched on the parents' faces as they asked the simple question, "Can we leave our son with you?"

The staff member was taken off guard. It was uncommon for parents to come with a child, and since it was a weekend, the representative from the Department of Civil Affairs was not there to do the paperwork. The woman told the parents it would have to wait until Monday.

On Monday morning, the mother showed up again, and again she asked if she could leave her son. The nurse on duty said yes. At that moment, the mother sat down with the child in her arms. She unbuttoned her blouse and nursed her baby for the last time at both breasts. Then she handed the baby to a staff member, who took him and bathed him and gave him the English name Adam. As the mother turned to go, she held out her hand, which clutched several crumpled renminbi—Chinese currency—in very small denominations. She said, "This is all I have." The staff told her to keep the money, that there was no need for her to pay.

Adam was already blind when he arrived from the pressure of the brain fluid on his optic nerve, and though he grew, he never learned to walk, and he required increasing amounts of care and energy from the child-care workers. "But when you ask our staff about baby Adam, they all speak of the sweetness of his disposition," Gary says. In light of the way other children with special needs were discarded and neglected across China, Gary found the commitment they had to Adam and the extraordinary care they provided for him "awesome to observe."

Adam's prognosis at the time was unknown, but over the years, Adam has remained as a central part of the Mother's Care community. On Gary's last visit to Mother's Care, in May of 2010, Adam was still living there. "He's one of the highlights for me," Gary says. "This last time, Adam was strapped into his therapy chair, and I sat on a stool beside him and held his hand for thirty minutes, just thanking God for his life. He has impacted our staff so profoundly—just exuding a sweetness and peace."

Adam will never win any competitions; in a true contest of survival of the fittest, Adam would have lost long ago. In fact, Adam is the type of child whose needs are so severe that a group home is probably his only option. He is the exception, the type of person who really needs an entire community for his care—a community in the form of professional child-care workers and medical staff at Mother's Care. A few years ago, Mother's Care opened a small group home for children like Adam with severe special needs who will probably never be adopted, and it is there that Adam still lives. And like the Adam Henri Nouwen knew, this Adam draws that community close to him, inspiring peace, removing the harsh competition of the world, the drive to get ahead, the barriers that arise when people, especially in developed countries, are self-sufficient, surrounded by wealth, success, and all that is capable.

"We are all frightened of the ugly, the dirty," Jean Vanier writes in *Becoming Human*. "We all want to turn away from anything that reveals the failure, pain, sickness, and death beneath the brightly painted surface of our ordered lives. Civilization is, at least in part, about pretending that things are better than they are. We all want to be in a happy place, where everyone is nice and good and can fend for themselves. We shun our own weakness and the weakness in others. We refuse to listen to the cry of the needy. How easy it is to fall into the illusion of a beautiful world when we have lost trust in our capacity to make of our broken world a place that can become more beautiful."

Vanier's vision is a radical vision, one that speaks to the tension in the modern world between competition and compassion, between the impulse to be an unfettered individual and the demands of a community, between the desire to reserve one's time and resources and energy for oneself and the paradox in the Prayer of St. Francis—"for it is in giving that we receive."

In his experience working with children with special needs, Gary saw one group that stood out among all others by consistently stepping forward to provide homes where those children would be loved, nurtured, and safe. One after another, it was Christian families in America who filled out applications to adopt children with health problems, physical disabilities, and developmental delays. Voices from secular sectors often criticize the motivations of Christians who are looking to adopt internationally as an attempt to proselytize. In April of 2011, *The Nation* published an article by Kathryn Joyce entitled "The Evangelical Adoption Crusade," an exposé on the Christian adoption movement. As a model of overzealous Christians, Joyce writes about Laura Silsby and nine other evangelical

Christians who stole Haitian children orphaned by the 2010 earthquake into the Dominican Republic to get them adopted by Christians in the United States. Joyce highlights preachers and orphans' advocates who speak of adoption as a way to share the gospel and to "bring children from the darkness into light," and people who, in their religious fervor, are willing to lie on visa applications, to bend and break rules in order to achieve this end.

The actions of Silsby and others who disregard international law in the name of "helping" children are unequivocally wrong and are a blight on the thousands who engage in the practice ethically. Yet to portray all Christians who adopt as exploitative evangelists, willing to go to any end for a modern-day crusade, is unfair to the vast majority—those who follow the rules, who adopt children out of compassion, and most of all who are stepping in and filling a huge void in the adoption of children with special needs. For the time, energy, and expense these families are willing to go to for the neediest, most vulnerable children in the world, they should be recognized instead of vilified; emulated instead of castigated.

Gary's vision of hundreds of thousands of people across the world stepping forward to open their homes to children who are truly orphaned and abandoned is an ideal—some might call it an idyll. But as Elizabeth Bartholet says in her *New York Times* blog post, "Five decades of social science demonstrate that institutions systematically abuse children. Children die at high rates in poor institutions, and even the best institutions destroy children's life prospects by damaging their intellectual and emotional potential." To abandon adoption is to abandon these children again. To decry the practice of adoption wholesale because of the crimes of opportunists is to leave millions of children without hope for a future. To say the issue is too complex or too difficult to solve is to ignore the rights of the child, to shirk our collective responsibility as members of the human family, to place a limit on what we can achieve in the name of justice, peace, and love.

In another book, *Compassion*, Henri Nouwen, along with two other Jesuit priests, points to another truth: that certainly there is much suffering in the world, and it's arguable that the more that people understand the scope and scale of this suffering, the more helpless they feel. Nouwen and his colleagues made this argument in 1982, before twenty-four-hour television and the ubiquity of the Internet, but now more than ever, people are exposed to countless and tragic stories—of natural disasters, of famine and earthquake and tsunami and tornado, and the cruelties of man-made disasters, of terrorism and poverty and authoritarian regimes. It's possible this access does not induce compassion and conviction to do something to help, but only numbness and a feeling that there's too much to be done, too many people suffering to make a difference, too much chaos to ever bring anything to order. There are hundreds of millions of children living at risk, in poverty, on the streets, exploited for child labor. There are millions who are truly orphans, without parents or kin to care for them, forced to languish in institutions. How can any one person help?

Very few people are going to effect the change that Mohandas Gandhi was able to effect, or Dr. Martin Luther King, Jr., or Mother Teresa. Yet even in her own mission, where she nursed thousands of sick and dying people from all over the world, Mother Teresa started small. "I never look at the masses as my responsibility," Mother Teresa said. "I look at the individual. I can love only one person at a time. I can feed only one person at a time."

It must begin with one person, and for children without parents, with one person's effort to give a child a home. "So you begin," Mother Teresa said. "I begin. I picked up one person—maybe if I hadn't pick up that one person, I wouldn't have picked up 42,000."

CHAPTER 9

THE MISSING BABY GIRLS

❦

So he bears a son,
And puts him to sleep upon a bed,
Clothes him in robes,
Gives him a jade sceptre to play with.
The child's howling is very lusty;
In red greaves shall he flare,
Be lord and king of house and home.
Then he bears a daughter,
And puts her upon the ground,
Clothes her in swaddling clothes,
Gives her a loom-whorl to play with.
For her no decorations, no emblems;
Her only care, the wine and food,
And how to give no trouble to her father and mother.

FROM *SHIJING*, OR *THE BOOK OF SONGS*

The People's Republic of China

Gary first saw a dying room in April of 1994 at the state orphanage in Shanjing,* a provincial city in Southern China. The room was a rectangle of concrete, ten feet wide by twelve feet long, with a closed door and two small windows that allowed a meager light to fight the heavy shadows in the corners but failed to ventilate the space. Instead, the smell of stale urine and sour bodies persisted. Against one wall, three or four wooden beds—more like tables than cribs—were pushed together, and on top, a faded comforter covered a lumpy mass.

---

*The name of the city has been changed, as have some peoples' names to protect individuals and works in China. Some specific details have been omitted.

Gary knew that babies were left in this room to die by attrition, to waste away without water or food until each little girl was so dehydrated and malnourished that her organs failed, she stopped sucking air into her spindly rib cage, and her heart simply gave up. He had heard the stories from Lian, a Mother's Choice employee and a dear friend of Gary and Helen's who had worked in the orphanage since the fall of 1992 and lived in a small apartment there, trying to fight the powerful tide of apathy and ignorance that led to the deaths of so many of these baby girls. He had heard of them from Helen, who had visited several times to offer Lian support and encouragement and returned to Hong Kong each time emotionally raw and physically exhausted.

But seeing it for himself was different. The room was quieter than he had expected, and the mass on the table was so still that Gary wasn't even sure there were children under it. When he finally pulled the blanket back to reveal a handful of dying girls, the sight of the sick and starving infants was a shock to his system. In that moment, when he expected to feel sorrow and indignation and compassion and grief, all he felt was numbness, as if the inhuman tragedy of the baby girls collapsed his capacity to think, to process, to respond, to react within the range of normal human emotions. Only later did the gravity of situation show its weight. "After we saw these rooms, there were big questions in our minds, questions about the government, the child-care workers, about society as a whole," Gary says. "It raised questions about eternal goodness and justice to see these innocent ones suffering. Many of these questions we couldn't reconcile very easily." Some still can't be reconciled, given the extent of the damage exacted upon the people of China through the one-child policy, damage that has taken physical, emotional, and ethical dimensions, damage that took a toll on the most vulnerable: infant girls and newborns with any sort of birth defect.

Since the policy was implemented in 1979, baby girls, who were referred to as "maggots in the rice" in the countryside because they cost money to feed, clothe, and educate but then left their families to live with their husbands, had become even more marginalized throughout the country. With China isolated from the rest of the world and information tightly controlled by the government, baby girls had been suffering, locked in a pocket of silence, for over a decade. It wasn't until the middle of 1993, only a few months before Gary's first visit to Shanjing, that the first news reports began to emerge about the wretched conditions in child welfare institutions across the country.

On a Sunday in May of 1993, the *South China Morning Post* spent its front page on the plight of the abandoned baby girls in Shanjing's state orphanage. The reporter's observations are similar to Gary's memories, but with the detail and immediacy of a dispatch from the field: "An old wardrobe stands in one corner. Soiled sheets are scattered on the floor. The paint is peeling from the walls," the reporter writes. "Four tiny bundles lie listlessly on a wooden cot waiting for starvation, disease, or sheer neglect to end their lives.

"That moment has already arrived for one," he continues. "A deep blue color has set across its face. The baby next to it climbs on top and sleeps, unaware that the playmate it is cuddling is dead."

Within months, other reports surfaced: in a four-thousand-word article in London's *Daily Mail,* in a 1995 documentary called *The Dying Rooms.* After the film premiered in England, the Chinese embassy in London responded with a letter to the producers of the documentary, denying the existence of such rooms. "Our investigations confirm that those reports are vicious fabrications made out of ulterior motives," the letter read. "The contemptible lie about China's welfare work in orphanages cannot but arouse the indignation of the Chinese people." High-ranking officials in China's cabinet also rejected the claims, calling them Western propaganda meant to discredit China's bid for the 2000 Olympics.

These state denials contradicted firsthand accounts like Gary's. They contradicted the photographs of aid workers and journalists, as well as documentation from the some of the institutions themselves. In 1996, Human Rights Watch/Asia published a horrifying 330-page report entitled *Death by Default: A Policy of Fatal Neglect in China's State Orphanages,* based on information they had gathered between 1988 and 1992. In the report, the authors claimed that the majority of children admitted to state-run orphanages had died.

"Many institutions, including some in major cities, appeared to be operating as little more than assembly lines for the elimination of unwanted orphans," the authors wrote, "with an annual turnover of admissions and deaths far exceeding the number of beds available."

At Shanjing, that assessment was apt. When Lian arrived in August of 1992, the infant mortality rate was nearly 100 percent; on average, the state orphanage received a baby each day, and on average, one died each day. Given the bleakness of the situation, it is difficult to understand how the caregivers made their way to work every day. Poor and untrained, without even basic knowledge of modern health practices or child development, they attended a job that they had been assigned by a local cadre. Some of the workers resented being forced to care for babies who had been thrown away, who were literal outcasts. But another reason for their callousness was a matter of numbers: there were just so many babies.

"How can you care when every day you have a new baby?" Lian would reflect years later. That apathy was something that struck Lian on that first visit to Shanjing, and her own response involved her—and by extension, Gary and Helen—in the welfare of the children of China for years to come. Lian had been compelled to visit by reports of the orphanage's conditions from some Western missionary friends. They had visited the orphanage in Shanjing and wanted to help, but were hamstrung by the significant language barrier. As a native speaker of Cantonese, Lian was better equipped to assist, so against mainstream Hong Kong opinion (which was to stay out of China completely), she made her way across the Bamboo Curtain of the Shenzhen River and into this growing provincial city. She showed up at the orphanage with two bags full of clothes as gifts—one with tiny garments for infants and toddlers, the other full of pants and shirts and dresses for adults—planning to assess the situation and return to Hong Kong with information for someone else. That changed when she found herself standing in a room full of sick and dying baby girls, where no one would help them to live.

Lian's paradigm for child care had been established at Mother's Choice, where each child received as much individual care as possible; where each baby had his or her own crib, clothes, and caretakers; where child-care workers took individual photographs of all the children and recorded milestones in baby books so that when they grew up, they could see they had been loved from infancy. At Shanjing, there were two rooms where babies lay five across on wooden tables. There were no mattresses, only a thin woven mat between the wood and the babies' backs. The infants were tiny, swallowed by clothes much too big for their emaciated frames, and some were so quiet that Lian didn't know if they were dead or alive. Their skin was mottled, their bodies covered in rashes and their scalps in sores, and their hair was in wisps from malnutrition. They had bloated bellies; their necks, arms, and legs were stick-thin and powerless. Because there were perhaps a dozen crying at once and only two or three child-care workers, the workers were simply ignoring them all.

But not Lian. Standing in the middle of a room that reeked of urine and teemed with neglect, Lian was overwhelmed, but when one baby beside her began to cry, Lian reacted instinctively. She reached down and picked the baby girl up. She rocked the infant as she passed into the second room, identical to the first. Within a few minutes, the baby girl fell asleep. Lian took her back to the first room and placed her on the wooden table, where she slept.

After seeing the dying room and being shocked by its reality, after playing with the older children in the courtyard, many of whom had been abandoned because of physical disabilities and were starving for attention, Lian made one last round before she left for the day. In the first room, the baby she had rocked to sleep was fussing again. Without thinking, Lian stopped and picked her up and began rocking her. Suddenly, she felt compelled to get the baby out, to take the baby with her.

"I didn't have a second thought," Lian says. "I went straight to the director and said, 'I have one more day in the city. I can take this little girl and care for her for the night. Then I will bring her back.'"

The director didn't ask for her information or where she was staying, but simply nodded and let her leave with the infant girl. Lian had hired a taxi for the day, and she returned to where he was waiting outside the social welfare compound and explained her situation to the driver. She asked him to take her to a store where she could buy bottles, clean diapers, blankets, and formula, which he did. He also told her that his mother was retired and that she would probably be happy to help care for the baby if Lian needed help.

Back at the hotel, Lian bathed the baby girl, put her in clean, dry clothes, and prepared some warm formula with milk. When it was time for her to return to Hong Kong, Lian couldn't bear to take the baby back. Instead, she decided that the driver's mother was the best option for temporary child care—that anything would be better than the orphanage where the baby girl would die by attrition. Lian contacted the driver, who picked Lian and the baby up and took them to his mother, and Lian gave the woman baby supplies and enough money to pay for formula and anything else the infant would need. Then she went and told the director of the orphanage that she had placed the child in good care and that she'd be back in a few weeks. Again, he simply said okay.

Lian returned to Hong Kong and used her contacts to locate a family in the United States waiting to adopt a baby. In September, the little girl left Shanjing for a family and a home in California. Over the next few months, Lian placed fourteen more babies for adoption internationally, and Mother's Choice began sending staff members to assist her in the care of the babies she was rescuing. By the spring of 1993, Lian was spending so much time at the orphanage that the director offered her an apartment, and Lian accepted. Reversing the migration that citizens of Hong Kong were making in droves—a move to Canada or

Australia or the United Kingdom, as far as they could get from the People's Republic—Lian moved into a shoebox of a room inside the social welfare compound in Shanjing and began working for no pay for the baby girls of China.

✤ ✤ ✤

By the time Gary visited Shanjing in 1994, millions of baby girls were missing across the country. An accurate number is unknown; the Human Rights Watch/Asia report cites the government's failure to keep official statistics on orphans as a major hindrance to understanding the full extent of the tragedy. Unsurprisingly, self-reported statistics from Chinese authorities were low: in 1995, an editorial in the People's Daily gave the figure of 100,000, while a Ministry of Civil Affairs report said 160,000. The ratio of male to female births told a different story, one that pointed toward a million girls missing each year, a number that emerged anecdotally and in news reports. The number is supported by the current gender imbalance, which in 2009 had men outnumbering women by 40 million. What happened to these baby girls, whether they were victimized by sex-selective abortion, killed immediately after birth, exposed, or left in orphanages to die by attrition, is a question that might never be answered.

Only slightly better known are the conditions that allowed for the one-child policy, which anthropologist and ethnographer Susan Greenhalgh describes as "one of the most troubling social policies of modern time." Beginning with the Chinese Communist Party's rise to power in 1949, the leaders' strong drive to prove themselves to the world, both as Chinese and as socialists, made them willing to go to great lengths for the advancement of the nation. In the late 1970s, the booming population of China, especially in poverty-stricken rural areas, became the newest and most critical focus of state control. Under Mao's rule during the previous four decades, the government had made almost no effort to control population, framing the growing number of Chinese as an asset. In fact, Mao spent those years silencing and dismantling the very institutions, the social sciences, that allow a country's population to be studied, tracked, and managed. By praising China's population growth as positive, Mao also labeled population a domain that was above critique, and population control became a politically dangerous subject.

What resulted from this countrywide, decades-long disregard was total ignorance of demographics in China. "In the early 1970s, solid statistics on China's population were virtually nonexistent," Greenhalgh writes in her detailed and incisive book on the development of the one-child policy, *Just One Child: Science and Policy in Deng's China*. Instead, leaders talked of population in general terms; "about 800 million" was the official report throughout the 1970s, even when the true number was inching closer to a billion every year. In truth, everyone—including Mao—was ignorant of the actual size and growth rate of the Chinese populace, and they would remain so until three years after Mao's death. Then, in 1979, the State Statistical Bureau finally gave a precise, authoritative figure: the citizens of China numbered 975.2 million.

Once the official number—so jarringly close to a billion—was in, the narrative began to shift. The growing population was no longer a source of pride; according to Greenhalgh, scholars from the People's University began arguing that the huge population was shameful and was preventing China from assuming its rightful place as a world power. How could China get ahead with so many mouths to feed? How could they rise to world power if the masses of uneducated peasants continued to produce even larger masses of uneducated peasant children, incapable of engaging in trade and commerce and industry with the rest of the modern world? And so a new phase began, where controlling population became the unquestioned answer to all of China's developmental woes. In a speech in March of 1979, Party Leader Deng Xiaoping urged party leaders to get population under control, using either administrative or economic measures: "Whatever brings population growth down."

It is important to remember at this point that China had no experienced population scientists or demographers. Greenhalgh explains that in the vacuum, two groups of social scientists emerged, proposing policies that were moderate and gradual, taking into account the realities of the subjects of birth planning: millions upon millions of human beings. One proposal was for a two-child policy with longer spacing between births. The second was for an *eventual* one-child policy, but only after several years of propaganda and education, which would allow people to adjust to and gradually accept the idea of significantly smaller families. Greenhalgh argues that both of these were viable options with significant political advantages for the party and significant personal benefits for the people. But like other Chinese social scientists, the designers of these two policies had suffered twenty years of political repression, deprived of scientific tools at universities and political connections that would confer status and sway in elite circles. Lacking these important assets, the moderates were never able to assert themselves.

Instead, the gap was quickly filled by a group of three natural scientists working as military researchers, men with no experience in birth planning but who had a strong personal interest in population, a belief in science as a panacea, and a desire to expand their usefulness. They were led by Song Jian, an aerospace engineer in charge of missiles at the Seventh Ministry of Machine Building. As part of the department of defense, these scientists had access to the newest science and technology, to conferences and publications where they could assert their claims, and to many friends in high places.

The Song group quickly capitalized on these advantages, Greenhalgh explains. Using control theory normally used to predict the behavior of missiles and machines, with the aid of the newest computer models and striking visual charts, the Song group devised a series of one-hundred-year projections using several different fertility rates, ranging from one child per woman to the 1975 level of three. If the 1975 rate were to continue, the Song group claimed, China would surpass 4 billion by the year 2080, on a landmass equal to that of the United States. The 1978 level of 2.3 children per woman would result in a constantly growing population, more than doubling by 2080. But in one hundred years, a one-child policy would cut the 1980 population by almost one third, to 370 million.

Greenhalgh points out that the data the Song group used was flawed from the beginning, given that the country had unreliable demographic data in general. Therefore, the projections were "highly precise—yet highly inaccurate." Additionally, such long-term projections are now considered essentially meaningless, since they undercut the human ability to adapt and change.

But the numbers—so "scientific" and technical—seemed indisputable, and they shocked China's leadership at all levels, heightening the atmosphere surrounding the already hot topic. If the economic outlook was bad now, how much more when the population was doubled or quadrupled? But the Song group also upped the stakes. Building on current (and ultimately unrealized) theories of population explosion from the West, the Song group argued that if China's population was not reined in, not only would the nation fail to thrive economically, but the effects of the natural environment would be even more devastating. Barring drastic measures, overcrowding would result in food shortages and starvation in China and would eventually cause damages to the planet's ecosystem that would make life on Earth untenable. Population would not only prevent China from modernizing. "It would also damage China's international reputation, as the explosion of Chinese numbers worsened the world at large," Greenhalgh writes.

With such hypotheticals looming on the horizon, China's leadership wanted to act. In order to convey their unwavering commitment to a modern and prosperous China, they applauded an immediate one-child policy and quickly reframed it as the only solution.

So between 1979 and 1980, one-child-for-all became official policy, and as a side effect of China's game of numbers, baby girls began disappearing by the tens, then hundreds, then thousands, then finally millions. When party leaders instituted the policy, they were convinced that, as a good socialist nation, the Chinese people would bend to their will. Like the Song group, they ignored the human component in the equation: that social, cultural, and economic realities would influence the behaviors of the peasant populace, which comprised 80 percent of the total population and was the main target of the program. Yet the reality of peasant life in China was highly structured around a specific design of family, one which included at least two children, one of which *had to be* a son. In *Governing China's Population,* a book Susan Greenhalgh coauthored with Columbia professor Edwin A. Winckler, Greenhalgh explains that this was already true traditionally but had intensified in recent years, first because Maoist policy had favored cities in the distribution of resources, leaving the already-poor peasants with increasingly poor conditions, then because reforms of the late '70s cut many social nets for peasants, a major one being support for the elderly. This left the nuclear family responsible to care for elderly parents and to fend for themselves on their newly private farms.

As they had been for centuries, family roles were clearly delineated. Parents invested in their children's health and education, and when the children grew up, parents provided dowries for their daughters and property for their sons. "Children reciprocated by demonstrating filiality, contributing to the family economy and, for sons, supporting the parents in old age," Greenhalgh writes. "As part of their filial duties, sons also had a moral obligation to pay respect to the ancestors and perpetuate the family line." Because the sons were a source of labor, provided old-age care, paid tribute to the ancestors, and perpetuated the family line, parents invested more heavily in their upbringing. In the traditional system, a daughter left her family to live with her husband's, so anything more than the basics seemed a waste to her parents. Couples typically wanted both a son and a daughter, but the son was the most urgent need, so much so that a common name for a baby girl was *Lai-Di* or *Zheo-Di,* which means "bring a baby brother next."

In their ideological fervor, party leaders underestimated this desire for a son, but they soon learned just how strong it was. Peasants resisted the one-child policy fiercely, hiding pregnancies, bribing officials and doctors, refusing to pay fines, and migrating to other areas to carry a pregnancy to term, among other things. This resistance could not be tolerated, as every illegal birth was a step further from their targeted numbers. Government crackdowns followed, one in the early '80s and another in the early '90s, during which central authorities gave local officials license to use any means necessary to enforce one child for all, including forced abortions and sterilizations—though the latter were almost exclusively performed on women. When Lian arrived in Shanjing in 1992, it was at the height of this second crackdown, when propaganda posters in the countryside proclaimed slogans such as "Deng Xiaoping says that any method that reduces fertility is a good method."

With only one opportunity to bear a perfect male heir, the pressure on women intensified, and having a girl brought shame, social ostracism, and accusations of mistakes in past lives, according to Greenhalgh. "I dare not go outside," one woman in a remote province said. "I just sit in my house, and carry my daughter with tears." Often, the parents could not bear the disappointment of a daughter; according to multiple and credible reports, cited in *Governing China's Population* as well as in the documentary *The Dying Rooms,* parents as well as doctors engaged in infanticide, suffocating infant girls or plunging their heads into buckets of water immediately after delivering them. Countless live infants were left in baskets and cardboard boxes, and the child inside was never a baby boy, unless the child suffered from some physical or mental disability. Baby girls were found in train stations, on doorsteps, and behind factories. Sometimes there were notes pinned to threadbare blankets giving a name or a plea for a caring soul to take her, but other times, the child was nameless. Many did not make it; research from this time period suggests that up to 50 percent of the abandoned babies died before they were found. Those tenacious enough to make it were placed in state orphanages, where the majority would die within days or weeks.

Casting aspersions on parents who would abandon their children comes easily, yet social pressures can pinch with a vice grip. Child abandonment, though not to be condoned, is a tale as old as Moses, stretching from an ancient past into the "enlightened" present. In nineteenth-century England, unmarried women who found themselves pregnant faced the harsh moral judgment of a prudish Victorian society that, because of the cultural insistence on inheritance and legitimacy, had no legal form of adoption. In his essay "What's Love Got to Do with It?: 'Adoption' in Victorian and Edwardian England," George Behlmer explains how many of these women felt that their only recourse was a booming baby trade conducted through newspaper ads, where they could find a foster family to take the child for pay. An investigation by the editor of the *British Medical Journal* revealed that many of the children died soon after these transfers, and that this was something the women knew would probably happen when they agreed to the arrangement. Though Parliament responded with legislation to prevent such "baby farming," both in the late 1800s and with a sweeping child welfare act in 1908, the practice persisted through World War I, after which adoption became a legal practice and society loosened its Victorian moral corsets. In the more recent past in the United States, forty-nine out of fifty states have passed safe haven laws since 1999, which allow parents to leave their children at hospitals or other designated places without fear of prosecution, all in response to reported increases in infant abandonment.

Of course, the scale and scope of infant abandonment in China in the early 1990s reached unparalleled numbers, moving away from an exception to a tragically normal circumstance. And though the government of China did not intend for infant girls to suffer these atrocities, once the realities of the one-child policy began to play out, there were political reasons that prevented intervention. One was that in theory, social welfare work is unnecessary in a socialist state. "Indeed, the entire concept of allowing 'social work' to continue in a socialist society was ideologically suspect, since it called into question the state's promise to eradicate the old evils of poverty and social marginalization," explain the authors of the Human Rights Watch/Asia report. After 1949, the Communist Party had seized charitable institutions countrywide and consolidated them into state-run social welfare compounds, which housed almost all *shehui san-wu*, or "social three-nones"—an Orwellian descriptive for people who had no home to return to, no one to depend on, and no means of support. The elderly, orphans, and people with intellectual or physical disabilities lived together in these all-purpose facilities for the sake of efficiency, hidden behind tall cement walls. "The strong ideological pressure to demonstrate that the need for 'social work' is indeed being gradually eliminated has led to wholesale denial of China's very real difficulties, including the problem of child abandonment," the Human Rights Watch writers explain.

In addition, the government did not do more to save baby girls because many of the babies who were abandoned were illegal births, born outside the lines of state birth planning laws. To intervene would add to China's population numbers and admit that people were disobeying the state policy. Maybe it seemed easier to pretend those little girls just didn't exist—and in state orphanages, that was quickly and overwhelmingly the truth.

It was happening all across the country, in rich regions and poor regions, in catchall social welfare compounds, and in the very few institutions dedicated solely to children who were orphaned and abandoned. Shanjing was only one of many such institutions where poorly trained child-care workers awash with apathy for their jobs watched as one child after another died from treatable illnesses and neglect. Specialized or skilled child-care workers were unheard of, and therefore child-care practices were subpar, to put it mildly. Gary says that at the state orphanage in Shanjing, instead of infant formula, they fed the babies *congee*, a watery rice gruel with very little nutritive value. The children were bathed once a week, all fifty in the same bucketful of cold water. Instead of using detergent to scrub the coarse cloth used as diapers, the workers simply rinsed them with water. Compounding the unsanitary conditions was the fact that there was no climate control in the rooms, so the sickly children suffered through cold in the winter, and in the heat of the summer, infections spread like wildfire. Yet when the babies were sick, child-care workers were not allowed to take the children to the hospital.

After relocating to Shanjing, Lian began training the staff at the state orphanage. She taught them to bathe the children on a daily basis in warm water, to use detergent to wash the cloth diapers, and to hang them to dry in the sun. Lian also began building up a network of foster parents, removing the smallest and weakest children and placing them in the care of concerned families in the neighborhood. The families were poor but could provide individual, high-quality care, and they were paid a modest stipend for their time. In the first few months in Shanjing, Lian lived and carried out her work with her own savings, but as the work grew, Mother's Choice began sending funds—Gary would hand carry thousands of dollars in Chinese *renminbi* anytime Lian called—to pay foster parents the same wage they would have earned in a factory. Lian also began traveling to other state welfare institutions across the province, hoping to save the weakest and most vulnerable from certain death.

Over time, her efforts began to succeed. "It was still a challenge to achieve a much lower infant mortality rate," Gary says, "but between the training and the foster care, babies started surviving." The intensity of the work was exhausting, physically, mentally, emotionally, and spiritually, and Lian needed regular breaks every six or eight weeks to plumb the depths of her experience. "We put a limit on how long she could be in Shanjing without returning to Hong Kong," Gary explains. "Lian would come stay in our apartment, and she and Helen would just sit on a down comforter on the floor and cry and grieve for what Lian was experiencing with these children. Helen, having been there, could understand some of the depth of what Lian was carrying inside her. They'd sit together for hours, and conversation wasn't necessary."

What Lian was doing inside of China was daring and bold. It was risky as well, and she learned to tread a quiet line and stay under the official radar in order to continue. When the dying room reports surfaced, Lian faced criticism from Chinese officials who accused her of participating in the exposés. Lian denied being involved; instead, she continued to focus on building relationships with local officials and maintaining a balance between the radical nature of her work and attracting too much attention, which could get her expelled and end her efforts to rescue baby girls from certain death. In this, she was incredibly effective. After two years of work in Shanjing, she was able to broker a relationship between the Civil Affairs Department of Shanjing and Holt International Children's Services, who hoped to begin facilitating the adoptions of infant girls and disabled boys who were languishing in social welfare institutions.

To show the outcome of adoption, Holt arranged a tour for the Civil Affairs officials to visit the homes of adoptive families in the United States, and Lian accompanied them as their translator. "They got to visit these children who were toddlers or maybe two-and-a-half years old," Gary says. "They saw the children in their bedrooms and their scribblings on refrigerator doors. They saw these Chinese girls were having the opportunity of a lifetime. They were being loved by their adoptive families like a birth family would love them. And it really opened these officials' eyes." Later, Gary and Helen learned there had been some suspicion that perhaps the children were being brought to the United States to be used for kidneys and livers. "But those rumors and fears were dispelled when they saw these children in their adoptive families."

Another pivotal part of the trip was a stop in Hong Kong. Gary and Helen had met with many of the officials on their visits to the state orphanage in Shanjing. Hoping to strengthen these relationships, Helen and Gary invited the officials to their apartment at Montgomery Block and also took them on a tour of the Baby

Care and Wee Care facilities at Bowen Road. There, the officials were able to see the number of children Mother's Choice cared for, as well as the quality of care they were receiving and how healthy the babies were. "I remember the term they used to describe our Baby Care unit was 'scientific,'" Gary recalls, which betrayed the officials' deference to science and their ignorance of modern child-care practices in the same phrase. "They said, 'You take care of the children so scientifically,' which meant the place was clean, that our care was hygienic and thorough. I don't think they knew how else to describe it."

"They were very touched by Mother's Choice," Lian says. "I remember that one official was in tears, and she was saying, 'I really believe there is love.' I think in the early days, for people who were in the government and of that generation, they were deeply touched by the love at Mother's Choice."

Seeing Mother's Choice was key to what happened next, says Lian. After they returned, several officials from the Department of Civil Affairs asked Lian if they could form a partnership, where Lian would open a home like Mother's Choice in Shanjing. It would be a stand-alone charity, a nongovernmental organization working to improve child care for the orphaned and abandoned children through both child care and staff training across the province. Lian was stunned—the very officials who had overlooked these baby girls for years were now asking her to be a model for the region, to provide the highest possible care. Floored by the prospect and somewhat overwhelmed by the potential responsibilities, she didn't know how to answer. She immediately called Helen, and excitedly, knowing what good could be done, Helen told her, "Say yes!"

Lian accepted their offer, and Gary began negotiations with the provincial Department of Civil Affairs soon after. He and the Civil Affairs officials began with a memorandum of understanding, outlining the partnership and the organization's two-pronged approach to child care: residential care of babies and training of child-care workers across the province. But the new orphanage also needed a building, and in the fall of 1994, Helen and Gary traveled to Shanjing to tour different properties.

"They first took us to a duck farm up on a hill on the outskirts of Shanjing and showed us the views, but there was no building," Gary says. "The second place was a fish farm. There was just a little building and concrete pits where you would raise fish. The last place was near a Peoples' Park, where on one side was a building complex that was three or four years old. It was built in the shape of a figure eight, ninety-six rooms, two stories, and it was empty. The officials explained that it had been built as a rehabilitation center for army veterans, but on the backside of the People's Park was a cemetery, and apparently the army vets of the Peoples' Liberation Army didn't want to be rehabilitated so close to where they were going to be buried."

They toured the inside and saw that the whole complex was built around two large courtyards, grassless and muddy, but spacious. And in the middle of the first courtyard was a white marble statue of a woman lying on her side with a young child leaning against her legs.

Gary and Helen and Lian were confused. "What is that statue doing in a center for army vets?" Gary asked.

"We have no idea why it's here," the officials answered.

"What does the statue mean?" Gary asked.

"For us," they said, "this statue means *mother's care.*"

"Now, they knew us as Mother's Choice," Gary says. "But six months previously, we had sat down in Hong Kong and discussed what we would call our work in China. We thought *choice* could perhaps be too political a word in China at the time. We had decided that our work in China would be called Mother's Care."

Gary told the officials that was the name they had recently chosen for the project, then asked, "How did it get here?" They shook their heads. One man began pointing toward the sky and said, "Only heaven knows."

Delighted and awed, they accepted the facility.

In early February of 1995, after almost a year of negotiations, Gary was back in Shanjing, signing the contract with the Department of Civil Affairs. In Hong Kong, they had secured a donation of HK $250,000 from the Rotary Club of Hong Kong Island. With it, they upgraded the facilities, outfitting the baby rooms, transforming the dirt courtyards into vibrant grassy lawns with delicate bottle palm trees as cheerful accents, and buying computers and copy machines to keep meticulous records on the babies. In May, Mother's Care opened its doors and immediately started caring for sixty babies. Gary and Helen and Lian were ecstatic—a year of negotiations had led to a rare partnership between a foreign charity and a government that had, up to that point, denied the tragedy befalling the baby girls of China. It was unheard of, a risk for the local authorities, even for those in Beijing who had approved it. Yet Mother's Care was up and running, taking care of dozens of children in residence, placing more in foster care, and adopting as many as they could overseas, to lives where they'd be loved and afforded dignity.

The first few years they were in operation, Mother's Care had almost three hundred babies in their care, and by 1996, they had seventy-four full-time employees, almost all local people. But over time, as workers in the state-run orphanages became more proficient through Lian's training, Mother's Care began decreasing the number of babies it cared for, allowing the state to take over. Now Mother's Care is no longer in operation as it was. Lian has shifted into working in HIV/AIDS care for children and families affected by the epidemic, which is quietly growing in China.

But seventeen years later, Lian is still amazed that Mother's Care happened at all. "It's all just a miracle," she says with a shake of her head, and in its context, it seems just that.

CHAPTER 10

JACOB AND FUXIA

❧

It's not what you look at that matters. It's what you see.

HENRY DAVID THOREAU

Shanjing and Hong Kong

At a train station near Shanjing, several people heard the child's cry at the same time. Almost two decades later, these people are nameless and faceless. Were they passengers waiting for a train, or had they just disembarked? Were they workers in the station? Whoever they were, they heard a child's cry and scanned the area for its source. Someone spotted the cardboard box. When they peered inside, they saw a tiny baby girl with a strikingly triangular face, with no note, no name. How long had she been in the train station? Were her birth parents close by, watching, around the block in a tiny home, or across the city in a crowded tenement? Or were they country people who had taken a train into town, left her in a busy place where she'd surely be found, and returned to their farm?

There was no way to know, and with all of the babies abandoned across China in recent years, it seems the people who found her knew very well what to do: contact the local police, who would take the girl to the closest social welfare institution. That institution took her in and named her Dang Fu Xia. *Dang*, as her surname, signified that she was property of the institution, but her given name was surprising considering her unlucky beginnings: *Fu Xia* meant "blessed, as one close to God" and "the beauty at dawn and dusk." She stayed—for how long? Twenty-three days, or a year? The records are haphazard, contradictory, giving different dates for her admission. The same confusion surrounded her age. Somehow, three different birth dates were assigned her on different documents, all in 1994, none conclusive, each a guess.

The only conclusive date is October 23, 1995, when she arrived at Mother's Care, a tiny waif of a girl in very poor health, unable to stand or crawl, over a year old but weighing only thirteen pounds. "Fuxia* arrived with her lungs congested," the Mother's Care social worker recorded in her file. "Her face was triangular in shape. It was obvious from the initial examination that she had fractures of her bones in her arms and legs. She did not smile for a very long time, preferring to sit on the play mat and watch what was going on. She seemed a very sad little girl." They wondered about the breaks, whether she'd been abused by previous caregivers or other children, and later Lian would recall that they weren't sure Fuxia would survive.

From the beginning, Lian had set about her new work at Mother's Care with force, recruiting workers and training them thoroughly, placing hundreds of children in nearby families for temporary care, and continuing to visit nearby social welfare compounds and orphanages to find the smallest and weakest baby girls to rescue. In October of 1995, she found Fuxia at one of these compounds and brought her to Mother's Care, knowing that such a tiny, sickly girl would be neglected by default; that if she hadn't been already, it was likely that she'd soon be placed in a dying room.

Fuxia didn't speak when she arrived at Mother's Care, even though the records they had put her at over a year old—possibly close to two, given the development of her teeth and what seemed like a comparatively mature emotional state. Instead, she attempted to communicate using signs. After a little investigation, Lian discovered that there was a school for deaf children in the social welfare compound where she had found Fuxia. Maybe those children had noticed that Fuxia was different, that she was weak, and they had taken an interest, bringing her food, signing to her to communicate, and without knowing it, keeping her alive. Given how small and weak she was, Lian's hypothesis would explain how she was able to survive under extreme conditions of neglect. It's possible that the staff didn't realize what the deaf children were doing, or maybe, because it was no skin off their backs, they allowed them to continue little acts of mercy that kept Fuxia alive. The theory is mostly speculation, but it seemed to Lian the most likely explanation for how a child with an obvious genetic disorder could have survived when her direct experience told her that children like Fuxia were immediately separated into dying rooms.

A few years later, Fuxia would be diagnosed as having osteogenesis imper-

*The spelling of Fuxia's name was originally two words. However, upon adoption to America, her parents combined them to make the name easier to spell in English.

fecta—commonly known as brittle bone disease—by a doctor in Hawaii, as well as a blood disorder called hemoglobin H-Constant spring disease, which makes her prone to anemia. But while she was at Mother's Care, they weren't sure why Fuxia was so delicate, why her face was so triangular, why her ribs protruded so noticeably, or why her tiny heart, which beat so rapidly, seemed to press against those ribs so close to the surface of her skin. In Shanjing, the local hospital couldn't diagnose her, and they refused to treat her, either because she was an abandoned girl or because they weren't sure what to do with her—or possibly both. Her caregivers at Mother's Care wondered if she needed more calcium or a better diet, and while those things helped her gain weight and improve generally, she still frequently fractured her bones. Lian did her best to splint, wrap, and immobilize Fuxia's bones when they broke, but soon her legs were so severely bowed that they tucked under themselves.

"Because of her condition, we were very cautious in handling her and held her minimally, doing only what was required for her care," Lian recalls. "I remember how her eyes would follow us from her cot." After some time, they learned how to hold her without breaking her, though fractures were impossible to avoid completely. The first time Carol Boyd, Fuxia's adoptive mother, saw the little girl, her arm was broken and was wrapped in a small blanket to keep it still. "And I could tell by the look of her legs that it would be a total miracle if she ever put weight on them because they were so curved," Carol recalls.

This was in early 1996, when Carol was visiting Shanjing to help Lian develop curriculum for a preschool at Mother's Care and also to train child-care workers. Carol and her husband, David, had been close friends with Gary and Helen for over twenty-five years; they had attended college with Gary's older brother, Don, at Bethany University, as well as the same Youth With a Mission training school in Lausanne in 1969. They were leaders during Gary and Helen's training school in 1970 and worked with them later in Germany. Helen and Don's wife Deyon, both nurses, had helped Carol and David deliver their first child in Germany in 1971, a blonde and blue-eyed baby girl they named Gretchen. In 1984, David and Carol moved to Hawaii to work at Youth With a Mission's University of the Nations. David became the chancellor, and Carol was the dean of the College of Education, positions they held until 2006.

Fuxia's records at Mother's Care from January of 1996, about the time that Carol first visited, provide a portrait of her growth, her intelligence, and her forceful personality. In her first three months at Mother's Care, Fuxia had gained weight, the social worker wrote, and she had good fine motor coordination. She was capable of placing rings on a stick from largest to smallest and could turn the pages of a book one at a time, which she loved to do, especially *Winnie the Pooh* with its brightly-colored illustrations. She could understand both Mandarin and Cantonese and had learned to say a few basic words. Though she couldn't stand or walk because of her weak bones, she could scoot herself on her bottom to get toys from the toy box, and she could stand with a walker and push herself backwards. Her personality had become much more lively and affectionate. Smiles and laughter were more common, even frequent.

"Fuxia can be described as being very smart, cute, and strong-willed," the social worker wrote. "She knows exactly what she wants, and she has a very cute mannerism of pointing with a flick of her wrist to demand it, which causes us all to laugh." She was adventurous with food, the social worker noted, eating spaghetti bolognaise with her caregivers, showing enthusiasm for anything in a packet or wrapping that she could open herself, and even enjoying cheese, a food typically reviled by Chinese people.

This was the Fuxia whom Carol first encountered, and though she was attracted to her, Carol was careful just to watch, not to engage too much or dote on Fuxia too deliberately. Carol knew that children like Fuxia watched as Westerners arrived, met their adopted children, and took the child with them, back to their homes in America or England. Carol wanted to avoid sending this little girl the wrong message. For Fuxia, this truly was a struggle, and as the days and months passed, as she watched other children being adopted by Westerners, Fuxia began drawing pictures of her future parents. Years later Carol saw a video where one well-meaning couple, there to adopt another child, saw Fuxia in her stroller and paused to talk to her, to coo over her, to touch her shiny black hair and smile at her as Fuxia broke into her own wide smile, which was bright and charming despite her crooked baby teeth. "They made loving comments on how cute she was and what responsive eyes she had," Carol recalls. "They gave her little trinkets and candies." Then as they stood up, waved good-bye, and walked away, Fuxia's face fell with the realization that they weren't there for her. "It was another one of those things she had to pick herself up from again," Carol says.

During her first visit to Shanjing, Carol had a fleeting thought: *This child needs adoption, needs a family.* But as a busy woman with a demanding schedule full of international travel, having already raised three children, Carol pushed the thought aside. Adopting a child like Fuxia wasn't something to do out of pity or on a whim.

Such a decision had to be made deliberately, fully aware of the commitment, accounting for the challenges that adoption would present. Carol left Shanjing with no plans to adopt, just a little space in her heart for a baby girl at Mother's Care.

When months had passed and Fuxia remained at Mother's Care, Lian and the other staff members began worrying about the lasting impact of seeing so many others adopted. A second concern was how controlling Fuxia was becoming, how she directed caregivers about their work and the daily schedule. She had picked up words of English that the caretakers used when they wanted to discuss a sensitive issue without the children understanding, but she had also learned each staff member's responsibilities and the typical routines, and she often corrected them if they deviated in any way. "She even attempted to do their jobs for them sometimes," Carol explains, "fetching the necessary diapers or directing how the infant should be bathed." Part of the reason Fuxia knew so much about the caregivers' routines was due to hypervigilance, a coping mechanism that children often develop when they have no consistent protection from a primary caregiver, when anything could be a threat. In the absence of a primary caregiver, Fuxia felt mostly fear; her world was mostly chaos. Therefore, she sought as much control over her environment as possible. These behaviors were symptoms of Fuxia's attachment issues, which presented themselves upon adoption, when the familiar surroundings and people that had helped her cope were removed.

So Lian and the others decided to move her into a foster care situation, but instead of placing Fuxia with a local foster family, several senior members of the Mother's Care staff, including Lian and two women named Au Pei and Mei Wei, decided to share the responsibility. Fuxia moved into the staff apartments, located in a second Mother's Care building less than one hundred yards away from the child-care facility. During the day, Fuxia attended preschool, which gave her the opportunity to learn and to socialize with the other children, though her activities were limited by her condition. In the afternoon, an older woman from the area would pick her up from school and stay with her in the apartment while her aunties finished the workday. Sometimes they took her to staff meetings with them, and she accompanied them on walks, to the grocery store, and when they made trips out to eat.

Yet Fuxia knew the arrangement was temporary. Often she would tell Lian and Au Pei and Mei Wei that she knew she had a mother and father. "She was determined," Carol says. "She really hung onto it, and she didn't get discouraged when other kids would go. She continued to believe that there were a mommy and a daddy for her."

✤ ✤ ✤

For several years after Mother's Care opened, Gary made frequent trips to Shanjing: to bring money for foster parents, to continue meeting with officials, to consult with Lian on important decisions about the direction of her work. The story of Mother's Care is truly Lian's story, a tale of her transformation: the story of how a timid young woman who thought of herself as only fit to follow grew into a mature leader full of self-confidence, creativity, practicality, and determination—into "the Little General," as Gary and Helen came to call her. But what Gary saw at Mother's Care had an immense impact on him. When he tells stories of children he has met over the years, they're often about the children at Mother's Care, children who suffered unbelievable tragedy and faced immense odds, children who taught him invaluable lessons.

It was a little girl named Si Bei who helped him articulate his belief in every child's desire to belong. Si Bei was several months old when she arrived at Mother's Care from another orphanage in the province, with purple hands and feet and medical records that revealed she had five holes in her heart. They tried to get her help in Hong Kong, but the doctor they spoke to said he couldn't help—that it would be too difficult to get her to Hong Kong. Instead, she stayed at Mother's Care, and as the social workers did for every other child there, they completed her adoption study and sent it to Beijing. They hoped she might be adopted to the United States, where she could live with her own loving family and get the medical attention she needed. Months passed; soon Si Bei was a toddler. She had a favorite dress, which was the color of lilacs and sprayed with a pattern of flowers. Though she was weak, she had learned to stand and walk by holding on to tables and chairs and walls, even to balance across short distances. Like Fuxia, she spent those months at Mother's Care watching other children leave with adoptive families. Finally, one day Lian was able to tell Si Bei that there was a family just for her. The James family lived in the United States and had been approved to adopt Si Bei, and within days they would be arriving in Shanjing to pick her up.

"The next day, Si Bei died," Gary says. "But the way she died is critically important. She didn't die abandoned. She was no longer alone. Instead, she died belonging. Somebody was embracing her." A few months later, the James family arrived in Shanjing to adopt a different child from Mother's Care, and in the tiny cemetery behind the building where the very few who died in their care were buried, the James family placed a marble cross engraved with her name—"In memory of Si Bei."

Through a little girl named Yun, Gary learned about a child's psychological and emotional threshold. Yun lived in the state orphanage before Mother's Care was open, in the earliest days when Lian was working in Shanjing. For some reason, Lian favored Yun; every day Lian paid special attention to her, bathing her, feeding her, and holding her, then placing her back in the bed with the other babies and continuing with other work around the orphanage. One day when Lian arrived, Yun wasn't in the first room where she normally was, or in the second. Instead, Lian found her on a bed in the dying room. Immediately Lian picked her up, bathed her, fed her, and placed her in the first room. Over the course of a few months, this happened six more times: Lian would arrive, find Yun in a dying room, and rescue her. Finally Lian got her out of the orphanage altogether and placed her in foster care with a British couple in the neighborhood.

On one of Gary and Helen's visits to Shanjing, they had lunch with Yun and her foster parents. "I just remember sitting in there in that restaurant, with Yun now a toddler, and she was running around," Gary recalls. It seemed she was growing strong and adjusting well. "I was just thrilled to see this." Yun was finally adopted to the United States, but there were, as Gary says, "significant challenges in attachment," a mild way of saying that she couldn't trust anyone, couldn't process her anger at being abandoned, her sorrow from being rejected, that being left to die seven times in her first year of life was just too much. The adoption failed, and Yun was placed in a small group home.

But more than anything, many of these children taught Gary what it means to be a survivor, how so many had a drive for life stronger than the odds against them. Gary first held Tiny Baby—an affectionate and very literal nickname—in Lian's office on one of his regular trips. She weighed only two pounds and was only the length of Gary's forearm, and her head nestled completely in the palm of Gary's hand. A caregiver had hand sewn a little blanket cocoon exactly the size of her body, and because her mouth was so small, she ate her few ounces of formula not from a bottle, but from an eyedropper.

Gary held her for half of the day, amazed that a tiny body like hers had enough fight in it to stay alive. When he returned over the next several years, he got to see Tiny Baby again and watch her grow and mature. Still much smaller than any of her peers, Tiny Baby was living with a foster family and attended school at Mother's Care. "What a bright button she was," Gary recalls. "At the tenth anniversary of Mother's Care in 2005, she was there singing and dancing and performing with the rest of the children, and she was an inspiration to me. We don't know how she survived. That's one of the amazing things that people who work with these children see. There are some who are just survivors, and that's why they make it."

Gary sees this in Fuxia, a girl who in her short seventeen years has eluded death five times. "She was left in the train station, and she was left to die in the Chinese orphanage, and there have been three other times where Fuxia has been sick, just at the point of death, and she has drawn back," her father David Boyd explains. These second chances point to a bigger plan in her life, he believes, a different intention, a different future for a little girl that has taken miracles to come to pass.

That future began in November of 1997, when Carol and David stopped in Hong Kong on their way to Shanjing, where they were going to do more curriculum development and child-care training with Lian. Gary and Helen had both met Fuxia early on in her time at Mother's Care, and like Carol and so many others who came into contact with this little girl, they noticed the verve and liveliness emanating from this diminutive child's broken body. But this was David's first trip, and Helen mentioned Fuxia to him the night before they left. "There's a little girl you need to meet," she told him gently. There wasn't any pressure from her, David says; in fact, it seemed like her words just held a certain peace.

David and Carol arrived in Shanjing and spent the day at Mother's Care, where they saw Fuxia in the preschool class they observed and during lunch, when they sat and ate with a whole group of children. That evening, however, she was the only child in Lian's apartment, where Au Pei and Mei Wei and the Boyds, as well as several other Mother's Care employees, had gathered to socialize. Though she was over three years old, she still struggled to sit on her own, so they had her tiny frame propped against the leg of a chair. She spent the evening pouring make-believe tea and passing it around the room, to the smiles and delight of all.

When it was time for her to go to bed, Carol asked if she could take Fuxia to her room. "I don't even know why I did it," Carol says now. "She only allowed certain people to hold her, and they could only hold her a certain way because of her fear of breaking—she was so delicate that she would break her own bones just with her muscles. So it was a real risk." But her foster aunties seemed okay with it, and they asked Fuxia if Carol could tuck her in. Carol says Fuxia looked at her with an expression that said, *Yes, you may.* "So I very carefully picked her up like I had seen the rest of them carrying her, where she faced out and you held her under her bottom, like she was sitting in a little chair. It was the only way you could carry her without holding on to an arm or leg and breaking it." As Carol left the room, Lian said to Fuxia in Mandarin, which Carol couldn't understand, "We're so sorry that David and Carol will be leaving tomorrow."

Carol took Fuxia to the bedroom that she shared with Au Pei and Mei Wei and very gently set her down on her sleeping mat. As soon as Carol let go, Fuxia began to cry. Carol, afraid she had mishandled the little girl, began trying to comfort her. Soon Au Pei entered the room and was able to ask Fuxia if she was hurt.

"No, no, no," Fuxia answered in Mandarin. "They're leaving tomorrow. Why are they leaving?"

"In her mind she was already projecting that we were her parents," David says. "No one had said anything about us adopting her, but she was not differentiating between us being consultants for Mother's Care and what she had in mind."

In truth, David and Carol weren't looking to adopt. They were just over fifty, had seen all of their children leave home, and were enjoying being a couple with an empty nest. They had busy lives, with settled roles in their personal and professional spheres. But that night as they lay in bed, David asked Carol if she thought they were supposed to adopt this little girl, and Carol admitted she felt drawn to Fuxia. They knew it wasn't a decision to make then and there, heady with Fuxia's delicate charm and extreme need, so they went home and bought a notebook that they began filling with reasons both for and against adoption. Their lifestyles were a con, as was the fact that they didn't have the money for the adoption. They were over fifty, and this little girl was only three years old. When they asked many of their friends for advice, almost all of them said they were crazy to even think about it.

But as the days passed, they felt a growing sense of rightness about adopting Fuxia. The next step was to broach the subject with their children, who were all away at college. Over Christmas, only weeks after their last visit to Shanjing, they sat down with both sons and their daughter, Gretchen, who had somehow intuited that they were going to adopt the dark-haired girl whose photograph was on the refrigerator before Carol and David even brought it up. They wanted the children's support, but they also wanted to know that if something happened to them, since they were older and Fuxia had severe needs, their kids would step in and care for her. All three, especially Gretchen, were supportive, and though everyone except their children told them they were crazy, they began the process to adopt Fuxia.

As with all adoptions, there were obstacles. They knew it would cost between ten and fifteen thousand dollars to complete the process, money they simply didn't have. They thought it would probably take a year or two, and they weren't even sure they would qualify, since it was their understanding that the combined age of an adoptive couple couldn't be over one hundred. Carol and David were fifty-one and fifty-two. But David loves a problem to solve, and in one weekend while Carol was out of town, he filled out all of the paperwork, comprising hundreds of documents. In the following weeks, he pursued the process aggressively, sending some documents overnight mail and filing all the necessary paperwork in person at the Chinese embassy in Washington, DC. They had just a few hundred dollars to start and used it for each next step, until six weeks in, some friends told them about some businesspeople they knew who set aside money to help adoptive parents finance the process. "Could we represent you to this associate of ours?" the friends asked, and the Boyds were more than happy to assent. After David and Carol wrote a letter about Fuxia and why they hoped to adopt her, the couple wrote them a check for seven thousand dollars, a timely and much-needed gift.

David and Carol worried about the layers of bureaucracy, the months the process could be delayed due to red tape and slow systems, but in April of 1998, the government official who oversaw Mother's Care e-mailed David. "I hear you are planning to adopt. When you have your paperwork, send it to me, not to Beijing," she wrote. David complied, and the official flew to Beijing herself to process the paperwork. Within two days, it was filed. (There were no shortcuts around rules or regulations; the official from Mother's Care simply pushed through the normal bureaucratic delays.) "We actually booked our tickets before we had approval," David said, "for the ninth of May. The day we flew, we heard from the official that we had been approved to adopt Fuxia."

Years removed, David views the process as part of an inevitable chain, one that began when he was a child. "When I was nine years old, I pleaded with my parents to adopt a dark-haired, dark-eyed little girl from China," David says. "I had an older sister, but I was the youngest, and I wanted more kids around the place. I begged for it, but looking at it in retrospect, I know that seed was for me, not for my parents. I just had to carry it for fifty years for it to germinate." He believes a connection existed between Fuxia and her adoptive family over fifty years ago, even though she is only eighteen. It's the same idea that many adoptive parents describe, and which those adopting from China call "the red thread" tying them together. The fortuitous events that allowed Fuxia to become part of the Boyd family just four months after they filed the paperwork were, in David's eyes, part of a greater plan of a loving God, who, in the words of the Old Testament prophets, is the defender of orphans and the refuge of the fatherless.

It seemed to happen just in time. By May of 1998, Fuxia had been stalwart in her conviction for almost two years, believing she had parents who would come for her. She had demonstrated an almost unshakable faith in what she saw as fact. But on the morning of May 9, Fuxia would not stop crying. Lian, Au Pei, and Mei Wei couldn't understand what was wrong. They asked again and again, but Fuxia just continued to cry. They decided to take her out for a walk in her stroller, and while they were out, the sullen little girl asked quietly, "Am I never going to be adopted? I know I have parents. Why am I never going to be adopted?"

Only that morning, Lian had gotten word that the adoption had been approved. She was able to offer Fuxia solace that, very soon, she would be adopted, and that her new parents, Carol and David Boyd, would soon be in Shanjing to get her. She would also have two brothers and a twenty-three-year-old sister named Gretchen, who was paying her own way to Shanjing to be present at the adoption, with small gifts and a card that Fuxia still has today.

The three arrived in Shanjing the next day, on Mother's Day of 1998. According to the birth date that Lian and the other foster aunties had chosen to celebrate as Fuxia's—of the three that were recorded in different government documents, they had chosen June 26—Fuxia was almost four years old. When Carol entered the room where Fuxia was, almost immediately Fuxia said, "Ma-ma," lifting the pitch slightly on the second syllable, leaving the word somewhere between a statement and a question.

"She said it with her Chinese accent and emphasis, but distinctly, 'Ma-ma,'" Carol recalls. "Then she looked at Lian, and with a question on her face again said, 'Ma-ma.' Lian said, 'Yes, this is your mama, this is your daddy, and this is your big sister.' But Fuxia just looked at us." She made no move toward Carol; it seemed instead that she wanted to remain in Lian's arms.

Fuxia eventually let Carol take her, but when she realized that they were going to leave the familiar building and the familiar faces, she began to cry. "She reached out for everyone, and we were so afraid she was going to break a bone," Carol says. "To anybody that would come by, she would say, 'Take me! Take me!' Even to the building manager whom she had hardly spoken a word to—she didn't like him. He was outside, and she was yelling at him, 'Help me! Help me!' And I thought, 'Okay, here it goes.'"

Carol says she knew enough about attachment disorders to know it would not be an easy road, but when Fuxia was still at Mother's Care, it was difficult to judge how extensive the challenges would be. "You don't see the way they will be until you take them out of what they know," Carol explains. "New adoptive parents are often under the illusion that these children are going to be so thrilled to have them. Even though the children have wanted and desired these parents, the whole process is so overwhelming to them. Many times they've simply replaced an attachment to their parents with a schedule or a building, with people they see every day who feed them. Even though it is not a secure attachment, it does provide a form of structure and security."

Having those things taken away is a shock, and the child often struggles with the change, as Jacob did when he first arrived at Wee Care Extension and then when he left Wee Care Extension to live with the Stephens family. Fuxia continued to cry as they left the building and got into a taxi. Carol was holding her as securely as she could without breaking any bones, but Fuxia was resisting her, trying to push her away and wriggle from her arms. After a few minutes of struggle, one of them suggested that it might help to sing, so Carol, David, and Gretchen began singing together in the taxi. It seemed to work. By the time they arrived at the hotel twenty minutes later, Fuxia had calmed down.

But as they lay in bed that night, with David's arm through the bars of Fuxia's crib scratching her back, they were both scared. They knew this was going to be difficult. As David says, the implications of their decision could only hit then, after they had signed the papers, when they were face-to-face with this delicate little girl and her many struggles. They had a difficult trek home, with five flights to get from Shanjing back to Hawaii, and on each one, Fuxia asked if the next destination was her home. While on the last flight, distraught and only able to see water outside the window of the plane, with tears she repeatedly asked, "My house in water?" It was only after she saw land that she calmed down and felt safe, but even today, Fuxia still refers to that day as one full of fear and uncertainty.

Over the next few months, Fuxia resisted and fought the changes and her new life, sometimes to the point that Carol was surprised at the force she could exert, at how fierce she could be without breaking bones. She often resisted Carol's attempts at closeness and caregiving to the point of violence, using teeth and fingernails to make her point, leaving bloody scratches and bruising bite marks on Carol's arms. But Carol was steady and close with her, holding Fuxia as she cried and fought and resisted. Carol found that gently holding her despite her resistance allowed Fuxia to verbalize her fear and pain and rejection. "I believe she began to understand empathy," Carol says, "because I could not help but weep over her pain and brokenness as I held and rocked her. I can remember some of the first times, she would reach up and touch my face and feel my tears, trying to figure out, 'What is this? What's going on? Why is she responding this way?'"

During this time, Carol began reading about the emotional, psychological, and neurological damage done to children in institutions. Soon she began graduate studies examining the process of attachment, hoping to assist other adoptive parents in their struggles with the post-institutional child. Based on her studies and personal experience, Carol views attachment as a spectrum, with the child who has a safe, secure primary caregiver on one end and the child who is institutionalized from infancy, without any secure base, on the other. Yet in the *Diagnostic and Statistical Manual of Mental Disorders* (DSM-IV), colloquially understood as the bible of psychiatric diagnosis, there is only one diagnosis—reactive attachment disorder (RAD). RAD is at the most severe end of the spectrum, characterized by disturbed and inappropriate attachment behaviors before the age of five. But children with milder attachment issues currently have no diagnosis at all. A forthcoming version of the DSM (the DSM-V) will include criteria for disinhibited social engagement disorder, which incorporates some of the behaviors attachment theorists identified as problematic—where children avoid their primary caregivers and show indiscriminate affection to strangers—a long half-century after John Bowlby and his colleagues identified the spectrum of attachment.

"A lag in acknowledging attachment theory in the psychological and clinical research has obviously influenced therapeutic intervention," Carol says. "There isn't a recognized therapy to date that deals specifically with attachment issues." Instead of receiving treatment to help children connect with their caregivers, children with attachment issues have been diagnosed and treated for things like attention deficit hyperactivity disorder, often with no benefit. Unorthodox therapies that deal specifically with attachment issues are shunned by the psychiatric establishment, but many parents of formerly institutionalized children seek "fringe" treatments after they've exhausted every other option.

The lack of appropriate treatment is intensely frustrating for the parent and the child and potentially harmful to both. Yet without a recognized diagnosis and treatment, delays are inevitable. One of the case studies in Carol's dissertation is on a Chinese girl who spent her first year in institutional care. She went straight from neglectful institutional care to the adoptive mother, who received no information about the effects of institutionalization or warning signs concerning a challenged attachment. But this little girl displayed classic symptoms of significant attachment challenges. As a toddler, she was unresponsive to affection and would stiffen against her mother's embrace, and she cried very little. She was indiscriminately friendly with perfect strangers but showed little concern or need for contact with her parent. Unsurprisingly, these symptoms do not register to parents as what they are, that the child has hardened and learned to get by without connections, but in later years, untreated attachment issues manifest in much more obvious ways, through violence, addiction, and psychopathic behavior. And even though the little girl's mother didn't recognize the symptoms at the beginning, she knew something wasn't quite right and began asking psychologists for help when the girl was three years old. The doctors she visited told her she'd have to wait until her child was seven. "So she waited until seven and then they started play therapy," Carol says. "There was very little accomplished in that. The therapies were more about helping the mom know what to do with her, helping to comfort her. But there was no lasting change."

Change happens when the parent builds a connection with the child, Carol says, when the child learns to trust the parent, that the parent will protect the child, comfort the child, and provide for the child what he needs. It's a paradox: that a child like Fuxia had such a strong desire for parents, that within her was an innate sense that the world would be right when she had a permanent family, but that when the time came, she was not equipped to accept it. It's the paradox of many attachment-challenged children. Some, like Yun who was left in a dying room seven times, resist the connection for years, maybe for a lifetime. But at some point, Fuxia had to relent. Because of her disability, she had to depend on Carol and David, she had to learn to trust them. "When she would try to stiffen and pull away, I couldn't let her," Carol says. "Her need to be connected was too great." After four or five months, the fighting began to subside and the process of learning to trust began.

"I was quite surprised at how quick and deep our emotions toward her were," Carol says, but true affection was slower for Fuxia. On the morning after the adoption, when they were in the hotel in Shanjing, Fuxia wanted out of the crib, and Carol lifted her out. Fuxia lay on Carol's chest and put her face right in Carol's face. "I love you," Fuxia said in English. Lian had taught the words to her, maybe as something she was supposed to say. "But it wasn't until months later that she said it in her language, that it just came out—*wo ai ni,*" Carol says. That's when Carol knew the sentiment was from Fuxia herself, unmediated and unmasked.

❀ ❀ ❀

Gary watched as the whole thing progressed. He had met Fuxia within weeks of her arrival at Mother's Care and knew that she was special—"a bright bundle of joy and energy," he called her. He was there the first time Carol met her, on the trip in early 1996. He vividly remembers one evening when they went out to dinner at a local Chinese food court with Lian and a few other child-care workers, who brought Fuxia along. "It was a maze, like a rabbit warren, going through all of the alleyways between several buildings to pick out the different foods," Gary recalls. "And there was Fuxia, so young, and already she'd suffered multiple breaks since she was in our care. But she had mastered chopsticks and was eating by herself, and it was so much fun, watching the dialogue between her and the women. Fuxia had all three of them wrapped around her little finger."

Gary had seen how David's first encounter with this little girl had made an impact, how just a few days with her had melted his heart and compelled him to act with only the vaguest notions of who she was, on the vaguest hopes for who she would become. Only four months later, Gary was privy to some of the Boyds' first days with their new adoptive daughter, as they stopped in Hong Kong. Having struggled with Jacob for months when he first came to live with them, Gary understood the struggles that the Boyd family faced as Fuxia adjusted to her new life.

In September of that year, Gary had his first opportunity to see Fuxia in her new home in Hawaii when David asked Gary to come speak at a conference in Kona to a gathering of businesspeople who were donors to the University of the Nations. Gary has forgotten what it was he spoke about, and in hindsight, it seems that speaking was only the ostensible reason he was there. More important than anything he said to anyone at the event, more important than the money they might donate or the people they might influence, Gary had a moment of clarity. It was during a time of meditation, when twenty people were gathered around a table with a few candles and a brass cross in the middle, with soft instrumental hymns in the background as a focus for their hurried minds. They were to cultivate a space for silence in a busy world, a contemplative moment to connect with God. During this time, Gary felt an impression—what in evangelical terms might be called a word or a message from God. There was no audible voice or shining light from heaven, only a simple command: *Change Jacob's status from foster son to son.*

"It was not earth-shattering," Gary says. "It wasn't, 'Open this mountain and walk through it.' It wasn't, 'Strike a stone and water will come out.' It wasn't even, 'This is my plan for you.'" To someone who was well versed in the stories of the Old Testament, where Moses and Noah and Lot and Job obeyed an ancient God with a flare for the dramatic, this moment seemed quiet, more natural than supernatural, more rational than not.

It's significant that Gary felt this shift while he was in Hawaii with the Boyds rather than at home in the middle of his normal life. This was his first visit with them since they had adopted Fuxia, and he was shocked at the ease with which David and Carol had made the commitment. As he says, "It rocked my world a little bit. I was thinking about how they already had three biological children who were almost grown, and now they had adopted a child who was forty-plus years younger than them, with special needs, and that this was going to be a work in progress for the rest of their lives. I internalized all of this, thinking, *What's the matter with you, Gary?*"

If, as David believes, Fuxia has eluded death five times because her life is meant for a larger purpose, that her life is to impact others, Gary is certainly one of those.

Two days later, Gary flew home to Hong Kong. "When I arrived back at the old Kai Tak Airport in Hong Kong, there was a phone at the end of the jetway," Gary says. "It was for security personnel, but I grabbed it and called Helen and told her we had landed. And I immediately told her that this was what I felt like we were supposed to do. She said, 'Oh, Gary. I'm so glad you're finally there.'"

Jacob had lived with them for eighteen months. His connection with Gary had been growing, slowly, as it had first with Helen. "We played this game that Jacob made up—we called it 'bop,'" Gary says. "It was like tag, but we would just be sitting together on the couch and he would reach over and poke me, and I was 'it.' But he was so subtle in how he did it. He would just lay down his hand beside you and reach one little finger over to touch you, to see if you were alert enough to know that it was your turn to touch him back." Jacob had also made inroads with his foster siblings, each in a special way. Katie was the only child still in high school when they began fostering him, and she was taken with him from early on. "Your laugh and smile are the absolute cutest I have ever seen or heard," she wrote in his blue notebook on his third birthday. And she knew how to incite his laughter too. She would pick him up, and he would throw himself backward so he was hanging upside down like a little opossum. Then Katie would hold on to his waist and began spinning in circles, and he would laugh hysterically until she was too dizzy to go anymore. If she tried to lift him upright, he'd fling himself back again, wanting more.

Andrew was the first to see him walk, and he also helped Jacob accomplish other firsts. For years, Jacob continued to be a difficult eater, and he didn't feed himself until he was almost five years old, when Helen put a peeled banana in his hands and he brought it to his mouth and took a bite, to her absolute astonishment. But with Andrew, Jacob was more cooperative. Even in the first few months of fostering, Jacob would eat, and eat well—first his soup of fish and vegetables and rice, and later different foods at home—but only with Andrew. Their family albums display several tender pictures of this, and one in particular conveys Andrew's gentleness with his new brother: they are sitting at a long wooden table that first summer in Colorado with the green foothills visible in the background, Jacob in Andrew's lap with a bowl of soup in front, Andrew's hand under Jacob's chin, delicately spooning soup into his young brother's mouth.

And with Amy, Jacob would try new sounds. She would make a noise or say a word, and he would mimic her. For a few years, Amy and her husband, Bob, lived in Colorado, just a few miles from Gary and Helen. "Sometimes Amy would have Jacob down at her house for a few hours to try to teach him new sounds," Gary says. "Down at her house he could say 'no' pretty clearly. Then she'd be at our house and hear him say 'nah,' and she'd say, 'Wait a minute, Lok Chi. You can say 'no' clearly at my house. You have to learn to say it at your house. And he did.'"

Of all the siblings, Shawna's bond with Jacob took the longest to form. Shawna was already married and living in the United States when they adopted Jacob, and he would only hear her voice for a few days every year or two. But after Shawna divorced, she and her son Joey moved in with Gary and Helen. "Now that she has lived with us, he recognizes her footstep coming upstairs," Gary says, "and before she even turns the corner to come into the kitchen, he says 'Duh *dah* duh'—I *love* you. And she says, 'I love you too, Jacob.'"

Though many of these connections began very early, in early September of 1998 Jacob was still a foster son, and from day one, Gary had been mindful about how he represented himself to him. "I called myself his buddy," he says. "I would say to him, 'You are my little buddy.' I felt like that was really an important way to position myself to avoid unfulfilled expectations. But when I got back from Hawaii and walked into the house, Jacob heard me come in the front door and had started coming toward me down the hallway in his little walker. And I knelt down and said, 'Come here, son.' Those were the very first words out of my mouth. It actually surprised me to hear me saying that because I had been so careful, but it was like I was suddenly extending myself into a commitment that he could hang on to. I was saying, 'I'm not going to pull this one back.'"

Because Gary and Helen had already been vetted as foster parents by the Social Welfare Department of Hong Kong, because Jacob had an unequivocal adoption status, and possibly because he had been in the system for so long, the adoption was processed very quickly. Gary and Helen filed paperwork in early September, and adoption went through officially on October 31, 1998. At a quiet ceremony in a high-rise office building in the Central District of Hong Kong, with Gary, Helen, Katie, and the social workers of the Social Welfare Department, the final stamps were placed on the thirty pages of adoption paperwork. In them, his name was officially changed to Jacob Lok Chi Stephens—though they would call him Jacob, Lok Chi, Jacob Lok Chi, and JLC interchangeably—and he became the youngest of five children in an American expatriate family living in Hong Kong.

In the years following both adoptions in 1998, Carol, David, and Fuxia were in Hong Kong and China several times, either for work with Lian at Mother's Care or with Youth With a Mission projects in Hong Kong. Very often, they stayed with Helen and Gary, and the two couples found comfort and support in one another, in the similar struggles they were facing, and even more joyfully, in the delight of their young children. Fuxia was so verbal, and normally chattering and noise disturbed Jacob, but somehow they gravitated toward one another.

"There was a rapport between them," Carol says, "and Fuxia would talk to him about everything, in the beginning in Chinese, then later in English." They played together well, though Carol says that often it was parallel play, where they sat in the same space and Fuxia chatted away to him but they stacked blocks or turned the pages of a book or pushed toy trucks across the floor separately. They'd continue peacefully for a while until Jacob would commence his favorite pastime, the same from doctors' offices and escalators in shopping malls, of popping out his prosthetic eyes.

"She would get so upset because he would pop his eyes out," Carol laughs, "and they would end up in one of the trucks she was playing with. And she'd say, 'Lok Chi, would you please keep your eyeballs in? Stop taking them out!'"

Their rapport might have been something intangible, a sense in both that they had a shared fate, the same wounds, a common bond. But Fuxia also saw a more practical connection as well. A marriage just might be in order, she explained to her parents when she was only seven or eight years old. When they asked why, she answered, "Because he could be my legs, and I could be his eyes, and we could get along just perfectly in life."

CHAPTER 11

A SIGHTLESS CHILD IN a CITY OF SOUND

❀

I could stop anywhere—bring to a close the walking I was doing and the think-ing that went with it—and suddenly the ambient noise of the neighborhood would open up around me. The ordinary street outside our suburban house was surprisingly beautiful with all its fractions of living. There were little reports of living going on in every quadrant.

STEPHEN KUUSISTO, *EAVESDROPPING: A MEMOIR OF BLINDNESS AND LISTENING*

Hong Kong

In the mornings, Jacob could hear birds. On the tree-covered hillside that was the Mid-levels, Montgomery Block was set amid a stand of trees, heavily canopied. It had not always been that way. When the British first arrived, local farmers and fishermen had been cutting down oaks and laurels for hundreds of years, for fire-wood, for furniture, and for shelter, and by the early nineteenth century, Hong Kong's hillsides were bare, exposing an underbelly of red clay and steel-colored granite. The British botanist Robert Fortune passed through in 1844, noted the scorched appearance of the island, and recommended that the British government cover the hillsides with trees as quickly as they could. It would improve the look of the place and save the colonists from the fierce and aggressive Hong Kong sun, the likes of which he had not experienced in all of his wanderings through the tropics. They heeded his suggestion and began an effort to reforest the denuded slopes, and in the 1860s, while the town of Victoria was being carved into the granite, avenues of trees were maturing into emerald lushness.

At the front door of Montgomery Block over a century later, a flame tree pro-vided cover with its low, wide umbrella. But it was also a spectacular sight, with brilliant red blossoms, five-petaled and large as a human hand, covering the entire crown of the tree through the spring and summer. And at every daylight, yellow-crested cockatoos would alight in its branches. Against the green leaves and red flowers, their white bodies and retractable yellow combs were striking. Like many of the trees—the flame from Madagascar, the camphors and the Brisbane boxes and other broadleaves that were used to green the hillside—these birds were transplants to Hong Kong. They had been brought from Indonesia as exotic specimens, décor for the homes of the British colonists and administrators. But according to local lore, in December of 1941, the British governor of Hong Kong, Sir Mark Aitchison Young, opened the cages of all the birds in the Government House just before surrendering to Japanese troops. Over the years, the cockatoos multiplied and eventually became a common sight in the trees above Victoria Harbor.

On the third floor of Montgomery Block, two stories above the flame tree, in a small alcove adjacent to the master bedroom, Jacob lay in his crib as outside the cockatoos cracked long, flat seedpods and emitted their harsh screeches and caws, interspersed with squeaks and short whistles. Just beyond Kennedy Road, more birdsong rose up from the aviary in Hong Kong Park, a semitropical enclave set back from the skyscrapers on the harbor front. In the shelter of the park lived dozens of songbirds, and the loudest calls made their way to the surrounding residences: the blue-throated barbet with three quick chirps, urgent and percussive; the great barbet with his longer ascending whistle, lonely and mournful but just as insistent; the white-rumped shama, its song undulating and calm; and the most melodious, the brook-like warbling of the straw-headed bulbul, an effortless fluting up and down, up and down, up and down, then up again.

Jacob could also hear the movements of morning, of Gary and Helen rising only a few feet away through the French doors. Sounds emerged from outside as social workers arrived at work, scraping open the wrought-iron gate, then releasing it to close with an echoing clang. A little further away, the light hum of cars faded in and out as they wound around the circuitous roadways of the Mid-levels, sometimes punctuated by the wail of a truck or ambulance emerging from a fire station on Cottontree Drive, only a few hundred yards below.

Because of his irregular sleep, Jacob rose at different times in the morning, but each day by nine o'clock he was on his way to preschool, located at the former British Military Hospital. Helen's office was next door to it in the ex-commodore's house, making the commute quick and convenient. From the third-floor flat, they made their way down two sets of metal staircases which echoed underfoot, then up the hill with its zigzagged series of concrete steps and landings, guided by low metal fencing on each side. Though the stairs might seem like a treacherous place for a blind child, this pathway up the hill was actually easy for Jacob to navigate once he learned the rhythm. Stairs are predictable.

"You never find a chair left on a stairway, or a bucket or a brick," John Hull writes in *Touching the Rock*—this in contrast to a wide-open space, which gives no signals and is full of unexpected obstacles. "For this reason, it is easier to find my way around a campus which is marked out by steps, little hills and valleys, low walls and lots of changes in texture, because I can mark out my route with sections." With its maze of sidewalks, stairs, and escalators, the city of Hong Kong gave this to Jacob, and the map was fleshed out further by the constant sounds of the city.

The concept of a rich and complex auditory map is somewhat foreign for a sighted person, for whom the world is constantly and immediately accessible through the organ of the eye, through the powerful gaze that acts on objects near and far, noticing shape and size and color and movement, discerning distance and position in relation to the viewer. But John Hull helps clarify the role of sound in placing the blind person within the world. In his memoir, he reflects on a Saturday afternoon in April of 1984, when he sat on a bench in Cannon Hill Park in the city of Birmingham, England. "There were groups of people walking together with different strides, creating a sort of patter, being overtaken now by one firm, long stride, or by the rapid pad of a jogger," he writes.

> There were children, running along in little bursts, and stopping to get on and off squeaky tricycles or scooters. The footsteps came from both sides. They met, mingled, separated again. From the next bench, there was the rustle of a newspaper and the murmur of conversation. Further out, to the right and behind me, there was the car park. Cars were stopping and starting, arriving and departing. Far over to the left, there was the main road. I heard the steady, deep roar of the through traffic, the buses and the trucks. In front of me was the lake. It was full of wild fowl. The ducks were quacking, the geese honking, and other birds which I could not identify were calling and cranking. There was a continual flapping of wings, splashing and squabbling, as birds took off and landed on the surface.

Within this auditory map, Hull discovered that the inhabitants of the world have to "scrape, bang, club, strike surface upon surface, impact, make their vocal chords vibrate" for him to know them. The world to him is one of action, and when the action ceases, the world disappears. Yet the dynamic, racing city of Hong Kong rarely stops. As in New York or London or Bangkok or Mumbai, the concentration of sounds—those of humans, machines, and nature—is a symphony of activity, filling the skies, roadways, and sidewalks.

Based on Hull's descriptions, the hillside would have been a distinct experience for Jacob because of the stairs, but also because of the particularity of its sounds. It was covered in ferns and moss, with short palms occupying the mid-space between the ground and the crowns of the taller trees, and the thick vegetation muffled the sounds of the city and even his own footsteps. Then they emerged from it, to meet the noise of traffic on Borrett Road. There Jacob signaled that he knew where he was by turning himself to the right at the top of the stairs, and they would head down the footpath, following it across the gated drive of a glass high-rise, home to China's foreign affairs department in Hong Kong. Past the driveway, the sidewalk sloped downwards, a few feet below and alongside Borrett Road, which curved to the left and up the hill. This was an in-between space, lower than the level of the road and the cars that slowed as they neared the 180-degree turn, above Montgomery Block and the ambient whistles of birds, above the bloated exhale of the air brake of a city bus, above the sounds of construction—the generic mechanical grinding, the regular pulse of hammer against steel—which floated up from several hundred feet below.

Then a wind might pick up, and suddenly one sound would become present and immediate: the leaves of the banana palms just above Jacob's head would flap against themselves, low and flat. He would turn his face toward the wind and pause as it blew across his face.

Wind was something he'd shown preference for from very early on. Elizabeth, the caretaker who had noticed that his time with Helen was calming to Jacob, discovered this one day by accident when she was taking him to a doctor's appointment in Central, the waterfront business district on the western side of Victoria Harbor. With Jacob in a stroller and time to spare, she took a few minutes to browse at a shopping center. But she stayed too long, and after realizing her mistake, she hurried out the door and literally ran down the sidewalk a few blocks. Then she stopped, fearful that Jacob might be scared by how quickly she was moving, and looked in on him in his stroller. To her surprise and relief, he was smiling.

Gary and Helen and others had noticed it too—how he loved being pushed in a toddler swing that hung beneath the metal stairs on the backside of Montgomery Block, and how he would open his mouth as he flew forward as if to swallow the wind. This was a preference that, because they were sighted, they couldn't entirely understand. As a child who had been blind from birth, his sensory experience was distributed differently, and even if he'd had words, he might have struggled to describe it. Or more likely, they might have struggled to understand him.

For sighted people, the comparison of being blindfolded or enveloped in darkness is often employed to describe blindness, but in truth, that's a vague and utterly insufficient attempt to inhabit the world of blindness, not least because for someone like Jacob, there is no such thing as darkness or any difference between light and dark—Jacob has never known either. But again, with his dual experience, John Hull helps the sighted person understand that the meaning of something as basic as *a nice day*, which to sighted people often means a blue-skied sunny day, is different for a person without sight, who cannot see the blue sky or the clouds or the glint of sunshine on rippling bodies of water.

"For me, the wind has taken the place of sun, and a nice day is a day when there is a mild breeze," John Hull explains in *Touching the Rock*. "This brings into life all the sounds in my environment. The leaves are rustling, bits of paper are blowing along the pavement, the walls and corners of the large buildings stand out under the impact of the wind, which I feel in my hair and on my face, in my clothes." For Jacob, when the breeze blew, it illuminated his own body in its entirety: the scalp and shoulders and the forearms and knees that he could never see. And when the wind tossed the leaves of the banana tree and they slapped against one another gently, he could know the tree and feel it as a canopy arching over him.

"The sighted person always has a roof overhead, in the form of blue sky or the clouds, or the stars at night," Hull continues. "The same is true for the blind person of the sound of the wind in the trees. It creates trees; one is surrounded by trees whereas before there was nothing." Maybe this is how Jacob would have described the phenomenon of wind if he had developed language, but even without that, his body conveyed his preference for it. At six, he stood on a tire swing with a grin as Gary pushed him higher, and years later, with arms and hands outstretched, Jacob would be openmouthed as he rode ATVs with Gary on the mountainsides of Colorado, still trying to swallow the wind.

After a moment, Jacob and Helen would continue, traveling about a hundred yards on this footpath beside Borrett Road, which reached street level at an intersection with Bowen. Jacob knew when they had reached the crosswalk, and he would stop, because cars, in perfect observance of the Doppler effect, rise in pitch as they near, then fall to a deeper register after they pass by. When traffic cleared, they would cross the street where Jacob's caretaker, Myrna, would meet them and accompany them the last few feet up the sloping pathways to the buildings on the promontory that housed both the preschool and Helen's office. On this last leg, Jacob could drag his hand along the brick retaining wall, where the roots of a Chinese banyan had pushed through and spread out like thick, leathery tentacles, forming a rough, irregular web. Once they reached the top, Jacob would help open a white metal gate, ornate with vertical bars and decorative Gothic points, which in the humid air was clammy to the touch. It brought them to a long hallway with tile floors, many windows, and high ceilings, and their footsteps, words, and movements echoed. The noises and textures would continue: the teachers' voices, children's songs, sitting knee to knee in a circle, feeling the softness of a cotton ball placed in his hand.

It had taken a while for Jacob to become a steady walker, so that he could make this trip to preschool himself without stopping and refusing to take another step. In January of 1999, a young woman named Sarah had enrolled in the Introduction to Children's Social Services course through Mother's Choice, which was divided between classroom hours and practical experience. For her child-care duty every day, she had requested to spend time with Jacob, who was now just shy of five years old. He was stubborn at first and untrusting, resistant to this young woman who was a stranger, and he would scream and cry and refuse to walk with her. "She worked with Jacob for two hours each afternoon to try to get him to a little children's park about a quarter of a mile away," Gary recalls, "and one day she came back and said they'd had success because Jacob went up twenty-seven steps before he stopped." But by the end of March, Jacob was taking the steps on his own, even the steepest: an unbroken set of seventy-two climbing the top half of the hill. He would even climb them backwards sometimes.

By this time, Gary had moved into the role of Mother's Choice managing director. After twelve years in that position, Helen had decided she wanted to focus her efforts with the infants and had moved into a position as the director at Baby Care. So Gary resigned from Youth With a Mission and took a corner office on the first floor of Montgomery Block to oversee the ever-growing organization as a whole.

He was home more regularly now, and he would often meet Jacob after his morning of preschool and take him for a walk around lunchtime. Until he was six or so, Jacob would ride on Gary's shoulders along Kennedy Road, but when he got too big to be carried that way, they would walk together. Because the footpaths were narrow and cars were close by, Gary gave him verbal cues to help him avoid other pedestrians, or the trunks or branches of a banyan that would protrude into the path. Jacob moved more slowly than others on the street, and he could hear the footsteps behind them become the footsteps beside them, then the footsteps in front, and then eventually disappear. Trucks would trundle by, engines downshifting around the curves, then roaring again to regain momentum on the straightaways, and the tunnellike shape of Kennedy Road amplified the noise. To their left, trees lined the hillside and reached out over the road, and across the street on their right, a stone-and-cement retaining wall kept the rocks and debris from spilling into the roadway. "I remember walking him along the street," Gary says, "and here'd come one of these lorries or a bus, and he'd just put his hands over his ears. They must have been excruciatingly loud for him."

It happened in dense crowds too, and in noisy restaurants. With so many sounds, Jacob struggled to synthesize, to block out the unnecessary ones and listen only to his father's voice. If they were going out for lunch, they would leave early to beat the crowds and hurry past the trucks and buses on Kennedy Road. "We're going up six steps," Gary would say as they arrived at the Hopewell Centre, a round skyscraper with a backside that opened into a brick-paved plaza on Kennedy. It was a convenient shortcut; because of the steep slope of the island, they entered on the seventeenth floor, but the ground floor opened on to the narrow, crooked streets and the bustling markets of Wan Chai.

Inside Hopewell was a set of concentric circles. Elevators formed the spine of the building, around which was a perfectly circular corridor, and electronics shops and tailors and travel agencies lined the perimeter. Sometimes they were alone, but other times the elevators were crowded, and Gary would guide Jacob back into a corner, hands on his son's shoulders. They'd hear the whirring descent, then the ding of the elevator as they reached the third floor, and he'd ask Jacob to wait until the others got off before they emerged. From there an escalator took them down to the ground floor, and Jacob became accustomed to the routine. "He'd grab the rail, and he had a sense of when we were getting close to the bottom," Gary says. As the clip of the stairs folding into themselves grew louder, Jacob's small frame would be rigid and alert, and he would lift his foot at the same time that Gary cued him to step off the escalator and onto solid ground.

By now, Jacob had shed his recalcitrant attitude toward eating out. On the contrary, he loved going out for dim sum, for pork and shrimp dumplings and spring rolls. He also loved Indian food, and Gary often took him to lunch at JoJo's Mess, an Indian restaurant with a weekly buffet only two blocks away through market streets. Between the Hopewell building and JoJo's, Jacob would hear the honking and idling of traffic and a storefront opening with the sound of perforated metal rolling up on itself. Open-air stalls held clusters of people, addressing one another in the rise and fall of a bargain, finishing with the clink of change and the rustle of a plastic bag.

Soon they would reach the small restaurant, mostly empty at the early hour, to be greeted by the gracious smiles and friendly welcomes of the proprietors. "They had the best curries and naan you could find," Gary says, "and I would sit Jacob at a table and then go fill a plate at the buffet, of chicken tikka, chicken curry, dal on saffron rice, and maybe some yogurt sauce on top." Jacob would eat his share of the fragrant and spicy dishes, and when people started filling the restaurant for lunch, Gary would guide him out to find a safer space, away from the cacophony of voices hemmed in by four walls.

Other times it would just be a walk to the children's park to spend a few minutes, providing an opportunity for them to be out and explore together. "We'd be walking along and he'd stop, and he'd turn his face in the direction of the wind. Then he'd cock his ear, and so I'd stop and tune my ears to what he was listening to," Gary recalls. He'd hear a shrill whistle—an *ee! ee!*—and look up to see a black kite, a common Hong Kong hunter, gliding up and down on the pillars of warm air radiating from the rocky isle. "And over time, he made me a lot more aware of what is going on in the world around me, of what I'm hearing, but also what I'm smelling, and what things feel like under my fingertips."

✿ ✿ ✿

In Hong Kong, sounds are varied but omnipresent, paradoxically intermittent and constant. For Jacob, the city manifested itself continually, whether in his bedroom, on the way to school, on weekday strolls, or on Sundays, when Hong Kong slowed but certainly did not stop. Each week, Gary and Helen would take Jacob with them to church, which met in a conference room at the Grand Hyatt on the harbor front. They took a taxi down, but they would walk home between the sleek skyscrapers of glass and steel in Central, through the towering apartment buildings, concrete and striated with shallow balconies, sullied by smog and weather, and wearing a tint of gray.

Sundays are mandated by the Hong Kong government as the day off for domestic help, so the city streets would be full of thousands of women gathered for a sort of potluck. There were so many that the government closed a central street for them where they could congregate freely. Yet they would spill onto sidewalks and under covered walkways a few blocks in either direction, and as they passed, Jacob would hear them speaking an assortment of languages, the lively and tonal Thai, as well as Indonesian and Tagalog. He would hear their laughter and singing as he and his mother and father traced their way back through the labyrinth of the city.

Halfway home, the tenor changed as they entered the sprawling shopping malls on either side of Queensway Road. One, named Queensway for its location on the thoroughfare, was also a major mass transit station. Once they crossed into the adjacent mall, a high-end complex of shopping and offices and hotels called Pacific Place, the echoes changed. They'd stop in the food court to buy Jacob's lunch, some Korean beef or a savory soup. As they waited, the space rang with the clink of forks against plates and spoons against bowls and voices in casual conversation. Next they took the elevator up to Kennedy Road, and where they emerged was a taxi queue, distinctive because of the frequent braking and the slamming of car doors and aggressive acceleration.

Once they climbed the stairs and were back in their apartment at Montgomery Block, Jacob might rest for a while; then Helen would sit with him at the piano. She'd play and sing for him, and over time he memorized the songs. "When he had a request, he'd give you the first five notes," Gary recalls. "You were then supposed to pick it up right there and sing all the verses and choruses straight through. If you left one of the verses out, he would go straight back to the top of the song, and give you the notes again, as if he was saying, 'I know all the words—let's put them all in here.'"

Other times, they would sit him on the piano bench by himself, where he would stay for an hour at a time, listening with his head cocked to the side as he ran up and down the keys with both hands. Maybe it was Helen's example, maybe it was the birds he heard outside, maybe it was music he heard in the city's organic orchestra, but his ears and fingers reached for sweet-sounding pitches, and he found harmonies that Gary and Helen were surprised by. When he tired of the piano, he would make his way to the small laundry room, close the door, and sit on the floor beside the dryer. And very gently, he would pound on the dryer door, over and over, boom boom boom boom boom, and listen to the sound as it bounced inside the hollow belly of the machine. He went there often. If they took their eyes off him for a few minutes, then looked up and wondered where he might have gone, all they had to do was what Jacob did in the middle of the sidewalk on Kennedy Road: stop, lift an ear, and listen.

Late in the evening, they would place Jacob in his crib, which he still preferred, though at six he was probably too old for it. There, before he fell into his fitful sleep, he would hear the night noises of Hong Kong. The traffic still hummed, but a different chorus would spring up, of frogs and cicadas and crickets, the calming strings of sundown. And there he'd stay until he heard the birds again, though often he'd wake in the night and call out for his mother, and her voice from the other room would assure him that she was still there.

CHAPTER 12

RETURN TO COLORADO

❧

Be grateful for whatever comes,
Because all of it has been sent
As a guide from beyond.

RUMI, "THE GUEST HOUSE"

Montrose—Hong Kong—Montrose

On March 28, 2002, Gary left Hong Kong for a short trip to the States. Exhausted from leading a twelve-week training school for child-care workers, Gary fell asleep before the plane left the runway and didn't wake up until it touched down in Chicago, his arms full of fiery pins and needles. There he had a short layover, but soon he was through Denver and into Montrose and home at the family's log cabin on Government Springs Road, high on a knoll several miles south of town, a high point amid a patchwork of fields and pastures.

The next day was Good Friday, a cool, sunny spring morning, but very quickly, the sun showed its force and the day turned hot. Gary was out early working on their forty acres of land, a low green crescent hugging the west side of the knoll. His aim was to secure a portion where they could keep their five horses close to the house instead of miles away on a friend's property. With his characteristic energy, he kept at it all day, digging postholes, setting posts, and stringing barbed wire, enjoying the clear air and the quiet, the brief respite from the city of Hong Kong.

That evening, he relaxed in the hot tub on the wooden deck of the log cabin. It was an opportunity, away from the teeming streets and the crowded offices, to let his mind go slack. There was no need to answer the questions of concerned social workers or adoption counselors or advise on a child, no meeting to attend about facilities or funding. No one was pulling him in five or six different directions. He was, for the moment, free to do as he pleased. When the warm waters had loosened the ache in his tired body, he got out of the hot tub, wrapped himself in a white terry-cloth robe, and found the couch in front of the television.

It was the end of March, which meant basketball, specifically the NCAA Women's Final Four at the Alamodome in San Antonio. Gary had played basketball for one semester in college, during his short stay in California with Don and Deyon, and he had coached his daughters in youth leagues in Hong Kong. American collegiate sports weren't widely broadcast there, however, so he was excited to see live action. That evening, he watched as Oklahoma took down Duke, then Connecticut began to pull away from Tennessee.

And suddenly he found himself staring at a screen full of snowy noise and no image. "I realized the second game was over," Gary says, "and I didn't remember the last few minutes. I thought that maybe I had just dozed off." He felt a tingling sensation on the right side of his head and all the way down his right arm, but as he looked over at where the arm stretched across the back of the couch, he thought he'd simply cut off the blood supply and it had gone to sleep. Whatever it was, he felt tired and wanted to turn off the television and go to bed. When he tried to stand up, however, his right leg, like his right arm, was unresponsive, and he crumpled to the floor. This didn't register as strange in Gary's mind; he simply rolled over onto his side, pushed with his left arm against the couch, and was able to stand. Though the remote control was still within reach—on the seat of the couch next to him where it had been throughout the evening—Gary walked over to the television and began running his left hand along the edges. "That part of my brain knew there was an on-off button," he recalls. "Where it was, I had no idea, but I knew there was one on there. I ran my left hand across the top and both sides, and I finally found a line of buttons. I started hitting the buttons, one by one, until I hit the power switch and turned it off."

Then the same part of his brain that had reasoned there must be an on-off button on the TV reasoned that it was time to go to bed. "Normally I would walk in a diagonal across the great room to the stairs leading to the master bedroom upstairs. But that evening, I walked through the French doors into the great room, and instead of going diagonally to the stairs, I walked along the front windows of the house and past the dining table, through the living room furniture close to the woodstove. I remember distinctly thinking, *This is a very unusual route to the stairs. I don't think I've ever taken this way before.*"

He reached the stairs and began to ascend them, but after three or four steps, he felt dizzy and began lurching backwards. The moment before he fell, he grabbed not the heavy log banister on the right, but the smaller rail on his left, which was attached to the wall with brackets at the top and bottom. "I gripped that rail so tightly with my left hand, with all of my weight, with all of my force, that I saw that rail flex like a fly rod when you're fishing for trout," Gary says. The railing held, and he pulled himself upright and continued upstairs.

Still Gary had no recognition that, besides the detour to the stairs, anything was off-kilter. He made his way to the master bedroom, climbed into bed, and closed his eyes. A few moments later, he thought he heard a sound, and worried someone was in the room, he opened them again. "Straight above me was an oversized hand," he recalls. "At first I thought it was someone else's hand, and that must have been the noise I heard. But it was my hand, my right hand, spread out, all the fingers splayed. I looked at it, and I thought, *Why didn't you go to bed with the rest of us?* So I grabbed it with my left hand and forced it down." Pressing his own hand to his chest, he felt terrycloth and realized he was still in his bathrobe. He sat up and began pulling and tugging at different portions of it, but he couldn't figure out how to untie the belt. After a few minutes of futile effort, he gave up and decided he'd just sleep in it. *This is the first time you've ever slept in your bathrobe,* he thought, *but okay.*

He lay down again, but before he could fall asleep, the telephone rang. He reached over to the nightstand on his left and picked up the cordless receiver and said hello in what he thought was a normal voice. It was Helen calling from Hong Kong. Jacob was upset, and after trying unsuccessfully to settle him, Helen had called Gary, hoping that hearing Gary's voice would help him relax. "Honey, did I wake you?" she asked.

Gary answered, "No," but what Helen heard was drawn-out and mumbled, low and slow, like the hello that had made her think he'd been asleep. She asked if he'd taken any medicine that evening, thinking that might have slurred his speech, but he answered again with the same drawn-out no. Helen's startled response seemed to calibrate Gary's sense of reality, and it finally began to dawn on him that something wasn't quite right. *I need help,* he thought. So he tried to tell her that, but he could only eke out the first two words: "I need."

"I couldn't finish the sentence," Gary says. "I felt like my brain was a disc that was spinning so fast I couldn't slow it down to find that word to finish, so I would start the sentence all over again, thinking maybe the next time I could get through." So again he said, "I need." He couldn't finish it. "I need."

"Gary, you're scaring me," Helen said. "I think you're having a stroke or a heart attack. I want you to hang up the phone so I can call somebody."

Gary protested, saying, "No-o-o, I don't want." But the rest of the sentence was lost, so he started it again. Maybe Helen understood what he was trying to say—"I don't want to lose contact with you." In any case, she put Katie on the phone and headed downstairs to call for help on another.

"I remember that Katie was very happy, very chirpy," Gary says. "A cheerful 'Hello, how are you? So Dad, did you watch basketball?'"

As he spoke to Katie, Gary got out of bed, got the bathrobe off, and began trying to get dressed. He awkwardly pushed his slow right arm into a T-shirt, then pulled his head through. He paused and pressed the phone up against his chest so he could put his left hand through the armhole. "In doing so, I discon-nected the call with Katie," Gary explains. "So I just set the phone on the floor in the bathroom, got some jeans on, put on some slippers, walked down the stairs, and went outside to my truck."

His truck was a rumbling diesel with a manual transmission. He was able to start it, to turn the key halfway and wait for the red light on the dash to go off before engaging the starter. He also found the switch for the lights, which flooded the back of the garage. But when he took his foot off the clutch, the truck moved forward instead of in reverse. Quickly he hit the brakes, then began trying every option presented on his left. He turned the lights off and on, sent the windshield wipers plodding across the glass, but he never even glanced toward the stick shift on the right—maybe because he'd just left Hong Kong, and in Hong Kong, the left side was where the gear shifter would be located; or maybe because the same issue affecting his right arm and right leg was affecting his entire conception of his right side. But he tried again, touching every switch and lever on the left side of the steering wheel, and unsurprisingly, met with the same result: a truck lurch-ing forward toward the back wall of the garage.

"Then it began to dawn on me that I was here by myself," Gary recalls, "and I couldn't even figure out how to dial the telephone to call Helen. I was thinking, *I'm alone, and I've lost contact with my family.*"

In that moment, before he had a chance to panic, lights appeared in his rearview mirror, and he felt a rush of relief. *Oh, somebody's here,* he thought. Gary turned off his truck and stepped out, cradling his right arm with his left. His neighbor Chauncey and his son Zane—"some very good Western Colorado names," Gary notes—stepped out of their truck and said they were taking him to the hospital. Gary acquiesced, climbing into their passenger seat, and they were off at a brisk pace. They explained that Helen had called David Horn, a close friend who lived in Montrose, for help, but because he was forty-five minutes away, David had called Chauncey and Zane, who lived only a quarter of a mile down the road.

"Of course, I knew who they were," Gary says, "but I couldn't say Zane, and I couldn't say Chauncey." He was also aware that he couldn't have made it to the hospital, that he wouldn't even have known where to turn to get there. In gratitude, Gary reached over and began patting Chauncey on the shoulder.

When they reached the emergency room, Chauncey ran in to get an attendant and Zane stayed outside with Gary, talking to him, trying to engage him, and slowly, Gary's words were returning. A few minutes later they were inside, and Gary could answer when the admissions personnel asked his name. He could answer "May 17" for his date of birth. But when they asked the year, he could see 1949 in his head, but he couldn't say it. So he said, "You guess."

And the attendant asked, "How old are you?"

Gary said, "Fifty-two."

The attendant said, "That's about the same age as my Mom. 1947?"

Gary shook his head no and pointed up.

"1948?"

Again, Gary shook his head no, and again pointed up.

"1949?"

Gary touched his nose with one finger and pointed at him. "I was using charade signs for 'You've got it: 1949,'" Gary explains. "Then he asked for my address, and I said Government Springs Road. But I knew I couldn't say the five-digit house number: 21671. I just couldn't put those numbers together. So I said to Chauncey, 'You tell him what my address is.' I already was becoming aware of how the brain begins to compensate when it can't deliver what is asked. You figure out another way to give the answer without having to supply it yourself."

So Chauncey gave them Gary's address, and they took Gary's vital signs, drew his blood, and performed a CT scan. In the meantime, David Horn, the friend Helen had called, arrived at the hospital and helped give the nurses information on Gary's family history and medical history. Afterward the doctors told Gary they were going to keep him overnight for observation; they thought he'd had either a stroke or a ministroke, called a transient ischemic attack (TIA). The doctors said they planned on doing an echocardiogram to check his heart, but they'd have to wait until the next day when the technician came in. So Gary spent a restless night at the hospital in Montrose. "Maybe it was the effect of shock to my system," Gary says, "but I didn't sleep the entire night."

In the morning, a nurse came in to check on him and explained that there was a slight problem, one that could only happen in a smaller hospital with limited resources. The technician responsible for administering echocardiograms was refusing to come in on a Saturday. But, she said, St. Mary's Hospital in Grand Junction, a little over an hour away, would be able to do an echocardiogram immediately. "If you were you, I would discharge myself immediately and get there," she said to Gary.

Gary followed her advice, and David Horn drove him to Grand Junction, where the medical staff administered the same tests as the night before. Gary's eldest daughter, Shawna, drove the three hours from Eagle, Colorado, and met them there, and somewhere around two o'clock in the afternoon, Gary was given an aspirin for the first time. "After the doctor had read all the tests, he said that I could get dressed, they were going to discharge me," Gary recalls. "They thought I'd had a TIA, they said. I could go home and resume life as normal."

Shawna knew her father too well to allow the doctor to give such advice, and quickly she pulled him aside. "Do you realize he was building a fence by himself the day this happened, digging postholes two feet deep?" she asked angrily. "And you're telling him he needs to return to normal right away?" When she finished, the doctor motioned to Gary as he was walking toward the desk to check out. In a soft voice, the doctor said, "Sir, if I were you, I'd do whatever my daughter told me to when I got home."

Gary left with Shawna and made the three-hour drive to Eagle, where he spent the night with her and her husband at their home. His sleep was fitful again, but Shawna had a few magazines lying around, and Gary read some articles to pass the time. Because he could read without effort or obstacle, he began to feel relieved. Things were back to normal, he thought. But during the Easter Sunday service the next morning, Gary struggled to keep up with any of the songs. Afterward they went out for Easter brunch, and though Gary wanted to order a tomato juice, he somehow misordered: the waiter brought him a mimosa. Gary pointed at his son-in-law's drink and said, "I wanted one of those."

"Dad, that's to-*ma*-to juice," Shawna said slowly. "To-*ma*-to juice." With his hand in front of his mouth, Gary practiced saying tomato juice in a whisper the entire drive back to Shawna's house.

Within a few days, Helen made her way to Colorado to nurse Gary while he rested. They stayed at the log cabin for several nights, but Katie and Jacob were back in Hong Kong without them, and work at Mother's Choice beckoned. By mid-April, they were on a return flight to Hong Kong, and as they traversed the Pacific, Helen woke Gary every few hours to have him pace the aisles. Later they learned that Helen's advice was good: a stroke specialist in Hong Kong explained that a blood clot could have developed when Gary slept for the entire flight to the States. The exertion of building the fence had likely contributed as well—the day in the sun at high altitude might have caused dehydration—and he believed Gary had suffered a stroke, not a TIA, which wouldn't have left lasting damage.

Though relatively mild, the stroke did leave lasting damage, and it called for an adjustment in Gary's way of life. After Gary returned to Hong Kong, he was able to resume his normal duties as managing director, but he found himself still struggling with language. He had completely lost hundreds of familiar hymns and classic songs that, as a strong, avid singer, he loved to sing. More distressingly, he would frequently find himself in midsentence at a loss for the right word. Other times, he'd insert an expletive into his speech without realizing it. This was a problem, since a good portion of his work revolved around public speaking— and at a charity for young women and children, no less. To compensate, he became more conscious of listening to himself, of slowing down and editing what he was saying before he spoke, which usually worked. But another effect was that Gary found himself easily fatigued, as if the stroke had knocked out his energy reserves. So in June of 2002, after Katie finished school, Gary and Helen returned to Colorado for their yearly summer rest. This time it would be longer; they planned a six-month sabbatical to give Gary a chance to convalesce.

Gary was quite active during those months. He spent a lot of time outside, irrigating the hay fields below his house and having the hay cut, baled, and stacked. He looked after the horses, and he chopped and stacked wood to use over the winter. But there was always the opportunity to rest if he wanted, to stop in the middle of the day and take a nap or head to Cobble Creek golf course on the south edge of Montrose proper. The pressure of operating a large, well-known charity was absent, their social lives were quiet, and the calm setting helped as well. "Just being in the peaceful, serene surroundings, just walking outside and calling my horses' names and having them nicker and run up to the fence, rub their noses, it was very therapeutic," Gary explains. But the healing was gradual.

"At the house, we had a large, three-person wood swing, and Helen and I would sit outside and gaze at the San Juan Mountains," Gary recalls. "We just had wonderful views—almost 360 degrees—and we could see two or three fourteen-thousand-foot peaks from our front deck. One evening, I was sitting with my arm around Helen, and we were watching the mountains turn purple as the sun was setting, something just glorious to observe. It was very pleasant weather, somewhere in the midseventies. We were swinging gently. And I looked deeply into Helen's eyes, and I said to her, 'Sweetheart, I love me.'"

Immediately Helen burst into laughter, and Gary sat confused, wondering what he'd said that was so funny. Little slips like this recurred for months, as circuits misfired, as blanks occurred, as other parts of his brain learned to compensate for the damage the stroke had done.

❀ ❀ ❀

That summer of 2002 was Jacob's sixth in Colorado. He had traveled there with Gary and Helen since the summer of '97, only a few months into foster care. When he was small, the trip itself was easy. Helen would place Jacob in the baby pouch, and he'd sleep for most of the flight. Once they arrived, however, it was a different matter completely. Each day, Jacob threw tantrums for hours on end, and a full month usually passed before Helen could even get him out of the house.

Yet these times in Colorado were important for the Stephens family. There were things they loved about Hong Kong: that it was a big city where they could walk to the market and church and school, where they had diverse friendships; that they could retreat to Montgomery Block, a secluded spot on a tree-covered, sun-dappled hillside with its own basketball court out back; that as the kids got older, they could be a part of their parents' work as volunteers at Baby Care. But during the summers in Colorado, they all rode horses and ATVs. They went fishing in chilly streams and had picnics with family and friends in broad open fields on mountainsides in Cimarron. The whole family reveled in the expansiveness of their summers, and when they were back in Hong Kong, they would gaze across the Pacific wistfully. The mystique of Colorado was so powerful that as middle schoolers, Amy and Andrew made a pact with one another: they wouldn't talk about Colorado on the bus ride to school. Otherwise they'd get too excited and wouldn't be able to concentrate on their work. Colorado talk was saved exclusively for the ride home.

For Gary and Helen, summer was critical in order to decompress from the responsibilities of Mother's Choice and Mother's Care. After the year's load of work and child care, they could step back from the weight of that work and concentrate on what was theirs—a cozy log cabin and the acres around it. For those six or seven or eight weeks, they could finally relax. So despite Jacob's displeasure at the change of scenery, they continued to go, and eventually he became accustomed to it. At intervals of calm during his weeks of protest that first summer, he would sit on the porch in the sunlight, either in someone's arms on the porch swing or scooting himself around in his baby walker. Family snapshots captured those contented moments—of Jacob playing with his feet as he lay on his back in a sun-strewn hammock, of him seated on a toy ATV in the middle of their dark green lawn with pastures and foothills in the distance, of Jacob in Helen's arms in a swimming pool, a small smile across his face as she lifted him in and out of the water, and one sweet photograph of Katie, Andrew, and Amy on the wooden porch swing, with Jacob on Andrew's shoulders, all four in wide smiles.

In 1998, the second trip Jacob made to Colorado, he had grown and was only a few months away from walking. A year had wrought many changes. Now Jacob would roll around in the grass with Katie and Andrew and even play with Blue, their black Labrador retriever. There are photographs of Jacob hugging Blue's neck, lying across Blue's back with his arms wrapped around the dog's torso, and wriggling his toes in Blue's fur. Jacob had learned to scoot his toy ATV across the porch, and he rode a real one in the mountains for the first time with Gary. As they moved up and down the hillsides in the crisp air, Jacob would open his mouth for the wind. Often he was tired by the end, and soothed by the rumbling of the ATV's engine, he would fall asleep against Gary's chest before they even got home.

In May of 2002, just after Gary's stroke, Jacob had turned eight years old. That meant that for the coming fall, he was no longer eligible for the early childhood intervention services at WatchDog, where he'd been receiving speech and physical therapy. That spring, Helen and Gary had begun looking for other therapeutic and educational opportunities for Jacob in Hong Kong. They had checked with the English Schools Foundation but were turned away; the schools could not offer services to a blind child who was nonverbal. They visited an English school program for children with special needs and brought with them Lois Harrell, a therapist for the blind from Sacramento, California. She pointed out that the entire school was built around sighted issues, that it was full of bright color schemes and other visual cues, but had no tactile or sound therapies. She felt that Jacob would not benefit from the setup.

During the restful summer in Colorado, Helen continued researching their options in Hong Kong, but when the summer began to wane and they still hadn't found adequate educational opportunities for Jacob in Hong Kong, Helen called the Montrose School District and asked what services they could provide.

Gary and Helen scheduled a meeting with Kevin O'Brien, an expert teacher of the blind, to learn more about the services in Montrose County schools. Kevin is a tall, athletic man with a short gray beard and a long gray ponytail, quick speech, and a profound gentleness. Because he is employed by both Montrose County and adjacent Delta County schools, Kevin spends many hours each week driving from one rural school to another. But impacting the lives of young people who are visually impaired is something he loves. When he recently sustained a stress fracture in his foot while training for the New York City Marathon, Kevin was not disappointed that he'd been running sixty or seventy miles per week that would not lead to a difficult yet fulfilling race under the skyline of the Big Apple. Instead, he was happy to be in a walking boot so he could continue his mobility routes with his students.

Kevin's passion wasn't always so well directed. He grew up in New Jersey and attended college at the University of Wisconsin, then moved to a small town called Leadville, Colorado, known for its high altitude and ski slopes. In his early twenties, he was living with some friends in a cabin at over eleven thousand feet, working odd jobs but mostly "kind of a hippie, kind of a ski bum," he says. In the back of his mind, he knew there was something more he wanted to do, but he didn't find it until a woman told him about her friend who taught the visually impaired how to use a cane.

"For me, it was an immediate, visceral, like-the-lightbulb-had-come-on moment," Kevin says. "Because I'm a very independent person, the idea of teaching other people how to be independent, to travel, to navigate, was extremely compelling." At the time there were only five programs for studies in visual impairment in the country, and one of them happened to be at the University of Northern Colorado at Greeley. He enrolled soon after, earning his master's in visual impairment in 1980. He did his student teaching at Perkins School for the Blind in Boston, a school Helen Keller had attended, as had her teacher Anne Sullivan Macy. Kevin then completed his orientation and mobility teaching at the Helen Keller National Institute outside of New York City, helping deaf and blind adults learn how to ride the subway into the city, how to navigate Manhattan and congested spaces like Times Square. Eventually the mountains of Western Colorado called him back, and he settled in Paonia, where he's been for the last seventeen years.

Despite his extensive experience, when Kevin visited the Stephens home on Government Springs Road, he met a student unlike any he'd ever known. A decade later, Kevin recalls the first encounter vividly: how Helen greeted him at the front door and invited him in, how immediately he could see Jacob standing in the doorway of an adjacent room about fifty feet away, bristling with excitement. For Kevin, these first few moments are telling. He may be saying hello and engaging in pleasantries, and to the parents and the child, it might seem like a typical first encounter. But for Kevin, it's much more. "I am 100 percent watching their movement, how they navigate, because just in a few moments I can gather information for how independent they are, how well they avoid obstacles, what kind of skills they use to move about.

"But Jacob wasn't moving," Kevin says. "I couldn't get him to take a step." Kevin began walking toward him, speaking to him from fifty feet away, from forty. "And then I was ten feet away, and he still wouldn't take a step. Then I was close enough that I put my hand on his shoulder, and he basically climbed on top of me in about three seconds.

"What floored me about this is that it showed me that he had no mobility skills," Kevin explains. "I had never seen a student like that. He was happy to have contact with me—he just climbed right on top of me—but he couldn't take a step toward me when I was three feet away."

Gary and Helen had tried to get Jacob help while in Hong Kong. Twice Lois Harrell visited from California—the same woman who had toured the special needs school with them. Both times she stayed with them for a week to work with Jacob. But because of Jacob's severe disability, a week wasn't long enough to leave a lasting impact, and though he could follow his mother or father up and down stairs and along sidewalks, he had not developed the skills to feel confident moving across spaces on his own.

Kevin stayed that day for over an hour, talking to Gary and Helen, and working with toys to see if Jacob would use his hands. Kevin noted Jacob's sensitivity to touch, how he didn't want to use his hands to explore any of the toys. After about twenty minutes, Kevin witnessed one of Jacob's tantrums. "It really might have been the overstimulation and the excitement, but he just had this major meltdown," Kevin says. "Jacob turned his back to me, and he was just screaming and screaming. Helen was trying to get him to calm down, but she was also explaining to me that for Jacob to lose it like this was not uncommon." He was still at it when Kevin left.

"I just remember that after an hour, I got in my car, and I thought, *This will test everything I've learned in my entire career,*" Kevin recalls. "*Then I'll learn a whole lot more than that.* Because I had never met a student like Jacob before. And just driving home, I was hoping that I would sometime make contact with him. I also told myself that it might take a really long time."

What Gary saw that day was a gentle man who came into their home and established a connection with their son within the first sixty seconds. "We observed a sixth sense between them," Gary explains. "Jacob and Kevin connected at that level."

From Kevin, Gary and Helen learned that the Montrose schools had a team of professionals—a clinical psychologist, an occupational therapist, a physical therapist, a speech therapist, and a physical education teacher with a master's degree in adaptive physical education—who would work with Jacob. Kevin recommended they begin an eight-week assessment of Jacob's needs, and Gary and Helen assented. Halfway through the eight weeks, Kevin met with them again and told them that their entire team would work with Jacob until he was twenty-one years old if he was enrolled in Montrose County schools.

"With all of the resources that were available to Jacob here in Montrose, we knew that we could not in good conscience take him back to Hong Kong," Helen says. So they made a decision. They enrolled Jacob at Northside Elementary in November of 2002, and Colorado became their permanent home.

It might seem like a sudden move—to leave Hong Kong, their adopted home, to leave their work and their friends and everything they had built for twenty-three years. But to Gary and Helen, it just made sense. "It seemed natural to us," Gary says. "It was almost like waking up one morning, and saying, 'Okay, we live here. We don't live there anymore.'" They were also conditioned to change. "We had spent the summers here for the previous ten years. Whether this is positive or not, I don't know, but we had learned that at the end of the summer, you just turned off the Colorado switch, and you turned on the Hong Kong switch," Gary explains. "When we found ourselves here in the fall of 2002, we had the Colorado switch on and the Hong Kong switch off, and we just left it that way. Maybe we unwired the circuit."

In hindsight, Gary feels that the stroke helped them close the chapter on Hong Kong and begin the new phase of their life, where Jacob would have a fuller and more comfortable existence.

"We never even thought we would leave there," Gary says. "We had lived there for twenty-three years, we raised our children there, and we saw ourselves living there until we were near retirement age." What's more, the Hong Kong community was recognizing the work of Mother's Choice in a big way. They had the support of the Hong Kong Jockey Club, an establishment of the Hong Kong social elite; the Community Chest, an organization like the United Way; and Hong Kong Rotary International. They had several major public relations firms working on their behalf. They had financial support from the business community of Hong Kong as well as the support of Hong Kong government.

In addition, Gary had received two major honors as the managing director of Mother's Choice just weeks before his stroke. The first was from the Singtao Newspaper Group, which presented an award called Leader of the Year. Its purpose was to "acknowledge the excellence and contributions achieved by outstanding leaders in Hong Kong, establish role models for younger generation, and inspire the public to strike for the best to help developing Hong Kong." One of six recipients, Gary was named their 2001 Leader of the Year in the area of Community, Environment, and Public Affairs.

Only a week before the stroke, on March 21, 2002, the man who had abandoned his undergraduate education in order to pursue a life of service was awarded an honorary doctorate from the University of Hong Kong. Gary's introduction by Dr. Elaine Yee-lin Ho, a professor of English at HKU, held little back by way of praise. "The refusal to turn away from those in distress, the determination to help the hopeless and despairing to regain faith in themselves, and above all, the unswerving belief in the right of the individual, and especially the child, to be loved—Gary Stephens has shown in his work how these cardinal principles of the good Christian can be practiced so as to live a good life and serve humanity," Dr. Ho said. She noted that for twenty-three years, he and Helen had worked tirelessly for disenfranchised communities in Hong Kong, the entire time without pay, earning respect both in Hong Kong and in mainland China. "Not only charitable in himself, he has also been a conduit and an encouragement for the charity of others, including all those generous members of the Hong Kong community who help to make his work possible."

Gary is quick to give Helen the credit: that she shouldered much of the load for the first twelve years as managing director, that the public recognition was an affirmation of their achievement together. "So we received these awards and it seemed like the sky was the limit," Gary says. "Then within a week of receiving the honorary doctorate, our life was changed." They were leaving Hong Kong, the friends they had made, and over two decades of work.

Gary returned to Hong Kong a few times in the fall: once in September for a leadership meeting for Youth With a Mission and again for a Mother's Choice board meeting sometime in November. But Helen stayed at the log cabin on Government Springs Road, trying to accomplish the herculean task of helping Jacob to adjust to his new life.

"When we returned to Colorado in the summer of 2002, he was raging a lot," Helen recalls. "Part of it was his loss of schedule, his loss of routine. He didn't have therapists or Small World Kindergarten to go to, and he raged four to six hours a day." Based on information they'd gleaned from the experts they had worked with over the years, they believed Jacob was again struggling with attachment issues, which were reignited by the move. It was important for him to have one primary caregiver to focus on so he could trust that his needs would be met. Helen became that primary caregiver: she was the person feeding him, changing him, and staying with him all day long. Now, Gary and Helen share in Jacob's care almost equally. "But in those days, it was more like 95–5," Helen says. "Those were really hard times. He was so upset, and he wasn't sleeping."

From attachment experts she'd met with, Helen knew she should be able to go out of the house for one to two hours, twice a week. "But if I ever tried to do that, when I came back, I got so much rage and unsettled behaviors for two or three days, it just wasn't worth it," Helen says.

Though Jacob was resisting the change, they knew that in the long run, this was the best option for him. So they struggled through the fall, finding solace in the peaceful moments, enjoying the sight of the cottonwoods turning vivid yellow on fence lines below their cabin. Gary began working at a church in Montrose that he and Helen had attended in the summers, and though Helen was fully immersed in Jacob's care, she also spent a few days a week with Gary's ailing mother in Olathe. They enjoyed the clear air, watched winter pass, and welcomed the thaw of a Colorado spring.

By this time, Amy, who had remained in Hong Kong and was working as a full-time volunteer staff member at Baby Care, had gotten engaged to a young man named Bob Strachan. Bob was a few years older than Amy but had also grown up in Hong Kong. After university, he worked in the business sector for a few years. He then took a break from business with the object of serving with a nonprofit. Because his father had been the director of Social Welfare for Hong Kong for several years in the '90s, he was familiar with the work of Mother's

Choice. In the spring of 2002, Bob signed on to work as a volunteer for a year and enrolled in their twelve-week training school called Introduction to Children's Social Services.

"During that time, I was a mentor to him," Gary says, "and I was just so impressed with the sincerity and the depth of this young man." But he and Helen left Hong Kong soon after, and it was only after they returned to the States that they heard Amy and Bob were seeing each other.

Amy and Bob were to be married on April 5, 2003, on the Chinese festival of Qingming—Grave Sweeping Day—and it would be Helen and Jacob's first return to Hong Kong since they left the city nine months earlier. Gary traveled to Hong Kong in early March, a couple of weeks before Jacob and Helen. He took care of some work at Mother's Choice and visited Lian in Shanjing to see how things were going at Mother's Care.

On the day Helen and Jacob were scheduled to arrive, Gary was anxious to see them. He borrowed a Mother's Choice vehicle to pick them up at the Hong Kong International Airport, built a decade earlier on reclaimed land in a northern inlet of Lantau Island, a few miles to the west of Hong Kong Island. Gary left the Mid-levels, fighting the congested roadways of the Central district, followed the tunnels and bridges that traced a circuitous path along the western edge of the Kowloon Peninsula across to Lantau Island, and then parked the car and made his way to end of the terminal where Helen and Jacob would emerge from customs and immigration. Soon enough he spotted Helen pushing a luggage cart, with Jacob seated in the small basket on top where people normally stow their briefcases or carry-ons. Helen was ashen-faced, and Jacob was facing her, slumped against her body. "He looked like he did when we first carried him in the sling," Gary says. "When I reached them, I spoke to Jacob, and he just lifted his arms so meekly. So I picked him up from the cart and just held him as we walked to the car."

Both Helen and Jacob were utterly exhausted, and Helen's arms were covered in scratches and dried blood. In the car, she explained how they had boarded the flight from Montrose to Denver without a problem. For the first twenty minutes, Jacob was fine; then he began crying and flailing. Because the flight was small and the plane held fewer than twenty passengers, the tantrum was particularly conspicuous. It lasted the duration and continued during their layover. In the Denver airport, Jacob was screaming and resisting her to such an extent that Helen was afraid they weren't going to let her board the second leg of their trip, the flight to San Francisco. In her panic, she even worried they would misunderstand Jacob's tantrum and arrest her for child abuse. Neither scenario occurred, but when it came time to board, Helen was at a loss. Her arms were full with Jacob, and she couldn't manage their carry-ons as well. Another passenger kindly offered to help and carried the bags onto the plane for her, helping her get settled into the first-class seats Gary had arranged for them so they could be more comfortable on the flight. (Gary's frequent flights during his years with Youth With a Mission had earned many free flights and upgrades over the years.) But because Jacob was still screaming, the flight attendants moved her to the back of the plane before it even took off.

Jacob raged during the entire flight to San Francisco, calmed down slightly on the second layover, then started up again on the flight from San Francisco to Hong Kong. For four or five hours of the twelve-hour flight, Jacob fought his mother, the noise, the space, the seat, and his own body. He raged against *what?* Helen didn't know—against the concrete objects surrounding him and against abstraction: against confusion and loneliness, against a world that had forgotten him, a world that filed him away out of sight and out of mind, a world that was filled with abundance but had offered him so little when he needed it the most.

Finally he wore himself out, went limp, and slept intermittently. It had been a fruitless battle, and he just didn't have the energy to fight anymore.

Helen and Gary returned to Montgomery Block and carried him up the stairs into the familiar old apartment. They placed him in the familiar crib in the alcove off the master bedroom, where he remained for the next two weeks, mostly in the fetal position. So Helen could attend the wedding and other festivities, a woman named Bing, who had been one of Jacob's caregivers, stayed with him, but he remained in that alcove in his bed through it all. On the return flight, there was no sign of fight from Jacob, but the trip had left a mark. "Once we got him back into school, the clinical psychologist asked me and Helen to come in," Gary explains, "and he asked us, 'What happened in Hong Kong?'" He said it was obvious that Jacob had suffered trauma while they were gone.

Gary and Helen were at a loss to explain what had been so difficult for him about the visit. "The only thing we could come up with was that Jacob thought we were taking him back to Mother's Choice," Gary says. "After that, I told Jacob that he never had to fly to Hong Kong again unless he said to me"—in his "dihs" and "dahs"—"'Dad, I would like to go to Hong Kong.'"

Almost nine years have passed, and Jacob hasn't asked to return.

CHAPTER 13

JACOB AND TEACHER

❦

I know the education of this child will be the distinguishing event of my life.

ANNE SULLIVAN MACY, "TEACHER" TO HELEN KELLER

Montrose

The moment Kevin opens the door, Jacob is standing in the middle of the empty classroom with his special education teacher at his side, pushing a button on a speech augmenter attached to his belt. Slowly and deliberately Gary's voice says, "I want to see Kevin." Kevin greets him with a booming "Hello, Jacob!" and Jacob moves toward Kevin's voice and embraces him. "Are you ready to go?" Kevin asks. Jacob says "Yeah" and heads to the back of the room, feeling his way along the shelves on the wall until he reaches the door, then grabbing his white cane that leans in the corner. He takes it in his right hand, turns the silver door handle, and steps out into the hallway.

This October, on his new medication, Jacob is calmer. It has flattened his effect somewhat—his facial expressions are muted, and he doesn't break into a smile as easily—but the benefits are substantial. His anxiety has decreased significantly, and his ritualistic behaviors are less frequent and appear to be less compulsive. He is much more manageable for his teachers, but still, Kevin pauses for a moment to explain their day and to establish his expectations for Jacob. They're going to City Market for some Band-Aids, Kevin says, for the cuts on his hands from working in a friend's garden. But because Jacob still pulls at the bottom of his shirt every few minutes, signaling his newest ritualistic behavior—that he wants to take the garment off—Kevin uses City Market as a reward as well as a way to practice walking on streets and sidewalks. They'll only go into the store if Jacob will keep his shirt on, Kevin explains. Jacob says, "Yeah," meaning he understands. "Then let's get started!" Kevin says.

Kevin lags behind as Jacob heads down the main hallway lined with metal lockers and glass trophy cases. This is new; for years, Kevin hurried down to the far end of hall to be Jacob's goal, but recently Kevin has let Jacob lead the way about half the time. Jacob doesn't like this development, and he stops periodically and calls for Kevin or begins to pull his shirt up to get Kevin's attention. But when Kevin doesn't respond, Jacob keeps going, all the way to the front entrance of the school. He opens the door for himself and steps out into the sunny, still October day. The morning started below freezing, but it's sixty now, and their path is a flat five blocks, moving between patches of warm sun and long shadows cast by the modest wooden homes and trees along Selig Avenue.

Kevin's excitement and patience are both palpable: excitement at Jacob's strengths and patience with his weaknesses. Jacob is arrow-straight when he crosses the street, Kevin says. Kevin has visually impaired students who are in the top levels academically but can't make it from one sidewalk to the other in a straight line, so to him, Jacob's innate sense of direction is astounding. Yet Jacob can't navigate traffic on his own. Though he has recognized the sound of cars since he was only a few years old and knows to stop, he has never crossed streets without someone leading him. On this quiet avenue in Montrose, he struggles to decide to cross, and when he does, he often stops in the middle of the street. That's a cognitive failure, something that isn't clicking, and for other students, such a decision would be plain as day.

So Kevin guides him each time. As they stand together at the edge of the street, Kevin asks, "What do we use to cross?"

Jacob lifts his left hand and touches his ear. "Dah," he says.

"That's right, your ears," Kevin says, and they listen. "Is it quiet?"

"Yeah," Jacob answers, and Kevin tells him to go.

A few seconds later, Jacob reaches the curb on the other side, but two feet to the left of the sidewalk. This is a rare error in Jacob's sense of direction, but Kevin is excited because it gives them an opportunity to practice righting the course. Recovery instructions follow, with Kevin guiding Jacob's cane: tap in front, which is grass, to the left, which is grass, and to the far right, which is sidewalk. "Now move that way, Jacob," Kevin says, and Jacob shuffles back onto the path to begin the next block. "Great job, Jacob. Give me five!" Kevin says, and Jacob brushes his hand across the top of Kevin's in a very soft five, then taps the sidewalk with his cane.

When he's walking, Kevin often closes his eyes—at a crossing or while he is stopped—to hear what Jacob might be hearing, to achieve a small sliver of under-standing of Jacob's experience. He focuses his attention on what Jacob might be feeling under his feet, on the difference between the smoothness of sidewalk and the rough asphalt of the road, and if he notices the pull of gravity on the ramps that lead from sidewalk to street level. "It's then that the world becomes multidimensional instead of just visual," Kevin says. "Normally our sight overpowers the richness of experience so our other senses don't play much of a role. Often people talk about how a blind person's hearing is heightened. Jacob's hearing isn't heightened. He just makes use of what he has, something a sighted person doesn't do."

Leaves cover the sidewalks intermittently, and the yellow maples rustle like tissue paper as Jacob shuffles through them. Jacob moves slowly in his wide-legged gait, his feet turned out. He holds his body rigid as he moves, and his whole person sways from side to side as he takes each step forward. It doesn't always look it, but his balance is almost infallible; Gary and Helen have never seen him stumble or fall in all of the years he has been with them, not at home nor in a store nor in a parking lot.

He makes it over areas where the path is uneven from tree roots and driveways, over sections that wind to the left around a thick tree trunk. He stops at the edge of the street on a particularly difficult crossing where the sidewalk and street are flush, unlike the others where the sidewalk descends to meet the street. Maybe he feels the gathering of leaves caught between the pavement and the asphalt, and he reads it as a barrier. "He has such good awareness," Kevin says. "He knows if there is a hazard. If there is a drop-off, he knows it. If he is walking and he perceives that there is something in front of him that is dangerous, he immediately puts his hand up in what we call upper hand protection." In the hallway at school, he never nears the walls, and he maintains his space even when dozens of other students are swarming around him as they move from class to class. Echolocation is another of Jacob's strengths.

Echolocation, explains John Hull, is an incredible phenomenon that Hull never experienced while he had even the faintest sight, but when he became completely blind, he developed this luminous tool of self-preservation almost immediately. "The experience itself is quite extraordinary," he says in *Touching the Rock*, "and I cannot compare it with anything else I have ever known. It is like a sense of physical pressure. One wants to put up a hand to protect oneself, so intense is the awareness. One shrinks from whatever it is. It seems to be characterized by a certain stillness in the atmosphere. Where one should perceive the movement of air and a certain openness, somehow one becomes aware of a stillness, an intensity instead of an emptiness, a vague solidity. The exact source of the sensation is difficult to locate. It seems to be the head, yet often it seems to extend to the shoulders and even the arms." It's the awareness of echoes, Hull says, and rather than an experience of listening with the ears, he feels it on the skin of his face, which might explain its older name: "facial vision."

This awareness is something Jacob has demonstrated since he was young. In middle school, the outdoor route he and Kevin took was a four-block walk to the hospital and back. Part of the route required crossing a bridge, and as Jacob approached it, Kevin wouldn't give him verbal cues unless absolutely necessary. And the route had pitfalls; at one point, the sidewalk fell away, but Jacob could sense that it fell away and never went near it. Similarly, he had to use a set of stairs when he was in elementary school to get from his classroom to the building next door for therapy. But one side had no railing, and Jacob sensed the danger; he never wavered from the absolute middle of the stairs.

Today, throughout the route to City Market, Kevin remains silent, knowing that if he speaks, Jacob's brain will switch from navigating each step of the route to simply following Kevin's voice. Jacob doesn't like Kevin's silence, and he'll call for help or press his speech augmenter, which will call out in Gary's voice, "I want to see Kevin." A few times along the way he begins to pull his shirt up, as if he's thinking, *If I do this, Kevin will have to answer me.* But Kevin is quiet, and sometimes Jacob simply continues forward after a few seconds. A few times, Jacob doesn't. Instead he stands still and swings his head, listening and listening, and Kevin knows they've hit a snag and walks up behind him to encourage him. "You can do this," he says. "You are doing so well, you are great at this." It's like helping a child develop the confidence to ride a bike, but this is teaching a boy to walk down the street.

Jacob makes it to City Market without taking his shirt off, and so they go in, leaving the quiet openness of the neighborhood, passing through the sliding doors and the immediate whoosh of climate-controlled air into a space filled with the rattling of carts, the voices of shoppers, and the click of footsteps echoing off tiled floors. Kevin gets a cart and holds the front of it as Jacob takes the handle and begins to push. They walk across the front of the store to the pharmacy section, and Kevin places his hand under Jacob's wrist and guides him toward the boxes of Band-Aids. "See how many there are?" he asks. Then he places one in Jacob's hand for him to feel, then says, "I think this is the right one." Jacob drops it into the basket, but it falls out through the leg holes of the child seat. "It's on the ground, Jacob," Kevin says. "You'll have to find it." Jacob bends down, feels for the box, and finds it, and a moment later, when it's safely in the cart, it's off to the checkout.

Kevin wants Jacob to pay, so Kevin hands him the money and guides his hand toward the cashier. The cashier takes the bill from Jacob, deliberately counts out the change, and places it carefully in Jacob's open palm. Kevin takes the money, then guides Jacob's hand toward the counter where the Band-Aids are sitting to encourage Jacob to pick them up and take them with him. He wants Jacob to understand the whole concept of picking out the Band-Aids, paying for them, and taking the newly bought bandages with him, but the cashier is overly helpful and in a hurry to check out the next customer. "Oh, here you go!" she says cheerfully and places the box in Jacob's hand. He takes it, Kevin sighs a little, and they leave.

On the way home, Jacob is a little less focused. He keeps stopping and saying, "Ma, Ma." Maybe he is sensing that the day is nearing its close. "Your mom will pick you up," Kevin says, "but first we go back to school and have your snack." Dad's homemade oatmeal cookies are the prize at the end of this leg, the incentive for him to keep his shirt on and to listen to Kevin's voice, to make his way back to Montrose High School.

Yet there's an unexpected twist. Halfway back, a wooden driveway gate that swings open like two barn doors has been opened since the last pass, and now it's blocking the sidewalk in two places. Kevin is excited to watch Jacob find a solution to his problem. It's one of the reasons Kevin loves working on mobility: he watches his students in a constant process of problem solving, the gears turning in their heads until they fit the pieces together, until they untie the knot. Sometimes it's difficult, but when they succeed, it's exhilarating. And here Jacob succeeds beautifully. When his cane hits the wooden slats, Jacob steps to the left onto the grass, around the gate, and back onto the sidewalk. A few feet later, the other side of the gate is an obstacle as well, and Jacob steps around that and continues on, unruffled.

And then they reach the last block before campus. At the end of that block, on the corner of 5th and Selig, is a large, two-story house, a light buttery yellow with white trim, which Jacob passes each day on his mobility route. As they near the house, Kevin is ahead of Jacob, encouraging him that he is almost there, almost back to the school. A woman standing in the yard stops Kevin to introduce herself. Her name is Cheri, she says, and she's been watching Jacob for almost two years and is so impressed by his progress. Can she say hello to him? she asks.

Kevin says of course and calls Jacob over. As Jacob approaches, Kevin puts his hand on Jacob's shoulder and turns his face toward her. "Jacob, I want you to meet someone. This lady has been watching you walk for a couple of years now," Kevin says, and Jacob's face slowly breaks into a big smile, the first real smile of the afternoon. After Kevin prompts him, Jacob says thank you—"*Dih* dah"—and also "Nice to meet you"—"Dah dah *dih* dah." Cheri looks on softly, with a gentle smile, and says, "Nice to meet you too."

Two years, and a world of difference, she says. He's so much improved from last year when he would stop and refuse to go on, when he couldn't focus enough to get all the way down the street, when his arms engaged in repetitive waving and his fingers braided themselves constantly. As Jacob walks away, Cheri watches him go with a look on her face that's at once hopeful, sad, and tender. Her mother had brain surgery some time ago, Cheri explains, and she spends much of her day in a chair, looking out on to Selig Street, at the gray wooden house across the street with a bay window and ornate gingerbread on the front porch, at the traffic that rolls to a stop at the corner, at the students who gather there for their parents to pick them up after school. But every day, she looks for Jacob, Cheri says, and watches him amble along the sidewalk on her side of the street, pausing sometimes to listen for Kevin or to rub his mouth with the side of his index finger. Jacob's walks, Cheri says, are what she looks forward to the most.

❅ ❅ ❅

It's hard to overstate just how changed things are on this sunny October day from when Jacob first enrolled at Northside Elementary in November of 2002. As with most new experiences, Helen started Jacob slowly, sending him for an hour every morning. But he was uncertain and afraid of the unfamiliar surroundings and of the strangers who wanted him to do new things, and his early patterns kicked back in. Helen says that at the beginning, he spent that full hour lying on the floor, screaming and kicking. What he needed—to feel safe and comfortable and in control—was impossible to achieve when his entire being was focused on refusing the new environment and people. And yet, this was the only way he knew how to respond; because of the early deprivation, he wasn't equipped for adapting, for openness, for change.

"It was probably not until the fall of 2003 that he was able to build up to more than one or two hours a day," Helen recalls. "Then he'd be able to go for three or four hours a day, and then he'd be able to stay for lunch. Then they started providing a quiet room for him, and they had a therapy swing for him in case he got too stressed."

From the start, Jacob saw Kevin several hours a week. They met in the quiet room, and Kevin had tactile books to read with him. Kevin brought blocks for Jacob to stack and battery-operated toys that would make noise and move, but they were for naught. Jacob would sit with his back to Kevin and refuse to touch anything. When he finally turned around, after five months of refusal, he was reluctant to engage, to explore the objects on the table with his hands, and if he did inspect them, it was always brief. Soon enough, he was overwhelmed, and a tantrum would ensue.

How Kevin handled these is what set him apart and allowed Jacob to trust him. One day Jacob was behaving as normal: refusing to participate, getting up from the table to stomp his feet and scream and cry. After a few minutes of wailing, Jacob walked over to a corner and sat down. Kevin waited for a moment, then spoke calmly as Jacob huddled in the corner.

"You know what, Jacob?" Kevin asked. "That's fine with me. Sometimes I feel like sitting in the corner too." He took the books from the table and put them away, and he went and sat on the floor in the corner beside Jacob. Then he said, "I have days like this too. If you don't want to do it today, we'll do it tomorrow. If you don't want to do it tomorrow, we'll do it next week."

"This is why Kevin is so perfect for him," Helen explains, "because when Jacob gets out of control and stressed and over the top, when I'm sure his brain waves are on red alert, like what someone else's would be like after a car accident, Kevin is just unfazed." Kevin's empathy and patience, which helped him look past the behavior and see that Jacob's brain was different from most, that he was easily overwhelmed by normal interactions and basic stimuli, were crucial in building a foundation and finding ways to move forward—even if it felt like sometimes they were moving backward instead. "I went through an entire process of figuring him out," Kevin recalls. "Many times I went home just thinking, *Wow, what am I going to do?* Because when Jacob doesn't get it, it's our issue. If he doesn't get it, we need to find a different way to explain something to him, a different way to work with him. In that way, Jacob is unconditionally right."

Those are the words of a determined teacher, of one committed and tenacious, of one who is willing to be introspective instead of placing blame. And that's important, because Kevin knows Jacob will pick up on that, that he'll sense Kevin's frustration if he allows himself to be frustrated. "When we interact with him, we really have to look at ourselves and say, 'If I'm having a bad day, I can't have that come across in my voice or my mood,'" Kevin says, "because Jacob is incredibly perceptive, and he might take it personally. Every time I see Jacob, I need to completely wipe my slate clean and start fresh. Most days, that's no problem. Some days, there could be something else on my mind, and Jacob is constantly reminding me of my obligation to be 100 percent with him all the time. And Gary and Helen inspire me to continually be that way because that's how they are with him."

It's this philosophy that has allowed Kevin to work through each of Jacob's challenges as they emerge. When Jacob resisted exploring with his fingertips to learn shape and size and texture, Kevin was baffled. *He's gotta use his hands,* Kevin would think. *How am I going to get him to use his hands?* With a different student, Kevin would use a technique called hand-over-hand, meaning he would encircle the student's wrist with his own hand and guide it to the object in question, but that was too much for Jacob, so Kevin adapted and began using a technique called hand-under-hand, where he placed his hand under Jacob's wrist to encourage him to reach in a certain direction. This style was less intrusive and respected Jacob's boundaries, and it had an added benefit: if it ever got to a point where Jacob was overwhelmed or stressed, he could extricate himself without a tantrum. Though he's still not as tactile as Kevin would like, Jacob did come to tolerate using his hands to learn about new objects within a couple of years. But Kevin still uses hand-under-hand with Jacob even now, and he has instructed all of Jacob's teachers to do the same.

Because of their unfamiliarity with blind students and Kevin's expertise with Jacob's particular challenges, most of Jacob's teachers defer to Kevin's advice and guidance. Over the years, however, there have been a few staff members who thought they could take Jacob and whip him into shape, could get him to follow their directions, and immediately. They'd had difficult students before, they said, and like those difficult students, Jacob would do things their way. "But Jacob's situation is so unique, given his background," Kevin says, "and that doesn't work with him. He ends up in a tantrum, but not because he is being disobedient or obstinate. He simply can't be forced into things."

And early on, he wouldn't be forced into walking around the school building without being arm-in-arm with a sighted guide. "When he started school here, his mobility was so lacking, it was stunning," Kevin says. Jacob may have known the apartment in Hong Kong, and he may have eventually learned the log home on Government Springs Road. But in the hallways of Northside Elementary, Kevin says, it was as if Jacob felt he was always standing on the edge of a cliff. One of the first things Kevin teaches a blind student is to walk along the wall with one hand on it as a guide. "With Jacob, he had to have his whole back and both of his hands on the wall, and he'd sort of shimmy along," Kevin recalls. "He was terrified not knowing what was in front of him or where the wall would end. It took about a year to get him off the wall to where he would trail it with his hand."

Kevin believes being institutionalized had a huge impact on Jacob's mobility, since he had no opportunities to move, to explore, to learn his world. "There were huge, huge critical periods in his life that any child who is blind would benefit from—learning to hold his head up, learning to smile," Kevin says. "When a blind child smiles, typically that smile is rewarded by the parents with a lot of praise and a lot of love and compassion and nurturing. But if you don't get that, or if there is not something out there that is exciting to crawl toward, or you're not encouraged to crawl, why move?"

So at Northside Elementary, Jacob continued with his back to the wall, and when his teachers tried to have him wear a little backpack so he could be like other students, he refused it, mostly because it separated him from the solid cinder blocks behind him. Finally, he made a breakthrough and began to walk forward and trail the wall with one hand. At that point, Kevin introduced the white cane, hoping Jacob would use it to discover what was a safe route and where there were obstacles, but another year passed before Jacob would hold on to it long enough for Kevin to teach him how to use it.

Accounts like this reveal why Helen calls Kevin one of the most patient men she knows. "He mirrors for me total acceptance of Jacob," she says. That patience and acceptance was critical then, and it's critical now, as an eighteen-year-old boy continues to struggle with an array of neurological, hormonal, cognitive, and behavioral challenges. "Sometime in November of 2010, Kevin was trying to get Jacob to walk into the high school library, and for whatever reason, Jacob did not want to go into the library," Helen explains. "Kevin worked with him for about an hour, trying to get him to go through the doors, but Jacob was having nothing to do with it. So they would go back and sit on the bench outside the door, and a few minutes later, they'd try again. And one of the teachers walked by and said, 'When do you think you're ever going to get that boy to go through the door?' And he said, 'Oh, maybe April. Maybe May.'"

Helen laughs as she tells the story, delighting in how Kevin understands and accepts her son, how Kevin has undergone the same change that she and Gary did years ago when they realized Jacob might never speak.

"When I think of where he has come from, just working with him is a joy," Kevin says. "Sometimes I think the school staff are too tough on themselves, and they are disappointed if they don't see progress every day. I just have to let them know, 'Folks, you are doing a great job.' I wish I had video of the first couple of years with him, because if they saw that, they would realize how much progress he's made in the past nine years." He advises them to let go of their plans for Jacob and the rigid schedules that rule the rest of the institution. They are on Jacob's schedule, Kevin says, because Jacob doesn't know how to trust their plans for him. "He just needs to have control of his environment, he needs to feel that he is safe, that *he* is doing the reaching out, and that he knows what's going to happen next," Kevin says.

In this way, Kevin is Jacob's advocate. He has the skills to help him, but more than anything, he has the patience to see it through and the humility to seek new solutions as new challenges present themselves. "The challenges have changed over time, and now he's going through puberty, and we don't know how it's affecting him," Kevin explains. "There are days that are a real success, and then there continue to be days that are a real struggle, where he is anxious and out of sorts, where he is aggressive and can't focus, where we don't know what is bothering him or what might be setting something off. So one day at a time is the general rule."

❈ ❈ ❈

Before school started this year, Kevin wrote a new education plan for Jacob. Previously, Jacob's team—Kevin, Gary and Helen, and the team of teachers at Montrose High School—attempted to integrate him into some of the academic classes that might benefit him. When the other students with special needs had music class or art, Jacob's teachers had him participate, hoping he'd enjoy making music, clay pots, or figurines. But he wasn't interested in any of it. He would lose focus in group activities and soon be up, walking away from the table, wanting to work on his mobility instead. Kevin spent years trying to teach him Braille, pouring himself into it, endlessly patient and hopeful. He thought that even if Jacob didn't learn to read, following the Braille letters would make his fingers strong or help him adjust to using his hands more. "I gave it everything I had," Kevin says. But before the 2011 school year began, he had a moment when the reality of Jacob's severe disability stood out to him, combined with the realization that this boy would soon be eighteen. "I spent a lot of time just staring at this school building. I spent a lot of time asking myself, 'What are we doing?' I had to look at my own expectations of his progression, and then I had to let them go."

Before school started in the fall, Kevin called Gary and Helen and said that he thought they needed to shred Jacob's current education plan and rewrite it—otherwise, they were just housing him in a classroom and babysitting him. They agreed, and Kevin developed a new one that nixed any academic subject and instead was based on community experience. Now, three mornings a week, Jacob goes with two instructors and a handful of other students to Sharing Ministries, a food pantry housed in a small warehouse beside some old railroad tracks only a few blocks from the school. The white aluminum building is sparse, with gray cement floors and a chill in the air, but there are a dozen people inside giving friendly greetings to coworkers or volunteers who have come for the morning.

For this one hour, the students sort bags of chips and boxes of cereal and help organize the food, which will later be distributed to those in need. They work in a large room in the back, with grocery store shelving along the sides and a long wooden table in the middle. A student named Miranda,* with a round face and long dark hair, has a black marker that she's using to cross through bar codes. A boy named Aaron, with severe Down syndrome, is holding a tennis ball in one hand and taking plastic packaging to the trash with the other. Jacob stands beside a teacher's aide, handing her bags of corn chips that she arranges in rows in a plastic bin. When the bin is full, she slides it onto a cart, then asks Jacob to push it toward a shelf, which he does as she guides the front around a stack of boxes. When they reach the shelf, Jacob places his hands on the bin as she guides it to the top, then they turn around to pick up a load of canned tomatoes.

He's calm at Sharing Ministries, as he helps sort food, and later as he moves deliberately between the table and the back wall, which leads him to the garbage can where he throws the plastic bags too dirty to be reused. That's his path the first few times, straight from the table to the back wall, then to the left to the garbage can. The teacher calls his name and gently taps on the table where the next bag sits, and he returns and feels for it, takes it in his left hand. After a few trips, he has mapped it, and he walks directly to the trash can instead of trailing

*Names have been changed.

the wall. But Jacob needs constant focus, and if he's not called back, he'll stand there, lolling his head from side to side, listening to the echoes of the open space, the voices of volunteers helping sort goods, the rustle of used plastic bags being flattened into organized stacks. A moment later, he'll take his shirt halfway off and hold it over his head before pulling it back down. But when a teacher calls his name, he moves back toward her, shuffling his feet with his arms extended to catch the table when he nears it.

When it's time to leave, Miranda takes Jacob by the arm and leads him out the back door, down a set of steps, and across a gravel parking lot to the bus.

Jacob goes to the Salvation Army and does similar tasks on Tuesdays and Thursdays. These activities are part of the school's program for students with special needs, and it serves a few underclassmen but is most concentrated in Step Up to Life, designed for eighteen- to twenty-one-year-olds. For most, the community activities help them acquire basic skills that might someday lead to employment. For Jacob, it's a way of learning to be among other people, to expand his experience of the world.

He still spends a good portion of his week with Kevin: Monday, Wednesday, and Friday afternoons. It's the most time Kevin devotes to any student in the Montrose and Delta County schools. Jacob needs it the most, and developing mobility means that he can now do very basic things that he couldn't before. For years, Jacob would wake Helen and Gary up in the middle of the night because he needed help getting to the bathroom. But now he has a bathroom in his room and can get there and back by himself, and Gary and Helen can sleep through the night. If Gary is working in his office or watching football on a Sunday, and Jacob calls to him saying "*toi*-le, *toi*-le," Gary can say, "Go to your room and find the bathroom." Jacob is more independent, and Gary and Helen are relieved of an hourly burden.

Kevin has helped Jacob improve his mobility significantly, but due to Jacob's impairments and compulsive behaviors, Kevin spends a good portion of his time managing Jacob—trying to keep him from licking the floor, his shoes, or the chairs, from yelling or screaming for no apparent reason, from taking off his shirt. During his first year at Montrose High School, Kevin spent a lot of time fighting Jacob's outbursts. Sometime in the spring semester, they had a rough week. On Monday, they were walking inside the school and Jacob squealed. Immediately Kevin returned to the classroom. The same thing happened on Wednesday: Jacob yelled in the corridor, and Kevin turned them back around. On Friday, Jacob kept it in check during the interior route, so they then began their outdoor mobility exercise, walking the few blocks to Walmart. They made it all the way up the walk to the front door, but as they passed through it, Jacob squealed again, maybe with delight, and Kevin had to revoke the trip for Monday.

But now that he's on new medicine, Jacob is calmer. Kevin can often keep him from acting out by giving him cues and reminders in a deep and slow voice and by redirecting him to something more productive.

Along with his inability to communicate, behavioral problems are what Kevin puts at the top of the things that trouble Jacob. It's there above his developmental delays and far above his blindness. Kevin believes that Jacob's blindness is simply an inconvenience—though he offers the caveat that that's easy to say because he can see. "Blindness is the loss of environs, it's the loss of space or distances," Kevin says, "but with the right tools or the right skills, a person really has pretty near full access." Yet Jacob's ritualistic behaviors are difficult for others to accept or understand, and his inability to talk to his classmates is another barrier. "He doesn't have a way to efficiently and naturally communicate with his peers," Kevin explains. "I know what he's saying because I know him so well. Sometimes I almost feel like Annie Sullivan with Helen Keller." But few others can make sense of his sounds, especially kids who only see him as he passes in the hall, on the arm of a teacher or with Kevin. And this brings in a third obstacle in relating to people his age: like many children with developmental delays, he's only known adults his whole life. He is so accustomed to being around adults or medical providers or therapists that those are the people he prefers.

Even still, walking through the hallways of Montrose High School, Jacob does impact his peers, and one can see this not necessarily through their reaction to him, but because they *don't* react. Jacob is not confined to a special school for children with special needs. Instead, he is out in the community, in the hallways of Montrose High School where other students are exposed to him and can observe his concerted efforts to move up and down the stairways and through the halls; and because of this, they don't point and stare.

Though inclusion is the preferred option in most of the Western world, opinions on special education are varied, with some camps preferring complete inclusion, while others fight for schools designed for specific subsets of special needs. After all, the different "needs" vary widely: there are some students in Jacob's special needs class who can attend mainstream language arts, the poorest fit imaginable for a student like Jacob. But people in favor of inclusion believe the question is not *whether* these students are included, but *how* to make inclusion most effective and efficient, and they see the benefit as a two-way street. Peter Farrell, a professor of special needs at Manchester University, argues that there's little evidence to show that isolating children with special needs in special schools is better. "What there is evidence of," Farrell says in an article in London's *The Independent,* "is that if children with special needs mix with others, it helps to make people in society more accepting of difference."

And this seems to be the case at Montrose High School. When mainstream kids pass as Jacob taps his way along the corridor, it's as if Jacob and his "dihs" and "dahs" were as typical as their "heys." Kevin never sees anyone mock or point or laugh. If anything, they are kind and say hello as they pass him in the hall, even though Jacob doesn't desire anything more than that superficial contact. Kevin wishes Jacob could interact more with his peers, but Jacob just abstains. He much prefers the company of his teachers to any student at Montrose High.

For Jacob, these student-teacher relationships are incredibly important. Further, they are a source of happiness, and he spends time at home asking about Becca, his occupational therapist, or talking about going to City Market with Kevin. But the nature of the school schedule—the short breaks on weekends, longer ones over holidays, and the veritable desert of summer—presents problems for him. In the beginning, it was as if the two-day break over the weekend reignited his attachment issues. "On Fridays, he'd ask, 'Are you coming back?'" Kevin recalls. "I don't think he would understand that absence. Maybe he thought I was just one of those people who was going to be there only periodically, but Mondays would come and he'd be a mess, throwing tantrums. And I started thinking about how insufficient our system is for serving kids like Jacob. Jacob needs a village. He needs this constantly."

Summertime is even harder. The first few weeks of the break, Helen notices a dip in his mood and an increase in his anxiety. Helen works hard to help him understand. She explains that it's not that they refuse to take him to: the doors are locked and no one is there. To help him understand that he'll be able to return, Helen runs through the months of the year with him. "This is the month of June," Helen will say, "and what comes after June?"

"Dah-*dah*," Jacob answers. That's Ju-*ly.*

"And then when do we go back to school?"

August, Jacob says. "*Dah*-duh."

Helen reads his school reports about what he did the last semester with Kevin, reviewing his schedule from the previous year and telling him how many more weeks before school starts again. After a few weeks, he seems to understand and settle in some, but it's always a relief when August finally arrives.

Kevin doesn't go the entire summer without seeing him, however. Several times between June and August, Helen or Gary will drive Jacob to Paonia, a small coal-mining town an hour northeast of Montrose, to visit Kevin and his wife, Nora, who recently retired from her position as a clinical psychologist with Delta County schools. The first time, Kevin was excited to show Jacob his garden, a substantial spread filled with vegetables and a large array of herbs. He hoped that Jacob would enjoy smelling the different plants—the fresh basil, the lemony thyme, the earthy oregano. Jacob's interest was brief, to say the least, but he did interest himself in other things. When Jacob found the stalk of an onion in white flower above the ground, he pulled the bulb from the earth and ate it on the spot, to the surprise of Kevin and his parents. Now they spend time doing activities inside, like sorting silverware, and often take walks: to a nearby park, to check Kevin's mail at the post office on Grand Avenue.

Last summer, Kevin took him to swim in Ouray, a town about forty miles south of Montrose. The town is small—the 2010 census reported one thousand residents—but it's idyllic, nestled in a narrow valley with steep mountain walls on three sides. People visit Ouray for typical Colorado activities, to hike and climb and mountain bike, to visit the Cascade Falls just on the edge of town and the Box Canyon Falls just a few miles further. But Ouray also has a large public pool filled with water from a nearby hot spring. "My only worry was whether he'd try to take off his bathing suit," Kevin laughs, "but Helen said that wouldn't be a problem. For Jacob, swimming in the spring was just so liberating. He's free of any mobility concerns, and all I can say is that for him, it's joy and it's freedom." He's like a porpoise in the water, Kevin explains, playful and full of laughter, exploring the edges and walls and bottom of the pool on his own, but frequently calling out to locate Kevin in space. These are Kevin's favorite times, these informal meetings where there are no time constraints or agenda. "Jacob is just a wonderful human being, and he's one of my best friends. He's very deep in my psyche, and in my heart as well."

Kevin has had a recurring dream in recent years where he and Jacob are at school, and suddenly, Jacob begins to speak. The conversation is always banal and everyday—simple "hellos" and "how are you?" But Kevin always feels elated in the dream, overjoyed that he can communicate freely and easily with his young student and friend, relieved at the thought that his speech has arrived. It's almost as if the natural order has been restored. "But one of the most interesting parts is that in the dream, he never gets his vision back," Kevin says, "and I couldn't care less."

When Kevin awakens from the dream, he's deflated, and when he sees Jacob later that afternoon, it's especially poignant. Their whole interaction is colored by the dream, made more vivid. Those days, the dearth of language from Jacob's lips is especially loud.

CHAPTER 14

FROM EAST TO WEST

❧

*I know that the experiences of our lives, when we let God use them, become the
mysterious and perfect preparation for the work he will give us to do.*

CORRIE TEN BOOM, *THE HIDING PLACE*

For both Fuxia and Jacob, their physical trials would have been enough. Being
born without eyes, with a hole in his stomach and septicemia, Jacob already faced
much to overcome. Fuxia's physical challenges were even greater.

Some of Fuxia's breaks were as old as her little body. "She had breaks in the
womb and in the birth canal," David says. "And when she first came to live with
us, she was breaking every four to six weeks. One of the first days we had her in
our home, Fuxia was just walking around the corner and lifted her leg, and
popped her femur." But her condition doesn't make the breaks any different from
a break for someone without brittle bone. "Her breaks are just as painful as other
children's, and they take just as long to heal," David says.

Though she had broken many bones before, that first break with Carol and
David was extremely traumatic. "I think that in her childlikeness, she thought
when she was adopted that this would go away," Carol says. "It was as if she
thought, *I'm going to be normal.*" The breaks continued, however, and Carol and
David looked for treatment options, though they proceeded slowly and allowed
Fuxia to choose whether or not she wanted to participate. "We didn't want to
start anything that would cause her pain in the early days of the adoption because
we didn't want her to associate her new family with pain," Carol explains.

"We also let her choose because she would have to endure the pain," David
adds. "So we just waited until she could say, 'Okay, I'm ready.'"

It didn't take her long. When she was seven, Fuxia opted for her first major
operation, a thirteen-hour procedure to place rods in her legs to reinforce and
strengthen the bones. By that point, her femurs had suffered so many fractures
and become so bowed that they had to be broken in five places to allow for the

rods to fit. "But there was no other way to keep her from breaking continually," David says.

Really, the procedure was more about minimizing the damages than precluding them. With the titanium rods, breaks can still occur, but the rods keep the broken bone in place, limiting the severity and allowing the fracture to heal more quickly. Yet as the years passed, Fuxia outgrew the original rods, and they've been replaced with additional surgeries, which weren't as extensive but still presented intense pain and extended recovery. Today Fuxia is still small for her age—she's 4'6" in the eleventh grade. Puberty has changed her bones on the molecular level, and she's not growing anymore, so for the first time in her life, she hasn't had a break in a year. Now she's working on developing muscle tone in her legs so she can use a walker, providing her with another option besides a wheelchair or the scooting she does around the house.

Some of Fuxia's most severe health struggles in the past few years have been related to her other condition, her blood disorder. She has always been more vulnerable when she got a cold or the flu, and David and Carol have had to be extra vigilant with any illness because she can take a turn very quickly. But in 2009, Fuxia contracted H1N1—the swine flu—and nearly died. "Within two days, her hemoglobin count dropped from 14 to 2," David says. "The doctor said that he'd never had a patient at that level who survived." At such a low level of hemoglobin, the blood is not able to carry oxygen to the necessary tissues, and most distressingly, to the brain. A hemoglobin count of four is usually fatal, and the Boyds feel that it was just a miracle that she survived at all, and especially that she survived with no brain damage.

Any parent struggles to see a child suffer, but David sees these trials as opportunities to lean on one another and grow closer. "You don't grow close to someone without pain, without embracing pain, and she has had scores," David says. "Fuxia probably has had sixty breaks, the majority of which were with our family. Those, plus the surgeries, plus the emotional challenges, have been opportunities to embrace each other emotionally."

David's reflection on his daughter's early struggles with attachment is only possible in hindsight and in the context of their success. It is a perspective he has reached years after they worked through the struggles, years after she learned to trust, after she stopped resisting David and Carol and lashing out at them for reasons that, as a four-year old, she couldn't possibly have understood. But Fuxia's successful attachment was not easy and was certainly not a foregone conclusion.

Their early intervention—the fact that Carol and David had done research on the abandoned child and that Carol devoted herself to Fuxia all day, every day, to help the young girl settle in to a new life in Hawaii—was effective in creating a bond between them. Carol also thinks that Fuxia's attachment problems could have been worse, that she benefited greatly from the quality care at Mother's Care and even more so from foster care with Lian and the other staff members, which served as a bridge between her institutional experience and a permanent family. Some typical signs of attachment disorder—indiscriminate affection, where Fuxia would try to move from one person's arms to another's, clinging to each, as well as her anger and rage—were combated by how Carol held Fuxia close, and they were careful to protect the growing bond in the first few months. "If Fuxia had the choice in the early months and couple of years of being held by someone else rather than me, she would try to move toward someone else," Carol says. "I would always go get her and bring her back and be really proactive in creating our connection and keeping our connection safe."

One of the most important parts of helping Fuxia adapt was discovering how important organization and structure and stability were for her, the same way they have been for Jacob. "She has always, always—categorically always—responded to routines and structure," David says. "It's like she calms down inside when she comes into structure." But in the first few years, if David or Carol had to be away from home for any period of time, Fuxia would lash out with tantrums, as if the separation had reignited her early landscape of abandonment.

The abandonment and subsequent trauma to the child's emotional and even physical landscape are what make Fuxia's and Jacob's experiences so much more unjust. It's not just that they were born in a world where they would be viewed through the condescending lens of pity, or labeled worthless or broken, or, at the very least, unfortunate because of their disabilities. They also suffered the consequences of institutionalization and deprivation, and the neurological, psychosocial, and emotional problems that presents.

Children with attachment problems live at a stress level that is much greater than the normal individual, Carol Boyd explains. "Their little hearts beat faster. They have more cortisone running through their systems. Anything that they are not used to is something that will frighten them, and any person that they are not used to. Everything is overwhelming."

So David and Carol looked for ways to make things simpler and to give Fuxia structure. Instead of a toy-filled bedroom, they pared back significantly, giving her only a handful of simple playthings and a few books to read, a few of which Carol had made for her. She loved one in particular, a story that touched on her roots in China as well as her connection with her new family, how her father had wanted to adopt a dark-eyed, dark-haired baby girl decades before Fuxia was born. In actuality, that one book would have been enough: Fuxia pored over it, turning the pages again and again until it was worn to tatters.

Their commitment to this little girl and the strategies they used were effective. "A year after we adopted her, we returned to Mother's Care, and she wouldn't get out of my arms," Carol says. "She kept telling the staff and everyone around us, 'This is my mommy.' She wanted to make sure she wasn't left behind."

But even with that attachment, the emotional terrain for Fuxia was riddled with the obstacles of facing her abandonment and all its implications. In 2002, David, Carol, and Fuxia returned to Shanjing to visit Lian and Mother's Care. Fuxia remembered her aunties and knew she had lived at Mother's Care, but David and Carol had waited until she was old enough to ask and to understand before they explained the more traumatic aspects of Fuxia's origins. That question came one morning, when Fuxia and Carol were on a walk at a familiar park in Shanjing. Normally Fuxia was cheerful on these outings. She would lift her feet alternately on the footrest of her wheelchair, as if she were walking as well. She would laugh as she prodded her mother to run, and when her mother complied, she would speed up her feet in time with Carol's. "But today she was curiously quiet," Carol wrote in her journal. "The smells of sweets, bean curd buns, and other treats being sold along the path did not bring a rise. The unrelenting stares, from those passing this *gwai lo* [foreign] mother and wheelchair-bound child, which always accompany our walk, were not responded to as she normally would—by glaring back. Her animated, unremitting chatter and normal posture were noticeably missing."

Carol did not press her daughter. Instead, she waited, matching her demeanor to the quiet of Fuxia's. Finally, a question came, timidly. "Mom, where did I come from?" Fuxia asked. Carol answered quickly that she had some information and would be happy to talk about it all, but that maybe that evening they could meet with Lian and her other foster aunties, and they would share everything they knew with her. "Buoyancy returned to her demeanor," Carol wrote. "She thought that was a good idea and played normally with a friend throughout the afternoon."

As the evening neared, Fuxia became quiet again, and when her foster aunties arrived, Fuxia climbed into Carol's lap. Carol looked down at Fuxia and asked if she was ready, but Fuxia looked up at her and said nothing. "I wanted to give her words for her internal struggle," Carol wrote. "'Is it so difficult that you would rather not ask your questions now?' I asked." After a few moments, Fuxia began quietly, addressing her questions to Carol, who related them to the aunties.

She first asked where she had been left. Lian told her that she was found at the train station and that the police report said she was lying in a little box; that passersby heard her and took her to the police. Fuxia began to cry silently, and Carol could feel the small girl's heart rate rise, and Carol wondered if her heart was beating the way it had when she was there in the train station, in the box—tiny, defenseless, alone. They waited silently as Fuxia recovered. After several minutes, Fuxia asked another question. "Who gave me my name?"

"This was a question I had hoped would not come," Carol wrote. "There was something about her name that she held on to with tenacity. I thought perhaps it was the one connection she felt with her birth parents, thinking perhaps they had named her." When they adopted her, Carol and David had chosen an English name for Fuxia, like most adoptive parents, but she refused to use it. "Upon meeting new people, she carefully explains, 'My name is Foo-sha,'" Carol wrote. "If they call her Fuchsia, she would quickly and often abruptly clarify, 'That is a color and a flower and I am not either.'"

Kindly but matter-of-factly, Lian answered her that the people at the orphanage had named her Dang Fu Xia. "I began to rock her as she quietly wept," Carol wrote. "I was at a loss, as was David. Her fast heartbeat had settled, indicating fear had passed, but resignation seemed to be setting in with a voiceless sobbing that forced her body to catch its breath."

A few minutes passed, and suddenly she shifted from resignation to anger. "How could they do that?" Fuxia asked, indignant, her body becoming rigid, her hands moving aggressively to her hips. "How could they just leave me? How could they leave me without anything to eat?"

"The words seemed to explode from her mouth, coupled with pain. I didn't try to stop her anger," Carol wrote in her journal. In fact, Carol shared her indignation. "But I knew that no matter what, she still shared their DNA. I was concerned her perception would be that if they were bad, she could be bad. Somewhere deep inside of her was an understanding that the parents who had left her were, in some unexplainable way, a part of her."

Fuxia has visited Shanjing on four separate occasions, and on another trip,

Fuxia again was moved to anger. The director of the orphanage where Fuxia was placed after she was discovered at the train station, where she had received her name, learned that Carol and David were interested in Fuxia's origins and invited them to visit. Worried that it would be difficult for her to see the place, David and Carol suggested she go to a park with David instead, but Fuxia was adamant that she would accompany them. Once there, she inspected each corner of the complex intensely. They toured where the children stayed, including the baby rooms where Fuxia had lived. "The babies were in their cribs, and the two staff standing at the wall talking to each other did not acknowledge our entrance," Carol wrote. "The babies were silent yet awake. Fuxia began addressing the staff after looking and touching each baby she could make her way to. In an irritated, high-pitched voice, she challenged the staff. 'Pick up those babies! Hold them! Why are you just standing there?'"

She had survived their neglect and had struggled through the physical challenges of her birth and much of the emotional trauma of her abandonment. But it was as if this young girl sensed how lucky she was, how narrow her escape, how unfair it was that these babies now suffered, and she was compelled in her very small way to struggle against the injustice of it all.

✤ ✤ ✤

In May of 2007, Carol was back in Shanjing, researching for her dissertation on attachment theory. In the hallway of her hotel one afternoon, she saw a blonde-haired, blue-eyed mother holding a Chinese infant. "I watched how the mother was holding the little girl—distant and restrained with a hint of fear in the mother's face," Carol wrote in her field notes. Carol asked the woman how long she'd had the baby, and the woman's reply of three days surprised her. To Carol, it seemed that the woman should have grown more comfortable with the child as days passed, yet this woman was timid with the child and seemed afraid. Carol asked her how old the child was. "Eighteen months," the woman answered with a quiver in her voice, but because the baby girl had been in an institution since birth, she was undersized and looked about half her true age.

"Then I asked the obvious: 'Is there something wrong?'" Carol wrote. "It was as if she had been waiting for someone to ask that question. Her words poured out intermingled with sobs and eyes streaming with tears, how she and her husband were so thrilled at finally having a baby, but within the first hour their little eighteen-month old had bitten her on her neck and clawed her arms. There were pronounced teeth marks still visible, now bluish in color, on the lower part of her neck, and scratches on her arm. As awful as they were, I knew they could not compare to the bruised spirit both she and her baby displayed and the body language of rejection that both wore."

Carol explained that she had adopted a child from the same city nearly ten years earlier and offered to meet with the woman and her husband the next day, to share her experience and advice. When Carol arrived at their hotel room at the appointed hour, she found not just the one couple, but five. They were all adopting through the same agency, and after some questions, Carol found that many were unprepared for the reality of adopting an institutionalized child. After she returned home, she continued to receive phone calls and e-mails from strangers who had heard that she was studying attachment and the abandoned child, that she and her husband had worked through their child's attachment challenges, and that maybe she could help. Carol sensed that this was a growing need, and her research shifted because of it.

"Adopting a child who has been in institutional care or foster care is a challenge, and you have to parent differently," Carol says. "But almost all of those that I have interviewed have had no preparation about what to expect from a child they have adopted. No coaching by the agency, no coaching by the institutions. One of the things I hope to do with this research is to make it useful, so adoptive parents understand what they are seeing, what to call it, what to expect, so they can start early and know what they are dealing with."

What leaves so many of these parents confused is exactly what this woman in Shanjing experienced: that their children seem to resist and reject them with such force. Like the infamous story of the woman in Tennessee who sent her adopted son back to Russia on a plane by himself, these adoptive parents often have good intentions but are unprepared for the potential challenges. They can't understand or deal with the displaced rage and aggression. They don't know that a trip to Disney World overwhelms the child who has lived in a concrete building deprived of color, sound, and activity. They don't realize that every minute a child with attachment issues sits in front of a television instead of interacting with her primary caregiver is another obstacle in building a connection. They don't recognize a common sign of attachment disorder, when the child is indiscriminate with his affection, sliding all too easily from one person's arms to another, as such. Like the child's infrequent crying, they misinterpret this phenomenon as a well-adjusted behavior, in this case seeing it as a sign that the child is outgoing and confident. Yet indiscriminate affection is the opposite of the behavior of a securely attached child, who prefers her primary caregiver over any other because she needs that primary caregiver to survive.

"One of my trips back to Mother's Care, maybe in 2003, one little infant really stood out to me," Carol says. The little girl had a cleft palate and a heart condition, and based on some of her bone structures—protruding ribs and a triangular face—Carol believed she also had brittle bone disease like Fuxia. "It seemed like everything that could be wrong with her was wrong with her. But this little girl had attached to one particular caregiver who had been the one giving her the earliest care and who also seemed to be gentler than the others. This baby was determined to live, and to live she had to connect." For this reason, she refused others who tried to care for her, and her infant demands were a perfect picture of what the child needed in order to survive.

"That's part of what attachment is—I need to be connected," Carol says. "Louis Cozolino, one of the neuroscientists whose work I've studied, says that there's no such thing as an isolated neuron. What he means by that is that the neurons in our brain don't develop without that stimulation of other neurons." The neuron, then, becomes a microcosm for human interactions, with parents and siblings and cousins and friends. In infancy, a child develops a sense of self by what she experiences through others. But if a child doesn't have a primary caregiver—be it mother, father, grandmother, foster parent, or any other stable, affectionate, responsive person—the child does not undergo the necessary processes of brain organization: of mirroring the mother's smile or the father's talk, of developing empathy through the parent's sensitive response when the child is hurting, of understanding cause and effect based on the caregiver's examples from day one. On a physical level, these processes develop as neural pathways in the brain, evolving into what John Bowlby called an "internal working model," structures in the brain that allow the individual to determine very quickly what is safe and what is dangerous, to organize the world and to navigate it easily. But without others, without parents who are deeply invested, without healthy, secure, productive relationships, these processes are thwarted. "These kids don't understand cause and effect," Carol explains. "They didn't develop that in the first year of life, and they didn't develop trust, and they didn't learn empathy, so you have to rebuild all of these pathways."

But it's also important to say that children who have been institutionalized are not lost causes. Children who have faced extreme abuse and neglect are surely the most difficult cases, but there is a spectrum. Many simply need adoptive parents who are aware of the challenges, who are equipped with the correct resources in the form of doctors and therapists, and who give them security and stability and unconditional love. "A really good social worker can play the very important role of preparing parents for what to expect," Gary says, "and a really good support group after the adoption can work wonders. That's where other adoptive parents can serve as references, recommending books to read, on attachment theory and bonding, and advising from their own experience."

But without the appropriate information, adoptive parents often enter the arrangement with unrealistic expectations and quickly become discouraged. In the most tragic cases, the outcome is a failure, both for the parents and the child. But just like poor adoption procedures call for reform, not a moratorium on adoption, poor preparation that results in failed adoptions calls for better practices, not for people to stop extending their homes to children without parents. A stable and loving family is something the child desperately needs, a fact supported by decades of studies, a value enshrined in international law. The United Nations declares this in the preamble to the Convention on the Rights of the Child: that the family is "the fundamental group of society and the natural environment for the growth and wellbeing of all its members and particularly children," and that "the child, for the full and harmonious development of his or her personality, should grow up in a family environment."

Adoption is not a panacea for the difficulties facing children. The factors that lead to a child being orphaned or abandoned—factors like poverty, which leads parents to abandon their children out of desperation; like the devaluation of certain babies, such as baby girls in China; or like insufficient support for parents of children with special needs like baby Adam—must be addressed on local and national levels, as well as by the global community. But in the meantime, children without parents should not suffer because the world is slow and lumbering in our attempts to solve these problems.

Based on their experience and the mass of empirical research, Gary and Helen are convinced that children do best in two-parent families, but that single-parent situations that are permanent are far preferable to foster care, and that all of these options tower far above institutions, which should only be used as a measure of last resort. There are just too many dangers in large institutions, Gary says, dangers ranging from the neglect that Jacob and Fuxia were subject to, all the way to physical and sexual abuse at the hands of caregivers and older, bigger children in the facility.

The number of children who are truly without parents is difficult to determine, but estimates range from hundreds of thousands to millions of children across the world—children in institutions and on streets—in need of the permanent solution of a family. In a 2004 report, UNICEF claimed that there were 16 million children who were truly orphans, without any living parents. But there are more than that who need homes. There are children who are physically and intellectually disabled who need homes, infants and older children who need homes, children in the United States and in Ethiopia and in Haiti and in Hong Kong. These are children of different races, without parents for many different reasons, like poverty or social pressures or war or natural disasters. In some of these situations, children can be reunited with their families, and they should be. But in others, the children who are not being placed in permanent homes, the children who are languishing in institutions because of bureaucratic inefficiency or regulations that prioritize the child's heritage over the child's healthy development or society's apathy toward the most vulnerable of human beings—those children are being failed by the international community, by the people that make up the human family. It's the responsibility of people all over the world to prevent that failure, to respond to these children's needs, to give them homes, security, safety, and love, and the opportunity to grow up as part of that human family.

It's because Gary and Helen responded to an obvious need that the infant boy abandoned at birth is almost unrecognizable these days. When Gary thinks of Jacob hanging limply in the pouch, then recalls an afternoon in Telluride with the seventeen-year-old on skis, on snow, on the slopes arm-in-arm with his father, he simply shakes his head. And when Gary thinks about the days in Hong Kong, when they couldn't find a school for Jacob or therapists to work with him, then sits through a meeting with all of Jacob's teachers and therapists and the vice principal of Montrose High school, hearing them speaking of their commitment to get Jacob more assistance, more individual attention, and better treatments, Gary feels full and grateful that the story has changed so much. When he thinks of how his son used to lie in a crib without no one responding to his cries, day after day, month after month, and then hears the developmental pediatrician at the Children's Hospital of Denver say to a colleague, "We are the ones who should have driven over to see this special boy in Montrose instead of him coming all the way to see us," Gary feels a sense of peace. It seems like, finally, people are responding to Jacob's cries. It seems like, finally, people care. Finally, there is a whole community attending to his needs.

In a way, the process has been a righting of the scales, a means of enacting justice, of setting things right in the world. It wasn't fair what Jacob had to endure, or what Fuxia or any children who are left without parents suffer. But what Gary and Helen did restored justice to one, which is all they could have hoped to do.

✤ ✤ ✤

Fourteen years ago, Helen had so many questions. "Can I do this?" she wondered. "How will I know how to care for him? What do I know about caring for a blind child? Am I too old for this?" She was forty-six when Jacob was born, with fears of failure, inadequacy, the unknown. It was an unfamiliar path, full of worries about how it would turn out, whether he would ever speak, and who their family would become. Now that she's down the path, she realizes that this is part of life. "By the time we figure out how to do something, then it is time for a new chapter in life," she says. "There are stages—parenting, caring for elderly parents, learning how to live on less money, how to adjust to a new job, to getting older." As soon as you master one, the next is upon you.

Helen's willingness to open herself to new challenges and to adapt as changes come is a type of wisdom, as is Gary's. Life moves from order to chaos and back to order, a discomfiting stretching and shifting like the tides or the seasons. "To live well is to observe in today's apparent order the tiny anomalies that are the seeds of change, the harbingers of order tomorrow," writes Jean Vanier. "Too much security and the refusal to evolve, to embrace change, leads to a kind of death."

Helen and Gary have always refused this stasis. Helen spent several years in Hong Kong figuring out how to help Jacob open up and be a part of their family, then spent a few more settling him into his new life in Colorado. As soon as that seemed to fall into place, she picked up a new mantle. One day, during a lunch meeting with some mothers who also had children with special needs at Jacob's elementary school, she learned about an organization called the Volunteers of America, which provides support and supplemental care for children with developmental and intellectual disabilities, along with a host of other services for communities and individuals. Soon Helen was renewing her nursing license, and she began working for Volunteers of America home health. She has been the case manager of the pediatric home health department, helping families in Western

Colorado secure the health-care assistance they need for their children with special needs. It's a stressful job, one that pulls her in several different directions, but one that makes use of her skills as an organizer and her experience raising Jacob.

Gary also began a new path around the same time Helen joined the Volunteers of America, also working for people in severe need of medical care, but halfway around the world. After working for a local church for a few years and overseeing the construction of a new building for its growing congregation, he was informed that his help was no longer needed. Within a few hours, Gary was invited to join Mercy Ships, a nonprofit that operates the world's largest nongovernmental hospital ship, the *Africa Mercy,* as part of their development team. This was in 2006, and Mercy Ships was trying to refurbish a newly acquired ship, trying to serve more people, and hoping to bring even higher quality medical care to the world's forgotten poor. The mission and work of Mercy Ships is to heal and to inspire hope in some of the most outcast and ostracized people in the world.

Each year the *Africa Mercy* settles into a port for ten months, usually along the West Coast of Africa—since 2003, they've provided their services to Liberia, Benin, Togo, Sierra Leone, and Ghana—to provide relief and development to some of the poorest countries in the world. The development aspect of Mercy Ships takes the form of capacity building in the medical sector, assisting communities in constructing medical clinics and digging water wells that fit their needs and their level of infrastructure, training villagers to grow more nutritious and productive crops with organic farming techniques, and providing mental health classes for community leaders and surgical training for local doctors. This work is important for lasting development, but the most compelling stories are related to their relief work: how Mercy Ships provides specialized surgeries that, due to a severe lack of medical infrastructure, as well as unreliable sources of clean water and electricity, are simply not available in the countries they serve. Instead, patients come to the ship, which is equipped with six operating rooms, to have cleft lips and palates corrected, to have benign tumors and goiters removed, to have burn contractures released, to have the clouded lenses of a cataract replaced with clear ones. They come to have clubfeet straightened and faces ravaged by the flesh-eating bacteria *noma* reconstructed. They come to have injuries from childbirth repaired and a new life restored, all free of charge. These are stories of people being reclaimed and are powerful acts to witness.

For the past six years, Gary has worked with the development department of the organization, where his skills in public speaking and storytelling and his history with promoting service-oriented causes are a perfect fit. The travel—visiting donors across the country, bringing them to the ship to see the work firsthand and to meet the four-hundred-member international crew who live on the ship and work there without pay—is vaguely reminiscent of his earlier career. But because Jacob grows more and more attached to him every year, and at eighteen is hungry for the connection with his father, Gary travels less frequently now, coordinating much of his work from his corner office at home, overlooking the cattle in Duckett's Draw. When he does travel, Gary limits any trip to ten days. It's the balance they have found, one that took time to discover, but which now seems fluid and workable—as long as they remain flexible, ready for the next challenge, open for the next call.

Over the last forty years, Gary and Helen have tackled countless hurdles together, and somehow, with steady commitment and faith, they've had the energy, the patience, and even the financial support to bring them through. At times, the challenges have seemed overwhelming, and they have faced resistance for their choices, even from friends and their closest family. But as Gary and Helen followed what they felt was right, what they felt they were called to do, the pathways opened up, and they found the support they needed. There are too many instances where this was true to attribute it all to luck or coincidence. When they decided to marry, they found the envelope of cash in Gary's mailbox that they used to buy their rings. In 1980, when they moved to Hong Kong as a family to work with Vietnamese refugees, Gary and Helen gave away their car, and people began calling almost immediately, donating hundreds of dollars to cover their airfare, and for over two decades, their family of six, then seven, lived rent free. In 1994, the government of China, at the time infamous for its fatal neglect of infant girls, helped open Mother's Care, saving thousands of little girls from deprivation and death. And after raising four children and working with thousands of others, they had the conviction, the patience, and the energy to see Jacob through the hardest times, to a place where he is swimming and skiing and at more peace than he has ever been. In each instance, they saw their good fortune as God's provision—that when they opened their hearts to serve others, to care for the least of these, they found the strength to do it and the resources to see it through.

Part of their energy with Jacob comes from the phenomenon that Henri Nouwen pointed out about his friend Adam: that far from being less than human because of his disability, he was fully human in a way that was challenging and enriching and poignant. The same is true for Jacob: something about him is magnetic. It's difficult to describe, and maybe it's as simple as the vibrancy in how he stands, as visceral as the intensity with which he is present for the sounds around him and the vibrations in the air, as illuminating as his attempts to connect with others in a way that pulls down their normal defenses and removes their usual fluidness and ease. Suddenly, things are on Jacob's terms, and one is humbled by that fact, but paradoxically uplifted by it at the same time.

In a very real way, and simply by being in his presence, Jacob reorients those around him. Gary becomes more aware of his environs, of the wind and the birds and the feel of snow beneath his skis. Kevin learns from Jacob, to be patient and to let go, and in this unlikely space, he finds a best friend. Helen discovers a new way to be a mother, to accept this son as he is, with no expectations of who he might become. "It's work," Gary says. "Undoubtedly it's work. But here we are fifteen years later, and we are looking at Jacob and the numbers of people he's impacted are in the hundreds if not thousands."

There are still worries about what will happen as Gary and Helen get older. "I don't think he'll ever be able to live independently," Gary says. "That's hard for me to admit. So if we are no longer able to care for him, or when we die, what does that mean?" Their daughter Amy and her husband, Bob, have committed to care for Jacob. They've seemingly internalized Gary and Helen's example. After the birth of two biological children, Anna, now seven, and Claire, age six, they adopted a little girl from Mother's Choice who was born with a congenital heart condition and a cleft palate. Ella was fortunate to be placed in foster care from a very early age, and Amy and Bob officially adopted her in August of 2009, when she was two and a half years old. She has thrived in her new home, bonding with her sisters, getting the care she needs for her heart condition, and gaining access to the therapies she needs for some difficulties she has with her speech.

Then in July of 2011, Amy and Bob decided to begin the process again. They applied with an adoption agency in Colorado and said they would consider adopting a little girl with a range of medical conditions. They chose a girl because it seemed easier; since they already have girls, they could share toys and clothes and bedroom space. But in a complete reversal of the Chinese son preference, most American families were requesting girls, leaving many boys with the same special needs waiting for adoption. "It just seemed so wrong," Amy wrote on a blog where she chronicled the process of adoption. "And yet here we were, one of *those* families who wanted a girl. So Bob and I got online, looked at some of the profiles of the precious ones who were waiting, and we were drawn to a sweet little boy with a cleft lip and cleft palate."

This boy had been living at a private orphanage called Maria's Big House of Hope in the north of China since he was six months old, where he had received quality care and medical treatment. Founded by contemporary Christian music singer Steven Curtis Chapman and his wife Mary Beth, the facility is housed in a six-story building with an industrial façade that was transformed into a whimsical sky blue dotted with clouds and is dedicated to caring for up to 124 children with special needs. By mid-July, Amy and Bob had filed their paperwork and been approved by their agency and by China's Center for Child Welfare and Adoption. They would name him Jonathan, but really, he'd be Jon Jon.

Then they watched the summer melt into fall. October passed, and along with it, Jon Jon's first birthday. In December, they had a big trip to Colorado for Christmas, where Gary gave the girls a new yellow Labrador puppy named Riley. Then spring came, and as it does for every adoptive parent, the waiting became excruciating, and every tiny step forward—a notarized document here, a notarized document there—became cause for celebration and excitement.

A great encouragement along the way was when Bob and Amy found out that Jon Jon had received a much needed corrective surgery at Maria's. Incredibly, this surgery was performed by a doctor who works at Vanderbilt University Medical Center, the very place where their daughter Ella receives treatment for her ongoing special needs. How amazing that this doctor, who performed Jon Jon's surgery during a short volunteer trip and then left China, never knowing what would happen to this young boy, would get to see him grow and flourish in ways he could never have expected.

In mid-April, they were finally granted travel approval, and on May 1, Amy and six-year-old Claire took a twelve-hour flight to Beijing as the first leg of an eighteen-day trip to bring Jon Jon home.

As adoptive parents of children with special needs, and as adored and adoring siblings of Jacob, Bob and Amy are aware of the commitment and the demands of their brother's needs. But there's also the worry that if Gary and Helen are gone, Jacob will again feel abandoned, that those first two years in various hospitals and facilities will be reignited as an adult, that he'll suffer again. It's then that the injustice of it all comes flooding back.

"I remember when I would think about what Jacob suffered in the early years, if I stayed there too long, I could get pretty angry," Gary says. Through his years of working to restore justice and dignity to people suffering all around the world, Gary has learned this is a dangerous place to linger, so he normally shifts his focus to what is joyful, to the high points rather than the valleys. But on the off day, climbing to the top of that hill is tough.

During the summer of 2011, when Jacob's ritualistic behaviors were becoming almost compulsive, when he was licking floors and electrical outlets and repeating himself again and again, Gary struggled with him. It was constant stress, and the anxiety in Jacob's body was a palpable presence like static on the radio or the heat from a fire or the vibrations of a jackhammer on a city street. There was no reasoning with him, no way to calm him or soothe him or just get him to stop for a moment so that things could settle down.

On one of these days, Gary sits with the thought of why his son was struggling, and how much difficulty it presented for everyone, but most of all for Jacob. And his eyes fill with tears, and his voice cracks a little when he speaks. "I have seen blind children with the same condition as him who were raised in families from birth, and they're verbal," Gary says, describing a video sent to him by a friend who works with blind children. "I've watched five-year-old blind children unloading the cans of groceries in the kitchen, stacking things in the cupboard. I saw a blind boy enter his school, how he navigated with his cane, and hung up his coat on the coatrack. His language was 100 percent. I was watching this and thinking, *I would have loved to have that for Jacob*. But that was robbed from him before he had a chance."

During those difficult days, that's the hardest part: for Gary, for Helen, for Kevin, for everyone who works with and loves Jacob. "We have no idea what his frustration level is," Gary continues. "But generally he's a happy boy. His tone in his voice is delightful, it's not angry. We know there is so much in there because he's been able to learn to swim and ski and count."

Gary then pauses a moment and gathers himself, pulling himself up a little, toward higher ground. In just a few weeks, the family will head to Massachusetts for his nephew's wedding, where Jacob will wade out into the sparkling blue bay in Wellfleet, with its calm, cool waters and coarse sand, and when his grown siblings look away, he'll pull himself out into the water thirty yards, looking for the edges like he does at home in his swimming pool, only to find they've expanded much further than he can imagine, into the "Duh-*dah*-duh *Dah*-duh," At-*lan*-tic O-cean, a new and exciting place. When they get back to Colorado, Gary will tell the story with pride in his voice, pride tinged with gratefulness for a son who, despite his early tragedy and current challenges, is slowly but surely making steps toward a fuller life.

"Here we are, and a lot of people who we know live in the 'what if,'" Gary says. "But the 'what if' didn't happen, and there are no do-overs in life."

Which makes it that much more important to live a life that does it right the first time. And for each of us to do our part, to work for a world where there can be fewer what-ifs.

AFTERWORD

❧

His Nineteenth Year

Jacob is approaching nineteen years old now. This son of mine faces profound challenges, and his mind, which is obscured from us by a language barrier, continues to amaze and confound me.

In some areas, his progress is still slow. He continues to try to communicate, but it's still in staccatoed, dash-and-dot speech. He still takes medication to calm his obsessive behaviors, and he hasn't fully kicked those habits. Yesterday evening I was in my office, and he was sitting at the bar saying, "Da! Da!" And I said, "Stop it, son! You're going to wear out my name!" He chuckled and then he said, "Da!"

But in other ways, he's come so far. His emotions are close to the surface, but whereas they used to be rage and fear, now he's joyful and excited. At school, there are encouraging signs. Jacob can walk out of the high school and to the car unaided. A few days ago, he went and found his augmentative speech device in his cubby at the back of the room, opened the lid, and pushed the button that said, "I want a drink." And his teachers fetched his lunch box and his thermos, and he poured himself a drink.

In these small glimmers, it just seems like he's getting it—that something is clicking. In the past, we'd give him the phone to talk to his siblings, but he would only say a word or two and push the phone away. Now when I am out of town, he's actually asking his mother—"Duh-duh-*dah?* Da!" And he'll touch his ear. "Telephone? Dad!" He wants to call Dad.

A few days ago I was in a meeting, and I walked out and saw I had three new voicemails just from the period of time I'd been in the meeting. The very first time I listened to a message from him, I was so moved I had to save it. It was this really tender, *"Da?"*—and what I heard was his heart saying, "I want to connect with you." Each message I've gotten from him tells me the same thing, and no matter where I am traveling, it brings a smile to my face and my heart knowing that he's reaching out to me.

I celebrate and am so moved by these phone calls and these voice mails, not because they're some overwhelming and obvious triumph, but because they are just so typical. When I am gone, my son wants to talk to me on the way home from school, again at supper, and at bathtime. He wants to know where I am and when he can expect me to get home. I talk to him like I would anyone else: "I'm in Tennessee, I'm with Bob and Amy." "Dah?" He recognizes and is excited to hear about them and about his nieces and nephew, all of whom I reference by name, even though he hasn't met his nephew Jon Jon yet.

In fact, when I spoke to Jacob from Tennessee recently, it was my first time to meet my newest grandson. He's an amazing little boy, so warm and affectionate, hugging my leg as we meandered across some of their property. I brought his father, Bob, a Stihl chainsaw and helped cut down some dead trees on their property to use as firewood. Jon Jon and Amy and the girls were watching this, and Jon Jon, such a typical little boy, loves anything that makes noise and has a motor. The day after we cut the tree down in rounds and pieces, Jon Jon had a new name for me. Instead of calling me Pop Pop, he says, "Vroom vroom vroom!"

It's just incredible to see him integrating so well with his new family and to witness the courage he has within him at only two years old. When he arrived from China, there was so much newness for him, so many things he had never seen. At first he refused to walk on the gravel driveway or the grass, and he'd cling to Amy instead. But now he's unafraid of either, and he loves picking up gravel from the driveway and throwing it, or plucking flowers from the lawn and chucking them as far as he can. Once terrified of Riley, the family's Labrador retriever, he now wants to play fetch with him first thing in the morning. Everything, including language and food and what it means to live with a mother and father and sisters, was a new experience to be integrated, and he has taken each one in stride and come out on top.

Obviously, Jacob's challenges have been more difficult to overcome, and we'll still have many struggles as he gets older. But there are so many ways that his life is rich and full, and for me, that's reason to rejoice. Just recently, I said to him, "Son, it's about time to go skiing at Telluride." And he responded excitedly, "Dah-dah-dah! Dah-dah-dah!" Tell-ur-ide!

In the past, we always stayed on green slopes, the easiest kind, but one day last year, we made it down an intermediate slope, and we even went over a few small jumps they have at the top of one run that allows people to practice jumping. We got a few inches off the ground, and as we were up, he was making the sound he makes when he is happy, like "Let's do that again!" So I'm confident that we'll be heading down blue slopes on a regular basis by the end of this year.

As each year passes, I look on his life with more confidence and more hope: that he will continue to bring joy to everyone whose path he crosses.

Hearing the Heart-Cry

As I said early in the book, I believe that if we, as willing and able adults living anywhere in the world, would open our hearts to children without parents, we could empty the orphanages of the world. I believe this fervently, with all of *my* heart, which for years has been heavy for children without parents.

I wrote this book to share my son's story, but also to bring awareness to the fact that children need homes. Maybe you have read this and feel an opening in your heart, the same opening that Carol and David Boyd felt when they first met Fuxia, the same opening Helen felt when she pulled Jacob to her heart over sixteen years ago, the same opening I felt when, in a moment of stillness and reflection, I knew that Jacob was my son.

If you've felt that opening, you've already made the first step. What happens next will vary by state and country, but you should start the official process by contacting a social worker in your area—either at the county or state level—who is qualified to do home studies.

For some people, opening your home as a foster parent might be the way to respond to this call. There are many children in our cities and towns who are in need of temporary care, and these children are vulnerable and hurting and could benefit hugely from your compassion. Local adoption is a pressing and important need, and I encourage you to be sensitive to that calling if it presses itself upon your heart.

If intercountry adoption is something you feel compelled to seek, the most important thing is to work with a respected agency that has a proven track record to ensure an ethical and legal adoption. There are many out there, but do your research and interview a few different agencies to see which ones you feel comfortable with. The journey can be challenging, but knowing the solace, comfort, and promising future you can provide to a child without parents, it's a journey worth making.

And Finally

For their inspiration, their kindness, and their support along this path, there are so many people I need to thank.

To the many who have already heard the heart-cry of children without parents and have opened your hearts and homes, including Adam and Kim, Andrew and Christine, Arthur and Missy, Bill and Susan, Bob and Amy, David and Carol, Doug and Deri, Elizabeth, Frank and Linda, Hans and Pascal, Harvey and Nancy, Jason and Carrie, Jeff and Gretchen, Jim and Barb, Jim and Pam, John and Carmen, John and Mandy, John and Nualla, Judy, Lawrence and Gina, Linda, Michael and Debi, Mike and Cathy, Mike and Paulette, Nury and Mary, Peter and Karen, Richard and Sheila, Rob and Joy, Roger and Val, Tony and Dru: I want to say thank you and God bless you.

To Polly, Myrna, Bing, Sarah, Gail and all at Small World Kindergarten; Lois, Nancy, Larry, Kevin; to each teacher and aide and all who have helped care for and train Jacob: Helen and I are so grateful for your investment in our son. To Cousin Ed, for your exuberance and excitement in teaching Jacob to ski at Telluride, we offer a very special thank-you.

To every person who was there at the beginning of Mother's Choice, especially our partners in founding, Ranjan and Phyllis Marwah: it was the right thing to do at the right time. Lives around the world are better because of all the efforts of so many. Thank you from the bottom of my heart.

To Shawna and Scott, Amy and Bob, Andrew and Alison, Katie and Ben: all of you have so deeply impacted my life and continue to surprise and inspire me. You each have such a unique connection with Jacob Lok Chi, and those bonds bring a smile to both my heart and face. I am so grateful for the way each of you has embraced him, and even more that he has responded and embraced each of you right back. Thank you for enriching his experience of the world by taking him swimming, riding ATVs, sledding, skiing, shopping at his favorite stores (What is it about Home Depot or Sam's Club that resonates so with him?), and of course, the tickles and hugs. Thank you for not seeing him not in terms of his disability, but rather his ability.

And to Helen: thank you for being the first to open your heart to him, for holding him close and letting your embrace give him a sense of safety, security, and self-worth. You are an incredible wife and mother, and your willingness to wait for me to get there on more than one occasion, trusting God to nudge me, is a testament to you and your relationship with the Father of All. I join other friends in ascribing "saint" to your name, because that is who you are to me. I love you.

GARY,
JANUARY 6, 2013

A Note from Carmen

I met Gary while working as a writer for Mercy Ships in West Africa. He visited the ship twice during my year onboard, and the second time, he asked if I would help him write a book. I said yes, but I was uncertain—of the story, of my ability to tell it, of how on earth we'd ever get it in print. Four years later, I am still amazed by our providential meeting. I am grateful beyond words that Gary and Helen opened their lives to me and allowed me to help share Jacob's story. I am better in every way for it—as a writer, as a daughter and a sister, as a friend, as a partner, as a human being.

Thank you to all of my teachers along the way, those who taught me to love reading and writing, especially to Peter LaSalle, Elizabeth Harris, Zulfikar Ghose, Joanna Brooks, and the very first and foremost believer in my writing, Cynthia Peveto.

Thank you to my friends and family for your encouragement and enthusiasm for this project, especially to Mom, Dad, Andrew, and Anna for your calm assistance in moments of seeming crisis; Noël, for reading and responding with kind words of support; and Malachi, for being a sensitive, esteemed, and in all ways remarkable reader and editor, counselor and listener, friend and partner. I love you all.

Carmen Radley

December 2012

Endnotes

Chapter 1

Dr. David Arredondo is quoted from an article on CNN.com by Karen Spears Zacharias, entitled "'Go the F*** to Sleep Is Not Funny," which appeared in June of 2011.

Discussions of Jacob Lok Chi Stephens's birth and medical history are taken from a series of medical records and child welfare reports transferred to his adoptive family upon adoption.

Information on the one-child policy is from Susan Greenhalgh and Edwin A. Winckler, *Governing China's Population: From Leninist to Neoliberal Biopolitics* (Stanford, CA: Stanford University Press, 2005).

The effects of deprivation on development are from a pamphlet written by Theresa Hawley, "Starting Smart" (Washington, DC: Zero to Three, 2000), and the information on the Romanian orphanage study was cited in Craig Smith's *New York Times* article, "Romania's Orphans Face Widespread Abuse, Group Says" (10 May 2006).

Descriptions of and conclusions about the film *John* come from Robert Karen's *Becoming Attached: Becoming Attached: First Relationships and How They Shape Our Capacity to Love* (New York: Oxford University Press, 1999) and from the book by the Robertsons themselves, *Separation and the Very Young* (London: Free Association Books, 1989), which includes still photographs from the films, Joyce's notes, and general reflections on the project. Reviews of the film also appear in the Robertsons' book.

Information and quotes from John Bowlby and the history of attachment theory are drawn almost exclusively from Robert Karen's *Becoming Attached*, where he cites the work of John Bowlby, Harry Bakwin, and Bill Goldfarb, as well as Anna Freud and Dorothy Burlington. However, some discussion of infant mortality rates in institutions and all discussion of John Watson and the impact of behaviorists on the child welfare establishment comes from Deborah Blum's *Love at Good Park: Harry Harlow and the Science of Affection* (Cambridge, MA: Perseus, 2002). Blum also aptly discusses how psychoanalytic theory reinforced the advice of behaviorists.

The Geneva Convention on the Rights of the Child, signed and implemented by the United Nations in 1989 and 1990 respectively, forms the basis of the last claim in the chapter.

Chapter 2

Discussions of the fall of Saigon and the stages of refugee flight are taken from a report by the United Nations High Commissioner for Refugees, *The State of the World's Refugees 2000: Fifty Years of Humanitarian Action* (New York: Oxford University Press, 2001). James M. Freeman and Nguyen Dinh Huu's *Voices from the Camps* (Seattle: University of Washington Press, 2003) provides more detailed descriptions of the impact of the Communist policies and effects in Vietnam, further flight, and comprehensive descriptions of refugee camps in Hong Kong. Bruce Grant's 1981 *The Boat People: An Age Investigation* (New York: Penguin Books) also details conditions of refugee flight.

The number of refugees arriving in Hong Kong at the time of Gary and Helen's move appears in Harold Chang's front-page article in the *South China Morning Post*, entitled "5,000 on way to HK in Vietnamese armada," 25 June 1977. Statistics for the total number of Vietnamese refugees, as well as the number that found safe haven in Hong Kong, come from the UNHCR 2001 report.

The history of ethnic Chinese in Vietnam and their subsequent flight are taken from Vo, Nghia M. Vo, *The Vietnamese Boat People 1954 and 1975–1992* (Jefferson, NC: McFarland & Company, 2006), and from Freeman and Nguyen's *Voices from the Camps*. Freeman and Nguyen's *Voices from the Camps* is also the source for information on a country of asylum's responsibilities toward refugees, and certain failures by those countries.

Chapter 3

Many of the insights on people with physical and intellectual disabilities throughout this book are from the philosophy of Jean Vanier, specifically his book *Becoming Human* (Toronto: Anansi, 1998). John Hull's *Touching the Rock: An Experience of Blindness* (New York: Pantheon, 1990) was useful in explaining what Jacob might have felt as a blind person in snow.

Dr. Anna Reisman's *Slate* article "Tender Young Minds" appeared on January 18, 2012, at www.slate.com.

Chapter 4

The news story cited in this chapter was Ophelia Suen's "Hongkong women fuel border abortion boom," which appeared on the front page of the *South China Morning Post* on June 9, 1986.

Discussion of the one-child policy comes from Susan Greenhalgh and Edwin A. Winckler, *Governing China's Population: From Leninist to Neoliberal Biopolitics* (Stanford, CA: Stanford University Press, 2005); and from Susan Greenhalgh, *Just One Child: Science and Policy in Deng's China* (Berkeley, CA: University of California Press, 2008).

Information about attitudes toward sex and sex education in Hong Kong was reported by Lin Sui Fung in a 2007 study entitled *Values & Attitudes of Adolescents on Sexual Behavior and Sexual Education: A Report* (Hong Kong: City University of Hong Kong). In 2008, the *South China Morning Post* also reported on the dearth of sex education in a Yau Chui-Yan article, "In the dark about sex," which appeared on June 15.

Chapter 5

Discussions of attitudes toward the transfer of Hong Kong to Chinese rule are from Frank Welsh, *A History of Hong Kong* (London: HarperCollins, 1994), which engages in a thorough discussion of Hong Kong's history but does seem to privilege English sources in the telling.

Information about the separate nature of English and Chinese settlements also comes from Welsh, who translates *Po Leung Kok* as the "Protect Virtue Association."

Letters from the pregnant girls are from the 1992 Mother's Choice Annual Report. Ranjan Marwah's letter about preventing teen pregnancy appeared in the 1992 Mother's Choice Annual Report.

Discussion of Fruit Chan's television commercials promoting awareness of the problem of teenage pregnancy appeared in an article by Matthew Scott, "Giving choice a voice" (*South China Morning Post*, 2002 March 7).

Chapter 6

The letter from Paul and Rose Kwa appeared in the 1991 Mother's Choice Annual Report.

Discussions of social welfare programs in Hong Kong are from Frank Welsh,

A History of Hong Kong (London: HarperCollins, 1994). The theme of business interests appearing to be ahead of social concerns is a major feature of the book, and seemingly, of Hong Kong's history.

Chapter 7

Discussions of the history of adoption can be found in Elizabeth Cole and Kathryn Donley, "History, Values, and Placement Policy Issues in Adoption," anthologized in *The Psychology of Adoption*, eds. David M. Brozinsky and Marshall Schechter (New York: Oxford University Press, 1990); E. Wayne Carp's introduction to *Adoption in America: Historical Perspectives* (Ann Arbor, MI: University of Michigan Press, 2001); and Madelyn Freundlich and Joy Kim Lieberthal, *Adoption and Ethics, Vol 3: The Impact of Adoption on Members of the Triad* (Washington, DC: Child Welfare League of America, 2001). The value of a child is discussed in Madelyn Freundlich, *Adoption and Ethics, Vol. 1: The Role of Race, Culture, and National Origin in Adoption* (Washington, DC: Child Welfare League of America, 2000).

Freundlich's first volume of *Adoption and Ethics*, which discusses race, culture, and national origin, is a comprehensive guide to the controversies over adoption and was my source for modern attitudes on international adoption, specifically the three loudest and largest camps: those who oppose international adoption in all cases, those who see international adoption as an unadulterated good, and those who feel that culture should be weighed alongside the child's need for a family. Gary and Helen Stephens would probably fall somewhere between the latter two camps; they insist that culture is secondary to a child's need for a home. Freundlich's book is also one of the sources for the history of international adoption in this book.

Sara A. Dillon's compelling and thoughtful article "Making Legal Regimes for Inter-country Adoption Reflect Human Rights Principles: Transforming the United Nations Convention on the Rights of the Child with the Hague Convention on Inter-country Adoption" appeared in the *Boston University International Law Journal*, Vol. 21, p. 179, 2003.

Madelyn Freundlich cites Michelle Hester of The Barker Institute, talking about the theoretical nature of heritage in the topic of child welfare. Hester's opinions are featured in Freundlich's *Adoption and Ethics, Vol. 1: The Role of Race, Culture, and National Origin in Adoption*.

Sharon LaFraniere's article "Chinese Officials Seized and Sold Babies, Parents

Say," published in the *New York Times* on August 4, 2011, is only one of many trafficking stories that can be found in newspapers and magazines from the past few decades. Like stories of failed adoptions, these stories receive ample media attention. Dr. Aronson discusses knee-jerk reactions to trafficking in her article "The Trouble With International Adoption Is Not Trafficking: It's the Global Orphan Crisis," published in *The Huffington Post* (2011 September 20). Her open letter to President Bill Clinton can be found online. Elizabeth Bartholet's entry in the blog discussion was part of a chorus of voices in the *New York Times's* "Haiti's Children and the Adoption Question," which appeared on February 1, 2011, at roomfordebate.blogs.nytimes.com.

Madelyn Freundlich's quote about the reasons for the decrease in Korean adoptions comes from her book *Adoption and Ethics, Vol. 1: The Role of Race, Culture, and National Origin in Adoption,* page 93.

Discussion of the "unadoptable child" can be found in E. Wayne Carp's *Adoption in America: Historical Perspectives* (Ann Arbor, MI: University of Michigan Press, 2001).

Jean Vanier's insights on the plight of persons with disabilities in the modern day and how to build a better, more compassionate world can be found in his book *Becoming Human* (Toronto: Anansi, 1998). The story of Henri Nouwen and his friend Adam is given in compassionate and full reflection in Nouwen's book *Adam: God's Beloved* (Maryknoll, NY: Orbis, 1997). Nouwen's reflections on the contemporary problem of compassion comes from his book *Compassion,* co-authored with Donald P. McNeill and Douglass A. Morrison, first published by Image Books in 1982.

Chapter 8

John M. Hull's memoir *Touching the Rock: An Experience of Blindness* (New York: Pantheon, 1990) was an incredibly helpful, insightful, revealing resource for the experience of blindness, especially because the subject of our own book could not share what his own experience of blindness has been.

Discussion of sleep disorders in children can be found in Robert L. Sack, et al., "Circadian-Rhythm Sleep Disorders in Persons Who Are Totally Blind," *Journal of Visual Impairment and Blindness,* Vol. 92, Issue 3 (1998), pages 145–162.

Chapter 9

The epigraph for this chapter is from Arthur Waley's translation of *The Book of Songs*, from "Minor Ode 189" (New York: Grove Press, 1996).

The *South China Morning Post* reported on the dying rooms on May 23, 1993, in an article written by Peter Woolrich entitled "China's unwanted children." There were follow-ups, in September 1995, with Tom Hildich, "A Holocaust of Little Girls," reprinted in *World Press Review*. Hildich's article contains the response by the Chinese embassy to the allegations of dying rooms. A major expose also appeared in London's *The Daily Mail* in 1994.

The history of social welfare in China, in particular illuminating the attempt to eradicate the need for social welfare under Mao, is covered by Robin Munro and Jeff Rigsby, *Death by Default: A Policy of Fatal Neglect in China's State Orphanages* (New York: Human Rights Watch, 1996). They also supply statistics, photographs, and first-person testimony from doctors inside Shanghai's premier orphanage about the policy of neglect that led to the deaths of so many infant girls.

Statistics from the *People's Daily* editorial and the government's reportage are cited in Robin Munro and Jeff Rigsby, *Death by Default: A Policy of Fatal Neglect in China's State Orphanages*. Exact numbers regarding the gender imbalance and lopsided male to female birth ratios are, understandably, difficult to find. Discussion of birth ratios and corresponding charts appear in Susan Greenhalgh and Edwin A. Winckler, *Governing China's Population: From Leninist to Neoliberal Biopolitics* (Stanford, CA: Stanford University Press, 2005). The gender imbalance is discussed in Daniel Shorn's 2009 article "China: Too many men," *CBS News: 60 Minutes* (February 11).

Susan Greenhalgh uses decades of research to explain in detailed and nuanced ways the development of the one-child policy in *Just One Child: Science and Policy in Deng's China* (Berkeley, CA: University of California Press, 2008). *Just One Child* is the main source used to explain how the one-child policy originated and is the source for most facts and statistics about the population of China prior to the implementation of the policy. The impact of the policy on Chinese society, which includes anecdotes as well as statistics and more general information, comes from *Governing China's Population*.

The translation of the names *Lai-Di* and *Zheo-Di* is given by a Chinese reporter interviewed in the documentary directed by Kate Blewett and Brian

Woods, *The Dying Rooms* (London: Lauderdale Productions, 1995).

Discussion of baby farming comes from George K. Behlmer, "What's Love Got to Do with It? 'Adoption' in Victorian and Edwardian England," in *Adoption in America: Historical Perspectives*, ed. by E. Wayne Carp (Ann Arbor, MI: University of Michigan Press, 2002).

Safe haven laws in the United States are available online through the US Department of Health and Human Services at http://www.childwelfare.gov.

Chapter 10

All of the early information about Fuxia's abandonment, health, and personality, and process of adoption comes from David and Carol Boyd, obtained through interviews and also through Carol's dissertation on attachment theory. Fuxia figures in as one of Carol's longitudinal case studies. (Fuxia elected to participate.)

Chapter 11

The ecology of Hong Kong and the discussion of flora and fauna in the Mid-levels is informed by Edward Stokes, *Hong Kong's Wild Places* (New York: Oxford University Press, 1995). The anecdote of Robert Fortune's travels is also in Stokes's book.

Again, John Hull's memoir *Touching the Rock: An Experience of Blindness* was instrumental in providing insight into the experience of blindness, especially in a city.

Chapter 12

A description of the Leader of the Year honor—the requirements as well as the purpose of the award—is available at the Singtao group's website, http://loty.singtao.com/loty_e_intro_1.html. Text of Dr. Elaine Yee-lin Ho's speech conferring Gary's honorary doctorate from the University of Hong Kong is also available online.

Chapter 13

Again, John Hull's insights are some of the best to help a sighted person understand the phenomenon of echolocation.

Special-needs inclusion is the subject of many studies and articles, but Peter Farrell's comments are featured in Hilary Wilce, "Special-needs education: Does mainstream inclusion work?" *The Independent* (London, 26 March 2006), online at independent.co.uk.

Chapter 14

Again, personal interviews with Carol and David Boyd are the source for much of Fuxia's history, and the stories of Fuxia's return to China can be found in Carol's dissertation on attachment theory.

The full text of the United Nations Convention on the Rights of the Child is available online. The preamble of the UNCRC is the source for the quotations in chapter 14.

Gary, Jacob, and Helen skiing in Telluride, Colorado, 2011.